# WORK WITHOUT WAGES

SUNY Series on Women and Work
Joan Smith, Editor

# WORK WITHOUT WAGES

Comparative Studies of Domestic Labor
and Self-Employment

Edited by
JANE L. COLLINS
and
MARTHA GIMENEZ

State University of New York Press

Published by
State University of New York Press, Albany

© 1990   State University of New York

All rights reserved

Printed in the United States of America

For information, address State University of New York
Press, State University Plaza, Albany, NY   12246

**Library of Congress Cataloging-in Publication Data**

Work without wages : comparative studies of domestic labor and self-
    employment / Jane L. Collins and Martha Gimenez, editors.
        p.   cm.—(SUNY Series on women and work)
    Bibliography: p.
    Includes index.
    ISBN 0-7914-0106-5.—ISBN 0-7914-0107-3 (pbk.)
    1. Domestics.   2. Housewives.   3. Informal sector (Economics)
4. Subsistence economy.   5. Women—Employment.   I. Collins, Jane
L., 1942–   .   II. Gimenez, Martha.   III. Series.
HD6072.W67   1990
331.4'8164046—dc19                                        88-37031
                                                              CIP

10   9   8   7   6   5   4   3   2   1

# CONTENTS

# ACKNOWLEDGMENTS

We have enjoyed the help and encouragement of many people as we edited this volume. By far our greatest debt is owed to Joan Smith, editor of the Women and Work series for SUNY Press. Aware that we were working on similar problems across arbitrary disciplinary boundaries, she brought us together and suggested that we pool our intellectual resources. Her foresight and intervention have led to a collaborative project that has been both intellectually and personally rewarding.

The papers collected here reflect lively discussions held in a number of contexts. These included—among others—a session of the 1985 meetings of the American Sociological Association on unwaged work, chaired by Joan Smith, and a session on labor processes and domestic production held at the 1985 annual meeting of the American Anthropological Association, organized by Jane Collins. Martha Gimenez would like to thank Michael Neuschatz and Jane Collins for their comments on her introduction. Jane Collins thanks Martha Gimenez, Randall McGuire, Michael Painter, and Joan Smith for their helpful suggestions and insights. Both editors appreciate the constructive criticism and ideas provided by the reviewers for SUNY Press. Finally, we wish to thank Kathy Martin for her careful translation of Susana Narotzky's article, and the editors of the *Review of Radical Political Economics* for their permission to reprint the article by Nona Glazer.

# PREFACE

The essays in this book seek to account for experiences of unwaged work, both in industrialized nations and in the developing world. They focus on Mexican women who plait palm leaves to supplement family income, on Spanish women who manufacture clothing at home for international corporations, and on men and women from small ranches in southern Peru who travel to Lima where they buy and sell fruits and vegetables. They are also about women in the United States who find themselves striking an increasingly difficult balance between waged work and work in the home. Each essay seeks, in its own way, to redress the invisibility of these forms of unwaged work in Marxist analysis. In so doing, many false distinctions between workplace and home, market economy and family economy, and public and private spheres are broken down.

As editors of this volume, we came to the problem of unwaged labor within Marxist analysis through different routes. One of us—Martha E. Gimenez—has written about domestic labor and its changing significance according to social class and a country's location in the world system. Her work entailed recognition that domestic work does not affect all women equally; how much domestic work women do, and what kind, depends on their level of income and on their social class. In her work, she has conceptualized housework as the reproduction of labor power on both a daily and generational basis. This reproduction process has both physical and social aspects; home workers meet the physical needs of family members, but they also perform expressive and nurturing tasks and socialize children in ways that reproduce family and class relations. The question of domestic work, and the household strategies that develop under advanced capitalism, are—in her view—not only important to our understanding of patterns of capital accumulation, but also are crucial to our understanding of political divisions among women and the limits of liberal feminism.

Jane Collins, in contrast, has written about the unwaged work performed by peasant families of the developing world, who are linked to the larger economy through labor and market transactions and occasional waged work. Attempts to conceptualize the unwaged productive and reproductive activities of these families have spawned a large literature on informal economy, self-employment, and petty commodity production. Many of these works have conceptualized unwaged production as "resistant" to capitalism, or as a remnant of former natural economy, rather than examining its reproduction within capitalist economy. They have experienced difficulty in linking the culturally specific processes by which families and communities reproduce themselves with the imperatives and constraints posed by capitalist classes and the state.

Part of what brought us together to edit this volume was the shared conviction that domestic labor—whether in the homes of industrialized nations or the farms and *favelas* of developing nations—had to be understood in relation to unfolding processes of capital accumulation. We believed that unwaged work was not autonomous from, but operated within, market processes and class relations. We also recognized that discussions of unwaged work in these two contexts (domestic labor and self-employed production) replicated each other in some ways, and that researchers working in the two contexts could benefit from a greater awareness of each others' work.

This was the inspiration for the present volume. The goal of bringing together the eight cases we have chosen is, in part, to compare the ways that the different authors have framed and analyzed unwaged productive and reproductive activities within capitalism. Despite their diverse settings, each of the essays reveals the centrality of unwaged work to family survival, and to the reproduction of relations of gender, class, and community.

Previous analyses of the social relations that structure unwaged work have had a functionalist tone. These relations are viewed either as being broken down by the encroachment of capitalist relations, or as being maintained by capital as enclaves of cheap labor. Most attempts to redress such functionalism have emphasized the autonomy of unwaged work, and have seen it as a site for the reproduction of anti-capitalist values.

Both of these approaches take a narrowly economistic view of capitalist society. They neglect both the multi-faceted ways in which people's lives are structured under capitalism and the variety of ways that people live within or contest those constraints. By focusing on case studies and accounts at the level of family relations, we hope that much of that economism can be dispelled and that the complexity of lived social relations will be revealed.

# Part I

# THEORIZING UNWAGED WORK

# Chapter 1

## Unwaged Labor in Comparative Perspective: Recent Theories and Unanswered Questions

### Jane L. Collins

The specialization of work to paid employment is the result of the development of capitalist productive relations. To be "in work" or "out of work" was to be in definite relationship with some other who had control of the means of productive effort. "Work" then partly shifted from the productive effort itself to the predominant social relationship.

—Raymond William
*Keywords: A Vocabulary of Culture and Society*

For the wage laborer does too little and knows too little. He can do only what he is paid for and what has been agreed upon by contract. . . . He works for too short a time and is exhausted too quickly. . . . That is why [he] is used so rarely.

—Claudia von Werlhof
*The Proletarian Is Dead: Long Live the Housewife*

In popular usage, the terms "work" or "labor" have come to imply the exchange of one's time and effort for wages. The intellectual trajectory of the last two centuries, as described by Raymond Williams above, narrowed the concept of work from the sense of all productive effort to that of productive effort performed for someone else. This "someone else" owned the means of work and controlled the conditions under which the work was performed. The narrower use of the term reflected an understanding of the underlying logic of capitalist productive relationships. It also made it possible, for the first time, to speak of women who labored for their families as "not working," or of cultivating a home garden as a "leisure time" activity.

Since the 1970s there has been a growing sense that an understanding of unwaged forms of work is essential to the analysis of the larger economic systems in which both waged and unwaged production operate. This critique has emerged from two specific intellectual projects—one, to understand the nature of women's domestic labor; the other, to understand the

3

variegated working lives of those we have called peasants in the third world. The labor of the individuals involved in both these cases is understood to be significant to larger economic systems. Yet, in both cases, the tools to analyze its "value," or its relationship to waged forms of labor, have been lacking. The present volume brings together a number of efforts by anthropologists and sociologists to grapple with this problem.

The terms that have been applied to "work without wages" are multiple and varied, suggesting the real variety in the structure and quality of these experiences. Domestic labor is a term that has been applied to a wide variety of productive tasks within the home—the cooking, food processing, cleaning, sewing, mending, and gardening that were characteristic of most U.S. households in the nineteenth century and of many rural households until quite recently. "Housework" has generally been used to refer to that more limited, and perhaps more highly technologized, range of activities performed (mainly by women) in homes today. Within Marxist analysis these activities, and some others, are understood to contribute to "social reproduction"—that is, the performance of tasks that are not remunerated by capital, but that are necessary to reconstitute classes and conditions of work from day to day and generation to generation.

Another set of terms has referred to unwaged activities that either come into contact with markets or substitute for market participation. "Informal economy" has been used to designate production of goods and services on a small scale, and in ways that do not make it into the official registers of bureaucrats and economists. It can also refer to forms of barter and non-market exchange that occur in times and places where cash is scarce. "Petty" or "simple" commodity production is a rather specific term used to refer to the small-scale, home or farm-based production of goods for market. "Self-provisioning" or "subsistence" production are labels that have been applied to labor invested in the production of food or other necessary items for direct consumption, thus avoiding market transactions and reducing market dependence.

More difficult to name have been the myriad small tasks performed on a daily basis by families dependent on the wage. These include the work involved in selecting and purchasing consumer goods, time spent commuting to work, the labor involved in complying with bureaucratic regulations, volunteer work, etc. Such tasks are not easily categorized. They have not traditionally been characterized as work—in fact, they are tasks that we most often perform in those blocks of time that people in industrialized countries have come to refer to as "leisure." Ivan Illich has called these chores "shadow work (1981)." Claudia von Werlhof refers to them as part of a feminine (not female) work capacity—"the healing-all-wounds, . . . the putting-everything-again-in-order, . . . the helping-out-in-all-matters, . . . the pulling-the-cart-out-of-the-mud. . . . '' (1984, 144).

## Empirical and Theoretical Issues

There is evidence that forms of unwaged work have proliferated and that their significance has increased as a result of the economic difficulties of the 1970s and 1980s. Portes and Benton, using data collected in connection with the United Nations Regional Employment Program for Latin America, have estimated that 60 percent of Latin America's urban labor force is in the informal sector (1984: 603, 608). With the debt crisis of the early 1980s, employment in this sector increased at an annual rate of 6.8 percent, compared with 2 percent in the formal sector (Roberts 1988, 5, citing data from PREALC 1987). De Janvry (1981) has argued that semi-proletarians—seasonal wage laborers who also work their own land and engage in petty trade or craft production—formed the largest rural sector in Latin America by the 1970s. The same trends appear to hold for much of the rest of the developing world (Portes and Walton 1981). A number of works have documented new strategic combinations of waged and unwaged work pieced together by both urban and rural poor (Bromley and Gerry 1979; Redclift and Mingione 1985; Mattera 1986; Perlman 1976; Long and Roberts 1978; Long 1984). New forms of outwork and sweated labor regimes, and the renewed reliance of laboring classes on a range of family and community-based strategies for self-provisioning, have also posed a challenge for theory. These trends are related in complex ways to the global restructuring of capital and to the fragmentation of the labor process in certain branches of production.

The significance of unwaged work in the industrialized nations may be growing as well. J. Smith (1984, 65) argues: "While such labor activities may be a good deal less common in the core than in the periphery, there is little doubt that in both, labor that is not directly organized by the wage is on the increase." This increase is reflected in such practices as garage sales, new forms of barter, and unregistered provision of services such as baby-sitting. It is also occurring at a more fundamental level, however. There is evidence that the total amount of time invested in unwaged activities necessary for the maintenance and reproduction of workers in the industrialized nations is expanding, as a result of the proliferation of new forms of consumption, the restructuring of consumption practices, and a decline in the availability of some services (see works by Smith, Gimenez, and Glazer in this volume).

Mingione (1985, 19) has related these increases in unwaged work to two parallel contradictions inherent in current processes of capital accumulation—accumulation accompanied by high rates of commoditization, which tends to increase the costs of reproduction of the labor force, and accumulation that goes hand-in-hand with disproportionate expansion of the surplus population (industrial reserve army), resulting in strong overproduction tendencies. He argues that in the industrialized countries, the intervention of the state has concealed these contradictions and postponed their disruptive effects during periods of high growth rates. They have become more evident, however, with the incapacity of the system to create "good" jobs and with trends toward the dismantling of the welfare state in western Europe and the United States.

Aside from their increasing predominance in times of economic crisis, there are important theoretical reasons for turning our attention to these unwaged forms of work. While they do not enter in direct and measurable ways into the "inner dynamic" of capital accumulation, they are integral parts of capitalist development. Like the state, they are essential to capitalism as a system of social relations. Unwaged forms of production stand in a dialectical and contradictory relationship to waged labor, and take their meaning from their relationship to the wage. Because of this close relationship, it becomes impossible to understand either the circuits of reproduction of capital or the reproduction of capitalist social relations apart from a consideration of the unwaged work that is performed within homes and communities.

Some social historians and anthropologists have examined the ways that unwaged work routines operate in contexts of family and community (see Segalen 1983, Long 1984, Scott and Tilly 1975, and several of the essays in Medick and Sabean 1984). This concern is in large part a product of/or response to the feminist critique of traditional approaches to the study of work, which argues that they overemphasize structural factors and the workplace while ignoring experiential features and the home. As Seccombe (1980, 36) has noted: "The proletariat as a social class is constituted at two locations, not one. It cannot live without working for wages. It cannot work for wages without living in a definite place outside capitalist production where it renews its capacity to work." Feminists have argued that this life outside the factory, and its implications for the working class and for gender relations, has not received the same systematic attention as have situations of formal employment.

Works that focus on routines and experiences of unwaged work in contemporary contexts demonstrate, among other things, that individuals find it easier to undertake unwaged work in some situations than in others. This depends in part on the availability of labor for the task—but also on the existence of networks to support the activities (through informal forms of credit, provision of advice and technical assistance, etc.; see G. Smith in this volume). Not only do these pre-existing relationships structure unwaged work, but the work that is done alters the relations themselves. The distribution of unwaged work across lines of gender and age may reinforce or challenge existing hierarchies within households or communities (see Cook in this volume).

The ways in which the routines and practices of unwaged work enter into the formation of class consciousness or class culture are less well understood. Different forms of unwaged labor clearly contribute to different ways of understanding one's class position. It has been argued that petty commodity production tends to generate the political contradictions traditionally associated with the petty bourgeoisie (Gibbon and Neocosmos 1985), although producers in this situation have at times engaged in powerful forms of collective action (Alderson-Smith 1976) and have even participated in revolutionary transformation (C. Smith 1986). The implications of informal activities such as scavenging, where considerable stigma is attached to the work, yet where workers in some sense control the conditions of their labor, have been contested (Birbeck 1978; Blincow 1986). Analysis of the class position of women who work within the home presents its own difficulties (West 1978). The class experiences of those engaging in unwaged work are always affected by the types of waged (or salaried) labor that they also perform, and the relationships they maintain with other waged and unwaged workers.

## The Diversity of Unwaged Relations

Unwaged labor is, in many ways, an awkward category. It does not emerge naturally out of the analysis of a particular phenomenon, but is comparative in intent. A few works have used a unitary concept of unwaged work productively. Wood (1981), for example, following Wallerstein, Martin, and Dickinson (1979), proposes that household income from a variety of unwaged sources can be calculated as a proportion of waged income, and households can then be scaled along a continuum from fully waged to completely unwaged. In this way, "part-lifetime-proletarian" households can be characterized with regard to the proportion of their income derived from waged and unwaged work at any particular point in time, and the relationship of income composition to shifts in the world economy can be analyzed.

For Wood, this measure provides a way of understanding how household decision-making (particularly with regard to migration) is conditioned by fluctuations in the larger economy. For Wallerstein, Martin, and Dickinson, it provides an index of the ''strength'' of labor markets, of the ways in which capital accumulation is proceeding in different parts of the world economy, and of the effects of these processes on laboring classes. A waged/unwaged dichotomy is useful in these cases in providing a simple measure of the degree to which a population is dependent on wages and the degree to which families must rely on their own resources to generate income or produce the goods that they need.

While for some limited purposes, unwaged labor can be treated as a unitary phenomenon, this type of analysis can be misleading if carried too far. Unwaged forms of work are organized by different sets of productive relationships in the contexts in which they occur. They emerge at different moments in the process of capital accumulation as a result of political struggle, the conditions of waged work created by capital and the creativity of workers. Comparative consideration of forms of unwaged work provides a way of examining processes of capital accumulation through observing their relative ability to absorb labor; it reveals the ways in which capital tries to restructure those social relationships that it does not convert into the wage form and in which workers respond to and resist these efforts. The goal of such analysis is to illuminate differences in forms of unwaged work through comparison—not to develop a monolithic or generic concept out of a diverse and heterogeneous set of experiences.

As previously mentioned, research relevant to this task has tended to focus on either the domestic labor of women or the unwaged work of small-scale producers. There are important parallels in the approaches taken by researchers engaged in these two intellectual projects, and in many cases they have benefitted from the use of the same theoretical tools. Part of the goal of this volume is to bring together work from both domains in order to illustrate these convergences and promote a ''cross-fertilization'' of ideas between researchers pursuing a similar problematic in different contexts. It should be emphasized, however, that such an endeavor is not based on the premise that housewives, peasants, and urban petty commodity producers share the same relationship to capital and capitalist classes. Such a position has been taken by Benston (1969), Bennholdt-Thomsen (1981), and von Werlhof (1984). Because she elaborates this view most fully, it is useful to examine Bennholdt-Thomsen's arguments to clarify how comparison can be useful, as well as to clarify the analytical difficulties that can result from pushing the similarities too far.

Bennholdt-Thomsen argues that housewives and peasants are integrated into capitalist economy in the same way because both are involved in subsistence production. In the category of subsistence she includes work related to reproduction and the education of children, as well as the production and processing of food and cloth and the provision of housing. While these activities are usually performed by women in industrialized countries, she argues that third world peasants—through their direct involvement in the transformation of nature to meet family needs—may also be seen as reproducing labor power (in the form of their families) for capital without compensation.

Bennholdt-Thomsen asserts that the capitalist mode of production can be conceptualized as consisting of two "areas of reproduction:" extended reproduction (or accumulation) and subsistence reproduction. Both peasants and housewives fall on the second side of this division, producing use values for direct consumption. The labor of peasants occasionally becomes subject to capitalist valorization processes when they sell some of their production on the market. More frequently, however, this is a result of the sale of their labor power. Thus, after a time lag, labor power nurtured by subsistence production becomes a commodity, and the private and concrete labor of both housewives and peasants becomes social and abstract.

The significance of the work of both housewives and peasants is disguised, Bennholdt-Thomsen argues, because of their attitudes toward their products. She suggests that even when they sell their crops, peasants do not consider themselves to be producing exchange values, but rather as retaining a "use value orientation." Nor do housewives see themselves as producing the commodity labor power, but rather as acting to meet the needs of their families out of affection or love. Thus, in both cases, ideologies mask the true nature of production and legitimize exploitation.

The problem that Bennholdt-Thomsen sets up is an appropriate one. Neither housework nor the self-provisioning production of peasants is directly implicated in the circuits of capital accumulation, and both lie outside value relations. Both are reproduced as conditions of the existence of the capitalist mode of production. Nevertheless, if one makes this argument (as Bennholdt-Thomsen does by placing both outside the sphere of accumulation), it is impossible to maintain at the same time that the labor involved is subject to capitalist valorization processes. This contradiction emerges most clearly when Bennholdt-Thomsen says of unpaid labor: "Capital does not assume any responsibility for it. It is unpaid work, which, in turn, is the exact definition of surplus labor." She is correct in saying that capital does not assume any direct responsibility for work performed under these conditions. It is in this respect, and this respect alone, that the unwaged labor of housewives and peasants are similar. But her equation of unpaid work with surplus labor represents a gross misreading of *Capital*. Surplus labor is not some essential quantity that can be appropriated in any context, but is a product of the particular social relationship that exists between the owners of capital and wage workers. In this relationship, capital *does* assume responsibility for work and dictates its conditions, and this is what makes the appropriation of surplus value possible.

Bennholdt-Thomsen's lack of clarity with regard to whether forms of unwaged work are internal or external to processes of capital accumulation, and subject—or not—to the law of value, is not the only source of confusion in her account. Her characterization of the activities of both housewives and peasants as subsistence production is also misleading. In fact, most of what these individuals do is not the direct production of goods for consumption. Housewives are mainly involved in processing and maintenance activities—they do not produce the goods necessary for the survival of their families, but change them into a usable form. While small-holding rural producers may engage in some self-provisioning, their participation in labor and commodity markets cannot be viewed as a simple diversion of use values to other purposes, as Bennholdt-Thomsen suggests. As Chevalier (1982) has demonstrated, even with minimal commoditization, producers become subject to market processes and their production is reorganized to reflect the market's dynamics.

### Unwaged Labor and Marxist Theory

Given these difficulties, why should a comparative analysis of forms of unwaged labor be attempted? Why, some might argue, is it necessary to reopen the protracted debates over the law of value that characterized discussions of domestic labor in the 1970s (which were finally abandoned without any real resolution)? At the end of this debate (discussed in more detail later in this chapter) many researchers argued that a reformulation of Marxism was necessary in order to include domestic labor within its analytical framework (Beechey 1977, 61; Bradby 1982; Sargent 1981).[1] Feminists, in particular, sought alternative formulations that would account for the widespread relegation of women's labor to a "private" sphere by patriarchal institutions, incorporating Lévi-Strauss' structuralist understanding of kinship relations and elements of psychoanalytic theory into materialist frameworks (Rubin 1975; Kuhn 1978; McDonough and Harrison 1978).

The question of the ways in which Marxist theory can be brought to bear on unwaged labor has not yet been resolved. There is a general recognition that Marx did not intend to illuminate relations between men and women, or the structure of the family, which he considered a "subordinate form" (Marx 1968: 40; see also Sayer 1987: 79). Historical materialism as most frequently practiced can answer some, but not all, questions about these relationships. As Seccombe (1980, 38) has pointed out: "The capitalist mode of production provides an historically unprecedented leeway to its laboring masses in arranging their means of subsistence." These arrangements are not dictated by capital and cannot be understood solely as a product of the dynamics by which capital reproduces itself.

On the other hand, as P. Smith (1978, 215) has noted, it is not the theory of value that marginalizes domestic production (or grants it leeway, as you prefer), but the capitalist mode of production. If such work lies outside the inner dynamic of capital accumulation, then we need to ask why it does, and how it articulates with that dynamic in specific times and places. The task for analysis becomes the exploration of the ways in which capital is supported by social arrangements that are not directly given as its conditions of existence, the ways these social arrangements are reproduced, and the contradictions that arise from their connections to capital. This does not entail subsuming them to the law of value as it is traditionally understood, but developing a rigorous and theoretically informed understanding of the more complex ways that they become intertwined with value relations. In its most radical form this understanding may require a rethinking and expansion of the law of value itself (Bradby 1982).

Such a task would involve discovering (1) the points at which forms of unwaged work articulate with labor and commodity markets (reproducing labor power, absorbing the labor of the unemployed, providing alternatives to the factory regime); (2) the social arrangements that control unwaged labor (home extension services, advice manuals for housewives, "assistance" programs and supervised credit for small-scale farmers); (3) the implications for class relationships; and (4) the contradictions that arise—in lived experience—between the "logics" and demands of waged and unwaged work regimes. While we can use these questions to structure our analysis of the unwaged labor of both peasants and homemakers, we cannot reasonably expect the answers to be the same. As Friedmann (1986a, 124) has emphasized, our success in conceptualizing real historical variability in labor situations depends on our ability to make adequate *distinctions* among the various "people who do not fit" capitalist social relations as narrowly conceived.

The ground that could be covered in reviewing treatments of unwaged labor is vast. For this reason, the discussion here will focus on the issues that have emerged from two debates—one concerning the proper way to conceptualize the production of small-scale farmers and craft workers, and the other related to the conceptualization of domestic labor (or housework) in capitalist economy. These are not the only debates of relevance (in particular, a large literature on informal economy and "marginalization" is being left aside), but they are illustrative of the theoretical issues that remain to be resolved. They also illustrate all too well the narrow way that problems have been defined and the failure of researchers working on similar issues to learn from one another.

## The "Peasantry Debate" and Simple Commodity Production

The persistence of small-scale or peasant production within capitalist economy has posed problems of analysis since the days of Chayanov, Kautsky, and Lenin (Banaji 1976; Chayanov 1966; Lenin 1899). In fact, the questions raised by these men—regarding the implications of the use of unwaged family labor in an agrarian enterprise and the long-term prognosis for such enterprises—remain central in the debates of the current generation of scholars. Lenin and Kautsky argued that small family farms were transitional and would be replaced eventually by fully capitalist farms employing wage labor. The continued viability of these enterprises in some contexts has been seen, by many researchers, as posing important questions about capital's ability to transform all class relations into the property : wage labor relationship and of the place of enclaves of unwaged production in an increasingly complex international division of labor.

A major critique of the concept of peasantry emerged in the 1970s, which argued among other things that the theoretical object of research on peasants had not been clearly specified in previous work. There was, in the words of several of the major critics, no "consistent economic and social content" to the category (Ennew, Hirst, and Tribe 1977, 308). They argued that what was required was a more rigorous specification of the social relations that bound peasants to capitalist classes. This critique led many researchers to attempt to develop more specific definitions of the relations of rural production relations. The concept of simple or petty commodity production was elaborated by a number of theorists as a way of specifying these relations, and of clearly situating the producers within capitalist economy.[2] Friedmann (1980) defined simple commodity producers as a class of combined laborers and property owners, operating in a context where generalized circulation of commodities prevails. The concept, as she developed it, refers specifically to enterprises, rather than to the livelihood-seeking activities of individuals; it refers to the production of goods for market, rather than to self-provisioning; it is not limited to agricultural production; and it specifies the combination of labor and property within the enterprise. Thus, the concept is reserved for a very specific form of participation in capitalist economy, and does not become an all-encompassing gloss for small-scale direct producer, as the term "peasant" had, in many cases.

While the analysis of simple commodity producers properly focuses on the nature of property relations and the dynamics of markets, insofar as these are family enterprises, it has been necessary to turn attention to how they obtain labor—that is, to family life cycles. If the form of the household is that of the nuclear family, the specification of labor dynamics is a relatively simple one. But in contexts in which simple commodity production has been studied, such simplicity has rarely been encountered (see Harris 1981, Collins 1986, and Roseberry 1986 for discussions of the difficulties that arise when scholars treat family economy in an ahistorical and unproblematic manner). In order to understand how labor is mobilized and deployed within the enterprise (and also how some property is transmitted) researchers have found it necessary to master the complexities of kinship, real and fictive; to come to terms with the meanings of key institutions, such as lineage and community; and to develop new concepts, such as "income-pooling units" and "survival networks." G. Smith's discussion of "confederations of households" in Peru and of the negotiation of neighborhood ties in Spain illustrates well the complex forms that such relationships can take.

Friedmann's work (1980) subsumes issues of family, community, and gender relations within a discussion of the ways that households reproduce themselves. She sets up a continuum between two ideal types. At one end are simple commodity producers, whose multi-stranded relations to other households have been replaced by market relations. For these households, "relations to outsiders progressively take the forms of buying, selling, and competition" (1980, 163). Reproduction is no longer dependent on social institutions outside the market. At the other end of the continuum are "peasants," for whom access to land, labor, credit, and product markets is mediated through direct and particularistic non-monetary ties to other households or classes. "If these ties are reproduced through institutionally stable reproductive mechanisms, then commodity relations are limited in their ability to penetrate the cycle of reproduction" (p. 163). Friedmann emphasizes that her distinction between enterprises that depend on the market for their reproduction and those that do not is neither an ideal nor a typological one. In practice, she notes, household enterprises exist along a continuum of market dependence, and all are embedded in complex networks of social relations, both market and non-market in nature.

Other authors have been less willing to discuss the internal dynamics of petty commodity producing enterprises. Gibbon and Neocosmos (1985), for example, reject attempts to describe the reproductive logic of petty commodity production because they believe it can lead to subjectivism—that is, focusing on the subjective calculations of the petty commodity producers themselves rather than on the social relationships that link them to capital. In particular, they insist that all petty commodity producers, as participants in capitalist economy, operate in a situation of generalized circulation of commodities. "Once peasants (or anyone else) *systematically* produce commodities, they are all controlled—by definite and precise forms of capitalist regulation which act as the absolute limits of their activity" (1985, 165).

As Bernstein[3] has pointed out, this means that, in principle, the diverse phenomenal forms of petty commodity production present us with issues that are "no different from (nor 'greater' than) the similar diversity of phenomenal forms of capitalist enterprises . . . " The features of such diversity ("levels of capitalization, productive forces, labor processes, size of product, etc.") remain a matter for concrete investigation, but the dynamics of the enterprise can be conceptualized as part of the essential relations of capitalism (1986, 19).

Bernstein, and Gibbon and Neocosmos, attempt to retain a distinction between the complexity of social relations as played out in historical contexts and the theoretical concepts we use to understand them. They try to avoid both subjectivism—which sets petty commodity producers outside capital because of a purportedly distinct rationality or logic of reproduction—and empiricism—which takes the fact that the phenomenal features of petty commodity production look different from those of other capitalist enterprises as evidence that they possess a distinct internal dynamic. The contribution of this approach is its refusal to confound historical phenomena with the categories of critical analysis.

Yet its confidence in the ability of laws of bourgeois economy to give an adequate accounting of petty commodity production apart from historical analysis is, perhaps, misplaced. Chevalier (1982), for example, argues strongly that the production of petty commodity producers is structured by the market, yet he demonstrates that the laws of capitalist economy are not *sufficient*, in and of themselves, to account for the functioning of their enterprises. He argues that goods and labor that do not enter markets directly still possess an exchange value in these contexts, and that their use is influenced by the potential for exchange. But Chevalier's analysis of real historical events in the Peruvian Amazon required a knowledge of the ways that kinship, community, and local power relations structured the availability of labor and land. An adequate conceptualization of a petty commodity producing enterprise need not specify the subjective rationality of producers—and it must locate the enterprise within the circuits of reproduction of capital. But, as Friedmann points out, it must also give attention to the family and community relationships that define access to resources and that organize the deployment of labor. As so many of the contributions to this volume reveal, subsumption into capitalist economy does not alter the fact that enterprises vary in the degree to which their reproduction is bound up with "direct non-monetary ties to other households and classes." Gibbon and Neocosmos' insistence on the generalized circulation of commodities within capital precludes an analysis of relationships crucial to these reproductive mechanisms.

Because of the embeddedness of these relationships and practices in networks of family and community; because they are often emotionally significant in ways that factory work relationships are not; and because they are not contractual, but are constantly being manipulated, negotiated, and rearranged, their analysis is no easy task. Students of petty commodity production, such as Gibbon and Neocosmos, in their zeal to eliminate all traces of analytical subjectivism and of arguments about survivals of traditional or precapitalist behavior, ignore the fact that significant non-commoditized transactions occur in even the most highly industrialized settings.

Another important, and related, issue that has emerged out of studies of rural producers concerns the ultimate transitionality of their unwaged labor. Friedmann attributes the continued presence of simple commodity production to its competitive advantages. These advantages—the lack of a structural requirement for profit, the flexibility of personal consumption, and the flexibility of decisions about the distribution of income—are not realized in all contexts, but only in certain conjunctural conditions. Friedmann clearly describes the waxing and waning of these conditions, for example, in her analysis of family wheat farming on the Great Plains (1978). Gibbon and Neocosmos, while they do not argue that petty commodity production will ultimately disappear in a process of class transformation,[4] note that it is unstable. They argue that it appears and reappears as a result of changes in the social productivity of labor. As capital abandons some branches of production in favor of more profitable ones, once-abandoned areas may be opened to small-scale enterprises. Neither Friedmann's answer for a specific case, nor Gibbon and Neocosmos' more general suggestion about opportunities created by variations in the productivity of labor, answer the question of how petty commodity production is reproduced on a worldwide basis "as an inescapable and integral part of capitalist development itself, and not as the outcome of policy, historical accident, nor of 'functional usefullness' for capital" (Gibbon and Neocosmos 1985, 157).

A final question raised by such studies is how the unpaid labor invested in household enterprises comes into contact with capitalist valorization processes, and the related question of whether we can speak of exploitation in these contexts. In Marxist analysis, the value of labor invested in the production of marketable goods is the average socially necessary labor time. For rural families using simple technologies and intensifying their own labor rather than purchasing more modern equipment or inputs, the actual labor time invested may be far greater than the social average. The fact that it is consistently greater, and that this strategy of intensification is made necessary by the structural disadvantages suffered by small-scale producers, has led some researchers to argue that this is one way that surplus labor is appropriated by outside interests—peasants and petty commodity producers sell goods more cheaply because they produce them with large quantities of their own unremunerated labor rather than purchased inputs. The average difference in the labor content of goods produced in different sectors (de Janvry 1981, 82–84) or the difference in prices received by peasant and "modern" producers (Vergopoulos 1978, 447) gives rise to a type of "unequal exchange" on a regional scale.

Friedmann has argued strongly against this position. She identifies two sources of error in the reasoning applied. First, it assumes that the price of production equals value, when there is no reason to believe that the lower prices received by agricultural households are further removed from value than higher ones. Second:

> Even if surplus value existed, it would have to be appropriated through a productive relation, from class to class, or redistributed within a single class through the equalization of rates of profit. Unequal exchange, even if its existence could be shown, cannot serve as a mechanism of accumulation between sectors. . . . Value has to be produced and appropriated through specific mechanisms for accumulation to occur. (1980, 169–70)

Peasants, on the other hand, may be exploited by precapitalist rent (what Wolf [1966, 49] calls "domain") and by interest, taxes, and terms of trade where immobility of labor, land, and credit create opportunities for monopoly, coercion, and unfree contractual relations (Friedmann 1980, 171).

Still, there are questions to be answered regarding the way in which petty commodity production enters world markets. Petty commodity producers participate in these markets as merchants, yet because of the small scale of their enterprises they cannot make the market responsive to their production costs. While it is incorrect to characterize this disadvantage as exploitation in the strict sense, it certainly gives rise to systematically unfavorable market linkages (de Janvry's point). The nature of these unfavorable linkages are relatively constant across contexts of petty commodity production. While some researchers argue that they are related to its historical emergence in a necessary way, others maintain that they are simply by-products of a more general process of marginalization and are not specified by, or necessary to, capital.

## Housework and the Domestic Labor Debate

Perhaps it is the failure to appreciate the different kinds of unwaged work that are combined in the category "housework" that has created major problems in understanding the significance of tasks performed under this label. Much of the daily work performed in the home (shopping, planning, cleaning, cooking, and sewing, for example) is responsible for the daily physical reproduction of the household members. Other tasks, such as childcare, reproduce the household generationally, while also reproducing class structure (see Gimenez 1978 for an elaboration of this model). Some tasks, such as home gardening, involve direct production. Most, however, are processing activities—transforming purchased goods into usable forms—or maintenance work—organizing, cleaning, and repairing household resources. All of these tasks restore or reproduce both the labor force and the family forms in which it takes refuge.

In addition, however, some of the work that homemakers do at least appears to be production "for" capital in relatively direct ways. Glazer (this volume) argues that women's activities in consumption pull them into the work process; that is, as consumers, they perform tasks that were once the province of waged workers.[5] The voluntary unpaid labor of housewives in community projects and activities, in many cases, substitutes for service provision by the state or employers (Pahl and Wallace 1985; Gershuny 1985). These shifts in the boundaries that define family, state, and corporate responsibility may not change the nature of domestic work, but they alter its intensity. Finally, in some cases, home workers combine their reproductive and restorative tasks with small-scale production or provision of services—laundering, cooking, or baby-sitting for others on a barter or informally waged basis.

The question of how housework relates to capitalist production (the "domestic labor debate") has occupied researchers since the late 1960s. Because the literature on this issue is immense, the discussion here will necessarily be selective, focusing on points where useful comparisons can be drawn with other forms of unwaged work. As indicated earlier, these include issues such as the points of articulation between housework and labor and commodity markets (and the related question of whether housework creates value), social processes that control labor performed within the home, and the degree to which the lived experience of housework has the potential to contradict the logic of capitalist production.

One of the earliest and most influential works that has addressed the role that housework plays within capitalism is Benston (1969). Benston viewed the household as a mode of production separate from and parallel to capitalism, and as a relic of precapitalist economy. The link between household production and capitalist commodity production was provided by the functions that the family performed for capital. These included serving as the "production unit for housework and childrearing," the "ideal consumption unit" for the products of capitalist manufacture, and the locus of satisfaction of the worker's emotional needs. Benston was one of the earliest to argue that the organization of the family guaranteed these as "free" services to capital—that is, their costs were not borne by capitalist enterprises, but by male wage earners.

Over the course of the early 1970s, these themes were explored and developed in a large number of works, most of which focused on domestic labor's role in the reproduction of the labor force. Harrison (1973) and others, for example, argued that surplus value was created by domestic labor and was appropriated from the household sphere through the male wage. The employer paid for one worker, in essence, but obtained the labor power of two. Gardiner (1975) and Gardiner, Himmelweit, and McKintosh (1975) followed a similar line in emphasizing the contribution of housework to family subsistence in ways that they argued enabled the wages of workers to be held low. Seccombe (1974) suggested that domestic labor could be considered a form of petty commodity production whose product was labor power; it was thus part of a "congealed mass of past labor" embodied in that product (p. 9).

These attempts, and others like them, were seeking to account for housework using the categories of Marxist analysis. They represented a dissatisfaction with a labor theory of value "in which the labor of half of the world did not take the form of value . . . " (Bradby 1982, 1), and with accounts that ignored the lives of the working classes outside the factory.

While the frustration of these scholars was well placed and their search for ways to conceptualize the social institutions involved in the "reproduction of immediate life" a necessary one, many difficulties were created by the attempt to locate reproductive work within the circuits of accumulation of capital. As Molyneux (1979) has pointed out, most accounts made housework seem "necessary to capitalist reproduction—as though capitalism itself would collapse if women were to leave their places in the home:

> The debate on domestic labour and the family has been suffused
> with what can best be described as functionalist assumptions.
> Housework is, for instance, variously referred to as "crucial,"

"necessary," or "essential" to capitalism; for its part, capitalism is sometimes seen as having "created" housework, and in some formulations even "depends" on it for survival. . . . There is no recognition that, however beneficial the domestic sphere might be in a given conjuncture, it is undergoing changes as a *result* of capitalism's expansion or of the class struggle, and might also generate contradictory effects for capital. The logical conclusion of this posited dependence of capital on housework and the family is, as some writers have suggested, that their abolition will bring about the downfall of capitalism. (1979: 20)

Historians have also pointed out that housework has not been an immutable feature of capitalism. The removal of women and children from the industrial workforce and the reconstitution of a "domestic" sphere were the product of struggles in which different strata of the working class and various branches of capital took different positions, and in which both church and state played a role (Humphries 1977; Barrett and McKintosh 1980; Curtis 1980).

As Briskin has argued, there was, in these works on domestic labor, a failure to distinguish between capitalism as a process of reproducing value and capitalism as a system of social relations. While there was a need to specify the integral role of domestic labor in the process of capitalist development, this could have been done without subsuming it under the category of wage labor (1980, 149). Both Molyneaux (1979) and Briskin emphasized domestic labor's role in processing and maintenance, and its ability to expand and contract with other demands on female labor. They argued that it does not produce the commodity labor-power, but participates in the process of the laborer reproducing him or herself.

Strictly speaking, domestic labor does not affect the value of labor power because this is based on the aggregate of commodities necessary to reproduce the entire working class; domestic labor cannot increase the value appropriated by capital because it cannot affect the socially necessary labor time needed to produce the workers' means of subsistence. Precisely because domestic labor is unwaged, it "cannot find its quantitative understanding in abstract labor and socially necessary labor time" (Briskin 1980, 159). Finally, domestic labor (with a few exceptions, such as home gardens) does not produce use values, but actualizes or transforms them (pp. 154–63).

Given this assessment, what then does domestic labor do, and how can its relationship to processes of capitalist accumulation be understood? According to Briskin (1980), Molyneux (1979), and P. Smith (1978), domestic labor, by working on the means of subsistence in a useful way, transfers its value to replenish labor power, but does not add to that value. It is one of the "external conditions of the existence of the capitalist mode of production which it continually reproduces (P. Smith 1978, 211). It is not necessary, according to these authors, to call upon the law of value in order to understand that "the capitalist family form—a family which owns no means of production, which is forced to sell part of its labor for a wage, and which therefore is dependent on commodities for its survival—is a structural component of capitalism," or that domestic labor is "that part of the family's labor that helps to maintain and procreate this wage labor force" (Briskin 1980, 143).

But the arrangements under which domestic labor helps to maintain and procreate are not "given" by laws of capitalist accumulation (as is the relationship between the owner of capital and the laborer, for example). They vary widely across time and space and among subgroups of the working class, and they can generate contradictions within capitalist social relations, as when women are pressured to enter the work force at the same time as they are trying to maintain the "traditional" family form. According to this view, gender oppression possesses a certain autonomy from capitalist social relations (although it has been reinforced by them in recent historical experience) and will not necessarily disappear with the end of these relationships.

Briskin's is perhaps the most radical expression of opposition to the more functional accounts of housework's relation to capital. While denying the place of housework within the "inner dynamic" of capital accumulation, she invites researchers to examine the historically specific connections that have existed between the two phenomena. Thus, she avoids the use of Marxist concepts as metaphors, rather than theoretical categories. On the other hand, Briskin may be somewhat too adamant in her insistence that domestic labor cannot affect wages. While Molyneux (1979) also argues that housework does not affect the value of labor directly, she does allow for the fact that societal expectations about who will participate in waged labor and who will stay home, and about what the home environment should be like, feed into the "historical and moral element" of socially necessary subsistence, and thus into the process (of class struggle) by which wages are determined.

The question of how housework affects the circuits of capital accumulation must be supplemented, however, by a query as to how these processes affect work within the home. In addressing this question, it is important to remember that women's work in the home has almost always been in combination with intermittent or regular periods of work in the public sphere. Young women of all classes have often worked outside the

home until they married; working class women have structured their participation in the labor force around childbearing and family responsibilities.
Women's potential position in a segregated workforce is a constant presence which shapes (and justifies or calls into question) their activities
within the home. In the workforce, women are recruited predominantly to
service positions that are defined as having low skill requirements and are
thus low-paid; these positions have no job security and few benefits, and
they are often part time (see J. Smith 1984). Positions of this type are frequently associated with a high degree of worker alienation (Feldberg and
Glenn 1982). Work performed within the home exists in contrast to options
in the workforce, and that contrast will be drawn differently for working
class women faced with service sector jobs with the features just described
and for middle class women whose options are likely to be more lucrative,
if less "flexible."

Women's compliance with highly alienating and insecure forms of
work is generated through complex cultural processes in which they learn
to accept a vision of themselves and their productive contributions as less
important and more expendable than those of male family members, a vision in which they view themselves as primarily, if not solely, responsible
for the well-being of other family members. This dominant vision of wom-
en's role and worth is reproduced within the family, naturalized by medical
practice, imposed by state institutions, and "sold" by the mass media and
advertising. No form of workplace domination could be as effective or as
difficult to contest.

Economic analyses (Marxist or otherwise) will not tell us how much
time a woman working in the home will spend on cooking, cleaning, or
childcare, or how she will go about these tasks. These practices are the product of a complex cultural determination reflecting the norms and expectations of a particular class position and the degree to which a woman
accepts, or is in a position to reject or reformulate, "expert" prescriptions
and societal expectations. Bradby has argued that domestic labor has, in
some cases, the potential to contradict value-regulated labor. In other words,
use values produced within the home are prized for having *more* time spent
on them, rather than less, as in capitalist competition: "A three course
meal has more 'value' in domestic terms than a quick snack, a carefully
ironed shirt more than one pulled directly from the tumble drier (1982,
126)." The implication here is that these spheres of activity may foster an
incipient resistance to the time economy of the commoditized world.

Precisely because women are caught between the social relations of
commodity production (through their real or potential participation in the
work force) and the non-commoditized logic of family relations in the

home, they feel the contradiction Bradby speaks of most directly. When a woman takes a job, it necessarily affects the work performed in the home. Home work may first be intensified (performed at a grueling pace on evenings and weekends), then prioritized, and ultimately it will in all likelihood be simplified through elimination of some activities. A commoditized logic takes over, as time spent in one activity is weighed against alternative uses with monetary value; activities that were formerly found rewarding are eliminated as too costly of time (see Friedmann in this volume).

One of the implications of these questions is that unwaged work may reproduce capitalist social relations, or it may take the form of resistance to those relations; it may, in fact, do both simultaneously. A family vegetable garden may support the daily and generational reproduction of a small part of the workforce; it may simultaneously occupy the labor of a family member who is then less willing to work outside the home; it may also give a sense of independence and autonomy to the family that throws into relief the alienating aspects of the waged work routine. The interplay between the economic and political forces that make unwaged work necessary, and the creativity of the working class in developing new strategies—the difficulties created by the restructuring of the work force and the ways in which livelihood is sought in the interstices of the employment structure—has often proved a stumbling block to researchers. There is a marked tension between accounts that focus on the forces that give rise to unwaged work and those that describe the "survival strategies" of the waged and unwaged poor. In the words of Roseberry, "A basic aspect of a capitalist social formation is that it is characterized by economic and political forces in part working behind the backs of the people who are most affected and in part working through the conscious activity of those same people" (1983, 201).

This is clearly not all that there is to say about domestic labor within capitalism. The point here, however, is simply to indicate the potential for a theoretically and descriptively rich analysis of labor that lies outside value relations, using familiar concepts of class and power relations, and grounded in an appreciation of lived social relations. It is to dispel the notion of the "autonomy" of unwaged activities in favor of an understanding of their position and meaning within capitalist social relations, at the same time that it rejects approaches which see them as rigidly determined by the laws of bourgeois economy.

## Conclusions

Attempts to conceptualize unwaged work have raised a number of issues that are of great importance to our understanding of recent changes in political economy. These changes have been engendered by the restructuring of capital and fragmentation of labor processes in certain branches of production, and they entail new forms of petty commodity production, outwork, and sweated labor regimes, as well as the reliance of laboring classes on a range of family and community-based strategies for self-provisioning. These attempts also push at the boundaries of much current Marxist thought, seeking to expand a materialist framework to account for forms of labor that lie "outside value." They call for recognition and theorization of the complexity of relations between capital and labor in contemporary social formations and especially of those forms of work that we are ideologically predisposed to ignore.

One of the goals of this volume is to indicate that, while we do not need to construct new theories from whole cloth to account for these phenomena, we need to enrich many extant versions of Marxism before they can adequately do the job. Unwaged activities—whether housework, self-provisioning production, or petty commodity production—are not an "autonomous" sphere. They are engendered by the contradictory character of production and social reproduction within capitalist social relations. While these activities are sustained and structured by highly localized, culturally specific processes of social reproduction, and while they cannot be understood apart from regional processes of class formation and class struggle, they continue to be linked in complex ways to global processes of capital accumulation.

As G. Smith (this volume) indicates, we cannot point to an historical period that was characterized by "pure" capitalism. Commodity production has never been completely generalized, and forms of less than free labor and non-economic surplus extraction have been features of many historical contexts. Yet some Marxist analyses—confounding historical phenomena with the categories of critical analysis—assume that there was (or will be) a society whose features could be completely accounted for by the "laws of bourgeois economy." Given such an assumption, unwaged work appears either as something "new" and inaccessible to Marxist theory, or as something that must be forced into pre-existing categories of political economy. The chapters that follow seek to avoid both these extremes.

Given the preceding discussion, the diverse ways that forms of unwaged work are related to capital should be apparent. When a woman produces weavings or straw mats for sale, the value of her labor power is realized through market transactions. When she makes tortillas for her wage-laboring husband or her children, this is not the case. The relevance of family and community ties to the reproduction of simple commodity producing enterprises is a product of the role they play in mobilizing labor, and

the labor process shapes, and is shaped by, these ties. In the case of housework, the labor process impinges less directly. What women do, or are able
to do, within the home is affected by alternative demands on their labor (the
strength of the labor market for women), by the standards set in a particular
period for housework and childcare, and by the way in which the consumption of necessary items is structured by manufacturers and retailers.

Women's domestic labor affects capitalist accumulation processes by
contributing to the body of unemployed who can be considered a particularly docile part of the industrial reserve army, thus providing not only a
welcome flexibility to capitalist enterprises, but also constituting a particularly vulnerable and "cheap" part of the work force; and by contributing to
division, hierarchy, and competition within the work force. While it supports capital in a variety of ways, it does so indirectly. It does not take the
form of abstract labor; the social relations of commodity production do not
obtain; it does not enter into surplus value, and it is not, therefore, value-
regulated. In this it is similar to self-provisioning production, to labor performed within the state sector and certain forms of scientific labor. This
location "outside value" is a product of the historically specific ways in
which public and private, family and work have come to be structured under capitalism.

The case of petty commodity production (and forms of petty commerce) is different. The labor that enters into these activities is indirectly
valorized by market processes. Analysis of petty commodity production has
clearly indicated its subordination to the effects of the law of value in capitalist competition and accumulation. While family structure, gender hierarchies, generational divisions of labor, and culturally defined interests and
motivations play a large role in structuring petty commodity production
(Friedmann 1986b), this is not so different from the social and cultural embeddedness of the shop floor, the typing pool, or the fast food restaurant.

A narrowly economistic Marxism does not work well, even when applied to "classic" problems within political economy. Even on the shop
floor, in a classic industrial setting, it is found wanting (Burawoy 1982, for
example). At the most fundamental level, this is because it confuses real
historical behavior and events with a logical account of the essential relations that structure them. Such economism cannot be expected to work any
better when applied to cases where capital and wage labor are combined
within the enterprise (as in petty commodity production) or where labor is
not directly subordinated to value relations. The pages that follow seek to
apply a socially and historically grounded Marxist analysis to forms of unwaged work—retaining a sense of the complex, and often contradictory,
nature of their manifestations in real social contexts.

# Chapter 2

## The Dialectics of Waged and Unwaged Work: Waged Work, Domestic Labor and Household Survival in the United States

### *Martha E. Gimenez*

Theoretically, the accumulation of capital on an ever-expanding scale entails the proletarianization of the population and the universalization of commodity production. This should lead to the centralization and concentration of capital in very few hands and the concomitant transformation of the rest of the population into a propertyless class whose only source of survival is its ability to sell its labor for a wage. Historically, this process is far from being completed and, within the world capitalist system, the degree of proletarianization in each country is determined by its unique insertion in the world economy and its corresponding place in the core or the periphery.

Proletarianization is least advanced in the periphery, where the presence of rural and urban subsistence sectors and relatively widespread cottage industries lowers the cost of labor power. Cheaper labor (and other incentives, of course) attracts capital from core to peripheral countries, where it is able to realize higher profits while maintaining the structural conditions that brought it there. Abundant unwaged labor engaged in the production of food and services (legal and illegal) keeps wages extremely low and profits high for those able to take advantage of these conditions. On the other hand, the flight of capital from core countries, particularly in recent years, has very important effects upon the quantity and quality of the demand for labor, and the relative input of unwaged labor in the reproduction of the labor force within core countries. Those effects have been intensified by the present crisis of accumulation and the adoption of economic and public policies designed to lower the labor costs of production regardless of social costs.

In this essay, I intend to explore the impact of this crisis, and the concomitant transformation of the economy in the United States, on the changing significance of waged and unwaged labor in the reproduction of the labor force. It will be my contention that the role of certain forms of unwaged labor in the reproduction of the labor force is relatively less important here than in the periphery because of the greater scale with which proletarianization proceeded in this country. I will also argue that the relative importance of unwaged labor as a source of household income and well-being in the United States varies directly with the value of the labor that is being reproduced. Finally, I will argue that the historically specific conditions that led to the structuring of unwaged domestic labor in the United States have been crucial for determining both the specifically capitalist basis for the oppression of working women and the conditions for generating the political and ideological awakening and mobilization of women. The dialectics between waged and unwaged labor are, after all, the empirically observable form—at the level of market and social relations—of the dialectics of production and reproduction under capitalist conditions; their study can shed light on the political significance of changes in the conditions under which unwaged domestic labor is performed.

## Forms of Unwaged Labor

The transformation of labor power into a commodity on a large and expanding scale is one of the essential features of the capitalist mode of production. Historically, proletarianization has been most advanced in the core countries, a fact that meant the near universalization of wage labor and the drastic decline in the proportion of independent producers. By 1974 in the United States, only 8.2 percent of all workers were self-employed, and only 8.8 percent were salaried managers and administrators; the rest were all nonmanagerial waged and salaried employees having no other source of income than the sale of their labor (Reich 1978, 180–181).

Unwaged labor, on the other hand, comprises different kinds of labor. It is, in fact, not always perceived as labor, given dominant ideologies defining as "real work" only that which is exchanged for a salary or a wage. The most important kind of unwaged labor under capitalist conditions is domestic household labor, which has been and continues to be the primary responsibility of women. Domestic labor is engaged in the physical and social, daily and generational reproduction of the labor force; it entails the daily and generational maintenance of the domestic worker herself, her children, and her husband and, sometimes relatives or friends (Seccombe 1974; Gimenez 1978). Households differ in size and structure, ranging from single-person households to urban or rural communes or "collectives" including more than one "nuclear family" and a number of unrelated people. Consequently, households differ in the amount of domestic labor at their command; I am referring here to the labor of children, husbands, and other household members who, in addition to the labor of the main domestic worker, can under some conditions become an important source of non-market income.

In addition to the production of goods and services for internal consumption, household labor may produce for the market. Unwaged labor—usually women's labor—can turn to the production of goods or services of varying quality which, although reaching a relatively unstable and narrow market, can become another source of household income, supplementing and sometimes replacing wage or salary income. Homes become small cottage industries supporting themselves on a regular basis or during times of low wages, unemployment, or underemployment. This kind of household activity partially accounts for the low level of wages in poor nations, where wages are seldom the major source of income ensuring the survival of vast sectors of the population.

In the core countries, there is a specific kind of unwaged labor that is becoming increasingly noticeable—empirically—although it is by no means a new development; what is new is the fact that it seems to be growing by leaps and bounds. I am referring to the work involved in the process of consumption: "The clear trend is for producers to work less and for consumers to work *more. The consumer, ultimately, will have to choose between hiring a robot and hiring himself*" (Burns 1977, 191; emphasis in the original text). "Self-service" in retailing entails work; food stores, discount stores, and department stores can sell at lower prices because customers do a great deal of work in the process of purchasing commodities. This work often includes evaluation, selection, weighing, wrapping, and carrying, and it almost always, of course, includes delivering the goods to the customers' homes. Self-service has become predominant in vast department stores and most clothing stores (except those for the very wealthy), as well as in gas stations; the proliferation of electronic tellers, catalogue showrooms, computerized and televised education, vending machines, salad bars and other forms of food self-service are just a few of the additional ways in which customers are forced to work in order to consume. Most of the shopping for food and clothing is done by women, although most people, regardless of sex, at times have to do this kind of work. Glazer (1984), whose research on the emergence of self-service in retailing is presented in this volume, has convincingly argued that this is "involuntary unpaid labor." Although it is perceived as privatized work done by women for the benefit of their families, it is work that benefits commercial capital by drastically lowering its distribution and retail costs. Under such conditions "women's unwaged work can be understood to be appropriated by capital" (see Glazer in this volume).

The notion that capital actually appropriates consumers' unwaged labor is, in my view, a powerful metaphor emphasizing the fact that capital unquestionably benefits from this primarily female labor. However, capital can appropriate surplus value *only* through the exploitation of wage labor; the effect of unwaged consumption work is to allow capital to lower the overall level of wages and increase the rate of exploitation, as the reduction in the costs of consumer goods made possible by self-service in fact cheapens labor power.

This kind of unwaged labor takes place, therefore, outside the household and entails—from the standpoint of capital—a process of *work transfer* from the realm of waged labor to that of unpaid labor. From the standpoint of households, on the other hand, it entails a transfer of unwaged labor from the "private" to the "public" sphere. This transfer, as Glazer points out, is part of a general process designed to lower both the costs of retailing and the cost and quality of health care and other services which were, in the past, performed by waged workers. Given that most of those services were performed by low-waged female labor, the present trend leading to their transformation into "family responsibilities" essentially means that it is the unpaid labor of women which will fill the gap in the necessary services needed for childcare, care of the elderly, care of the sick in hospitals, etc. As is obvious, this process of transformation of waged into unwaged labor generates unemployment, lowering the bargaining power of workers and contributing to the ability of capital to lower the level of wages. Growth in unwaged consumption work, therefore, allows capital to reap greater profits through two channels: the cheapening of labor power, and the increase in its ability to discipline the labor force and impose lower wages.

Another form of work transfer takes place when manufacturers not only reduce the costs of distribution but also the assembly costs; increasing numbers of household goods (furniture, exercise equipment, toys, etc.) require not only that the customer work at the place in which the goods are sold and take care of their delivery, but also that they be assembled at home. The high cost of paying wage workers a living wage is thus reduced for manufacturers, while customers must spend some of their "free time" doing unpaid assembly and finishing work under the guise of consumption.

Renting equipment to do some kinds of household work or home improvements, instead of calling for the services of a company, is another form in which people perform unpaid labor; in this case, however, it is for themselves, not for capital. Only exceptionally wealthy households can afford to pay a living wage for services; those who can pay only for equipment, tools, and other materials use their own labor to produce many of the goods and services that enhance their standard of living. The home improvements industry has thus become "a subcontractor to the producing household" (Burns 1977, 43).

## Waged Labor as a Necessary Condition for Unwaged Labor

In the United States today, what is the economic and political significance of the process whereby paid labor is replaced by unpaid labor? How does it affect the reproduction of various kinds of labor power? How does it affect workers' ability to struggle for higher wages? Can unpaid labor be a basis for the sustenance of households, as some would want to believe in their celebration of "household capitalism" (see, for example Burns 1977, particularly ch. 3)? Could workers turn to their useful labor as a source of subsistence in these times of high and persistent unemployment? Could unemployed workers, in other words, use some of the survival strategies of workers in the periphery, transforming their households into small commodity-production units or small-scale food or services providers? Could the intensification of unwaged domestic labor contribute to stretch low wages?

The present crisis of accumulation has reduced millions of persons to poverty or near-poverty levels. The poverty rate reached 15.2 percent in 1983, the highest level since 1966, while the number of people below the poverty level, over 35 million, was the highest since 1964 (O'Hare 1985, 8). By 1986, the poverty rate had declined to 13.6 percent and the number of people below the poverty level reached 32.4 million (U.S. Bureau of the Census, 1987b, 1). The persistence of high unemployment rates in many parts of the country during the last few years, however, has had a devastating impact upon millions of families and their communities (Bluestone and Harrison 1982; Buss, Redburn, and Waldron 1983; Piven and Cloward 1985; Patton and Patton 1984; Congressional Quarterly 1983). Sluggish economic recovery has been accompanied by the increased immiseration of the working classes. This is reflected primarily in the decline in real wages, especially among young male workers (Dollars & Sense 1987, 10), and the enormous increase in the labor force participation of married women, particularly those with small children—54 percent of women with children under six were working in 1985, up from 34 percent in 1976 (O'Connell and Bloom 1987, 7) and 12 percent in 1950 (Baldwin and Nord 1984, 18). In 1984, 53 percent of all married women and 65 percent of all married women with school age children (ages six to seventeen) were in the labor force, up from 24 percent and 28 percent respectively in 1950 (Baldwin and Nord 1984, 18).

The greatest declines in employment during the late 1970s took place in the manufacturing and construction industries, which offer the best wages for blue collar workers. As the economy slowly recovers, it does so through sectoral changes and changes in the division of labor which offer relatively few opportunities for most of the presently unemployed. A recent study by Bluestone and Harrison (1986) indicates that over 50 percent of the eight million net new jobs created in the United States between 1979 and 1984 paid less than $7,000 a year, well below the 1983 official poverty threshold of $10,178 for a family of four (O'Hare 1985, 6). The decline in the demand for skilled blue collar labor has been accompanied by some increases in the demand for technical and scientific labor and for relatively unskilled and low-paid production and service labor. According to the Bureau of Labor Statistics, for example, the fastest job growth between 1984 and 1995 is likely to occur mainly in occupations at the top (e.g., lawyers, physicians, and surgeons) and bottom of the occupational hierarchy (waiters and waitresses, janitors, cleaners, etc.) with very few jobs in between (U.S. Bureau of the Census 1987a, 384):

> Between 1973 and 1986, the number of blue collar workers . . . increased by only 4.4 percent. In contrast, men's employment in service occupations—for example, security guards, orderlies, waiters, day care workers, and janitors—increased by 36.7 percent. (Dollars & Sense, 1987, 10)

Consequently, large numbers of men are unable to find jobs similar in pay and skills to those they have lost and thus are unable to support their families as in the past. Most working class households today need the wages of at least two adults to keep above the poverty line; the "family wage" is no longer a realistic possibility for most workers. This problem has been exacerbated by the fact that employers, to cut labor costs, impose wage cuts at the time new contracts are negotiated and/or demand a lower starting salary for many blue and white collar jobs. Working class poverty is further intensified by cuts in the federal budget which affect badly needed social services. In turn, these cuts generated enormous pressures on state and local budgets which now have to cope with substantial increases in the demand for their help.

The effects of these changes on the lives of millions of people is shown by the evidence beginning to emerge from a variety of reports from special interest groups, research institutes, and congressional documents. Most waged and salaried workers have few if any savings, and their major assets are their homes and cars. Unemployment forces them to cut expenses in food, medical, and dental care. Once unemployment insurance, compensation, and severance pay are exhausted, many go on welfare or have to rely on food stamps; they use up their savings and, eventually, after missing payments on cars or other credit purchases, they lose these goods. Many also lose their homes when the new jobs they are able to get do not pay enough to keep up mortgage payments. A new category of poor appears in the soup lines; the "new poor," who until recently had been relatively prosperous, now join the ranks of those in need of food and shelter. The estimated national total homeless population ranges between 240,000 to 1,000,000 (Congressional Quarterly 1983, 135). Long-term unemployment also has devastating effects on people's physical and psychological well-being; domestic violence of all kinds, alcohol abuse, insomnia, depression, and suicide increase under these conditions (Congressional Quarterly 1983, 129; see also Buss, Redburn & Waldron, 1983).

I have described in some detail the consequences of unemployment to highlight the vulnerability of working class households in this country. Among vast sectors of the laboring masses in the periphery, households may be appropriately conceptualized as "income-pooling units" only partially dependent on a wage for their survival (for a thorough exploration of the theoretical significance of this concept see Smith, Wallerstein, and Evers 1984). In the context of the United States, the degree of proletarianization of the population has led to a situation in which the concept of "wage-dependent households" might be more appropriate to characterize the conditions under which most workers live. Given that all households—regardless of class—include as a component of their total income goods and services produced by domestic labor (which is paid labor in its entirety only in the households of the very wealthy), there is a general abstract sense in which all households can be viewed as income-pooling units. But the experience of the unemployed in the United States shows their virtually *total* dependence on wages for basic survival. This is exactly what advanced proletarianization means: the separation of the vast majority of the population from any access to viable means of production which, unavoidably, generates total dependence on wage income.

While some households may have some resources which allow them to survive without a wage or salary input (e.g., rental income, income from farms or from other businesses), it is unlikely that the vast masses of the unemployed will be able to pull themselves up by their bootstraps through the use of their own labor. It is the case that when real wages begin to fall, some households can stretch their wages through an intensification of domestic labor. Women work harder, things are repaired and mended, and all household members make do with less. This is contradicted, however, by the fact that drastic declines in real wages, such as those that have taken place in recent years, have been reflected in the enormous increase in female employment and "dual-paycheck" families. As is obvious, women's employment, especially when it is full time, reduces women's ability to intensify home production of use values to stretch the wage (Waite 1981, 11–12; J. Smith in this volume). Furthermore, while women's wages keep households afloat while their unemployed husbands seek work, their lower salaries are frequently not sufficient, in the long-run, for mortgage payments and other debts. Once unemployment benefits are exhausted, households are left in a desperate situation unless other members can find paid employment.

The preceding discussion highlights the fact that, in the circumstances created by advanced capitalist development, the sale of labor power by at least one wage earner is *the* major condition that allows for the productive use of unwaged labor in the household—for the production of goods and services for internal consumption and for the market as well; "reproductive activities are possible only insofar as they come in contact with the capitalist wage relationship" (Smith 1984, 67). In wage- or salary-dependent households, waged labor is the condition for the productive combination of unwaged labor and means of household production (Gimenez 1982). A second important condition for the productive use of unwaged labor is the possession of skills. Proletarianization, as Braverman (1974) and others after him have shown, entails a constant process of skilling and deskilling of workers. As new skills emerge commanding high wages, in time they are fragmented into their component elements, lowering workers' skills and wages.

The universalization of commodity production also implies, at this level of analysis, the relative deskilling of domestic workers. While what Cowan (1983) has called the "industrialization of housework" entails the learning of new skills to use modern household technology, it also entails the loss of skills that could have been used to turn domestic labor towards market-oriented production. What is more important, the cheapening of some basic subsistence goods—food and clothing—through mass production, self-service, and the availability of cheap imports makes it impossible for home-produced goods to compete in the market with mass-produced goods, even if people still had the necessary skills. Most working class households in the United States could not become cottage industries when unemployment strikes, not only because of the lack of financing the household's wages could initially provide, but also because market conditions and the relative lack of skills of most people would make that transition extremely difficult. This is in clear contrast to the countries of the periphery, where cottage industries continue to flourish as a crucial source of supplementary income. In the United States, even if unemployed workers have skills (furniture making and repair, auto repair, dressmaking, etc.), the average salaried or waged household cannot afford such services and opts for mass produced goods or the use of domestic unwaged work to repair cars and some appliances. The very high (from the standpoint of working class households) hourly wages of service people have pushed more and more people to learn how to do those things themselves. The peculiar dialectics of waged and unwaged labor under conditions of extreme proletarianization as in the United States have thus led to the relative economic uselessness of unwaged useful labor. The production of use values (for household consumption or for the market) via useful unwaged labor is thus subordinate to the production of exchange values via waged or salaried labor.

The rule of capital is thus manifest in the subordination of unwaged to waged labor, of useful labor to abstract labor. Unemployment would not be a threat if households were only partially dependent on wages or salaries and could switch their income from wage to non-wage income when unemployment strikes. The success of proletarianization is the stripping of households of their income pooling capacity insofar as it could be used to ensure economic survival outside the wage relation. Production, therefore, determines reproduction in ways that vary with employment status and location within the various strata in which propertyless workers are distributed. Total dependence on a wage or salary to survive means that employment and wage/salary levels condition the ability of households to engage in some or all the forms of unwaged labor previously discussed:

a) domestic labor engaged in the production of use values for household consumption (i.e., labor that enters in the process of physical and social reproduction at the daily and generational levels),

b) domestic labor engaged in consumption work (shopping, self-service, and transportation of purchases),

c) domestic labor engaged in the production of use values for home maintenance and improvements (i.e., labor that reproduces households' "infrastructure"), and

d) domestic labor engaged in the production of goods and/or services for the market (e.g., "cottage industries" of all kinds, word processing, childcare).

## Class and Intra-Class Differences in the Use of Unwaged Labor for the Process of Physical and Social Reproduction

How does the differential ability of households to take advantage of their unwaged labor affect the reproduction of the capitalist class and of the various socioeconomic strata (i.e., "poor," "working class," "middle class," "upper-middle class," etc.) in which the working class (i.e., the class of propertyless waged/salaried workers) is fragmented at the level of market relations?

Recent economic changes in the United States resulting in declining living standards in the working class have been accompanied by an increase in the concentration of income at the top, the growth of a small but privileged "upper-middle class sector" (with incomes above $47,000), and the "shrinking of the middle class" (Rose 1986, 9–11). Upper and upper-middle class sectors represent a growing market for specialty stores; for hand-made, labor-intensive and relatively unique goods (e.g., pottery, "wearable art"); and for expensive personal services. Those who can use type $d$ unwaged labor to take advantage of these narrow markets are generally persons with specialized skills from "middle class" background; they may be suddenly unemployed professionals or skilled workers who can successfully use their skills, often blessing the day they lost their jobs. But my major concern in this essay is not with the small "cottage industry" sector catering to the needs of the privileged. Instead, I am concerned with the conditions that affect the ability of wage-dependent households to use their labor resources to survive, to engage in the tasks of physical and social reproduction, and to improve their quality of life.

The dialectics of waged and unwaged labor among the steadily employed and more affluent sectors of the working class are quite different from those which obtain among the poorer sectors, particularly those afflicted with periodic lay offs, unemployment or underemployment. Among the employed and relatively affluent working classes, households have the ability to use types $a$, $b$ and $c$ unwaged labor to produce a standard of living that would be unaffordable at market prices. As indicated earlier, because of market conditions that make it difficult for most households—except those of the very wealthy—to pay a living wage for labor needed for household repairs, cleaning, improvements, etc., and because of manufacturers' and retailers' cost-cutting strategies, most adults in the United States engage in increasingly larger quantities of unwaged labor inside and outside their homes. These forms of unwaged labor are wage or salary-dependent; the amount of unwaged labor time households can generate to their advantage depends on their levels of income and the amount of labor time already exchanged for that income. There is, in other words, a direct relationship between income level, the quantity and kind of unwaged labor households can generate, households' standard of living, and the quality of labor power they reproduce.

Given that women are the major providers of types $a$ and $b$ unwaged labor, their employment lowers the amount of housework they do, as time-use surveys show (Waite 1981, 11–12). When real wages fall and married women enter the labor force, and when single mothers work, the quantity of type *a* unwaged labor available falls (e.g., fast foods replace homemade meals); type *b* declines in some respects (e.g., food shopping); and the overall quality of life may decline, particularly for single mothers. Depending on the size of their combined income and stage in the life cycle, working couples might experience a decline in the quantity of home-cooked meals and housecleaning, and increases in types *b* and *c* unwaged labor resulting in home improvements and repairs. In low income dual-earner working class households, the quantity of waged-labor time required for basic survival increases without providing the monetary basis for the use of unwaged labor to their advantage. Under these conditions, the quantity of types *a*, *b*, and *c* unwaged labor these households can use is likely to decline, especially type c labor because it requires money for the purchase or rental of tools, materials, etc. While affluent "dual-career" households can simply purchase domestic labor and other services, low income "dual-paycheck" working class households have to make do with less, sacrificing standards of consumption and childcare. "Dual-career" households and, in general, affluent upper-middle class households are able to substitute services purchased directly from individuals (e.g., servants, baby-sitters, gardeners) or from companies that provide services (housecleaning, lawn care, childcare, repair of household appliances, etc.), for some of the socially necessary labor time that would have to be spent in types *a* and *b* unwaged labor. At the same time, they can increase the quantity of time spent in less arduous and more appealing forms of *b* and *c* unwaged labor, thus improving considerably their home environment and their quality of life. On the basis of the preceding discussion, it is possible to make the following generalizations pertinent to households of waged and salaried workers who are, in terms of their location in the relations of production, propertyless workers (i.e., they do not own income-producing property or capital):

1) Dual-earner households—given time constraints and women's primary responsibility for domestic labor—are likely to experience a decline in the quality of life if their ability to use type *a* unwaged labor to their advantage declines, without being accompanied by the ability to substitute market services.

2) The higher the total household income, the greater the ability of households to substitute (at least on a part time basis) purchased services for type *a* unwaged labor and to use types *b* and *c* unwaged labor to their benefit.

3) The higher the socioeconomic status (i.e., ranking based on levels of income, education, and type of occupation), the greater the ability of

households to substitute purchased services for most or all of the most arduous and less creative forms of types *a, b* and *c* unwaged labor, and the greater its ability to use all three types of unwaged labor primarily for the considerable improvement of their quality of life.

The ultimate product of unwaged domestic labor, in its three forms, is the physical and social reproduction of social classes on a daily and generational basis. As income levels rise, householders tend to relieve themselves of the labor that enters into physical reproduction, by purchasing services through the market, or through relations of personal dependence with servants. In other words, the greater the household's income level, the greater the ability of people to spend "quality time" with their children, and the better able they are to concentrate on the pleasant tasks of social reproduction through enhancing their personal development, social life, and home environment. This process of structural and functional differentiation[1] in the context of unwaged domestic labor relations is fluid and its outcome fluctuates, in propertyless households, with socioeconomic status, the number of adults who work, and marital status.

Unless income levels are high, single parents—especially single mothers—are less likely to be able to focus on the social dimensions of domestic unwaged labor. In very affluent single- or dual-earner households, women and men are unlikely to engage in unwaged labor, except those types dealing with social reproduction. And in very wealthy households (i.e., capitalist households), in contrast to what takes place in working class households, even household management can be left to butlers and housekeepers, while the lady of the house is concerned exclusively with the tasks of social reproduction on a daily and generational basis (and even those are likely to be shared with social secretaries, governesses and tutors; see Gimenez 1978, 315–319).

Among the propertyless classes[2]—regardless of their "socioeconomic status" at the level of market relations—waged/salaried labor is the necessary condition for people's access to the material conditions required for their physical and social reproduction on a daily and generational basis. The class that controls the means of production also controls people's access to the conditions of reproduction. At the level of market relations, this means that employment conditions the exercise of unwaged labor; in the absence of a wage, unless the state intervenes, people are left to fend for themselves in ways that vary according to the place of their countries in the world-system.

In core countries, there are welfare systems that make it possible for the unemployed, and those unable to participate in the labor force, to survive at a minimum level of subsistence. The welfare state intervenes to pay for the physical (but not the social) reproduction of the labor force at substandard levels—so that many households are forced to reproduce the unemployable layers of the reserve army of labor. Even when the welfare check and other government transfers are combined with domestic labor, they are frequently insufficient to allow for the economic recuperation of households, and for the reproduction of labor power in a marketable form. In fact, an important effect of long term unemployment and welfare dependency in core countries is the stripping of a large proportion of poor households from their last important economically productive role: the reproduction of labor power. Instead, they simply reproduce people; and people, in themselves, without marketable skills, have no value under capitalist conditions. Each crisis of accumulation increases the population of the unemployed and the unemployable by expelling from the work force—sometimes forever—millions of workers and their families. Their numbers are augmented also through natural increase, thus presenting a problem insurmountable within the parameters of the system.

## On Domestic Labor and the Oppression of Propertyless Women

As shown so far in this essay, the dialectics of paid and unpaid labor in the propertyless class are such that unpaid labor is thoroughly dependent on paid labor for its utility to the household. By propertyless class I refer to the vast majority of people in the United States who depend on wages or salaries for survival; this propertyless class is stratified on the basis of income, education, and occupation. It would be out of place here to enter into the debate about the class location of the so-called middle classes. For the purposes of developing my argument, I will point out that it is possible to differentiate strata at the level of market relations (e.g., working, middle, upper-middle classes), based on individuals' income, education, type of occupation, place of residence, and overall standard of living. On the other hand, at the level of relations of production, these "classes," insofar as they share a similar relation to the means of production (i.e., they are propertyless), are subject to the constraints inherent in the nature of domestic labor. All households, regardless of socioeconomic status, are faced still with the fact that domestic labor is socially necessary and cannot be indefinitely postponed, particularly in the case of childcare or the care of the sick or elderly.

Feminist thinking to date has been focused primarily on the fact that domestic labor is defined as *women's labor* and has, as such, important and real negative effects on the lives of women and on their ability to attain economic and social equality. Even when working full time, women continue to be responsible for most of the housework and childcare. To change this situation, feminists have advocated, in addition to equal opportunities for women in the economic sphere, childcare services and changes in the sexual division of labor in the home. Some have perceived both waged and unwaged women's labor as labor controlled by men for their benefit—the material basis of patriarchy (see, for example, Hartmann 1981, 18).

The origins of the oppression of women today cannot be sought in primordial relations between the sexes or in male conspiracy theories, but in the historically specific ways in which the relationship between men and women are structured as agents of production and reproduction in different social classes and strata within classes. Under capitalism, the class that controls the means of production also controls and determines the relative access of the propertyless classes to the means and conditions for their social and physical reproduction. The development of capitalism, the tendency towards the universalization of commodity production, and the proletarianization of the labor force have indeed structured the relations of physical and social reproduction between the sexes and, therefore, domestic labor, in historically specific ways (see Gimenez 1982, 1987; see also G. Smith in this volume). One important dimension of these processes has been the "industrialization of housework" (Cowan 1983) and the erosion of the ability of working class households to use domestic labor for stretching the wage. A second and relatively overlooked consequence of those processes, with momentous significance for most propertyless women, has been the relative eradication of the servant strata as a stable and widespread participant in the relations of physical and social reproduction. In countries of the periphery, domestic service is still one of the major sources of men's and women's employment, particularly in Latin America (Boserup 1970; Rollins 1985, 38–48). Not only the rich, but also middle and working class families have access to domestic servants often on a full-time, live-in basis. The rich and the affluent can afford skilled servants; others can have as live-in servants, in exchange for board and room, orphan girls or the daughters of the rural or the urban poor.

In the United States, on the other hand, "at no time . . . have even half of the households in the nation been able to have such help full time" (Cowan 1983, 119). In the nineteenth century young unmarried women and immigrant women worked as maids, and the 1870 census shows that about one million women—half of the women employed for wages—were domestic workers. During the early twentieth century, decline in immigration and growth in other employment opportunities led to a decline in the number of white women willing to do domestic work: from white and single, the domestic labor force became black and married. The inclusion of domestic work under government regulations requiring the payment of income taxes, social security, and contributions to unemployment funds, increased the cost of domestic servants beyond what most households could afford, pushing such employment underground and making it hard to estimate accurately the number of participants. While having at least a full-time maid was the acknowledged symbol of middle class status in the nineteenth century, today the number of domestic servants has declined drastically (from 28.7 percent of the female labor force in 1900 to 5.1 percent in 1970, and a maid is certainly not required for middle class status (Cowan 1983, 120–122; Rollins 1985, 53–57).

The hiring of domestic workers on a part-time basis, however, is relatively widespread in the United States. Part of the supply of domestic labor comes from people who work on a temporary, part-time basis (e.g., teenagers, students, housewives who might need extra money for while, etc.), in addition to those who support themselves through such work. Domestic work is also provided by commercial enterprises who hire wage workers to provide housecleaning services to those who can afford them. Only the very affluent and the capitalist class, of course, can afford full-time, live-in servants. Furthermore, there is a qualitative difference between the hiring of temporary and sporadic domestic help (e.g., baby-sitters, biweekly cleaning women, etc.) and the practice, common among the affluent and the wealthy in core countries and vast sectors of the population in periphery countries, of having live-in domestic servants, or servants who come daily and stay from morning to night.

The examination of the dialectics between waged and unwaged labor sheds light on the fact that *domestic labor*, widely held as one of the material conditions that determine the oppression of women, has a *dual nature* grounded in the material conditions in which it takes place in different social classes. As structured by capitalist development in core countries, *domestic labor is unwaged labor among the propertyless classes;* it is not only one of the historically specific material conditions that determines the oppression of propertyless women under capitalism, but *owes its specificity to the fact that capitalism has eroded the material basis that made possible the existence of a servant strata catering to the needs of vast sectors of the propertyless class during the early stages of capitalist development.* This fact, which is the inexorable outcome of the process of capitalist development as a whole, is also one of the crucial *structural determinants* of the emergence of the women's liberation movement in core countries, of the positive reception of the movement among middle and upper-middle class upwardly mobile, career-oriented white women, and of the directions taken by the feminist analysis of the family and the sexual division of labor.

The women's movement of the late 1960s and 1970s, like all political movements, had in addition to political and ideological determinants, structural, objective determinants. The latter had to do with demographic and economic changes resulting in the presence of a larger-than-ever number of adult and young women in the labor force and in higher education, higher divorce rates, and the military draft which pushed many married women to the labor force. *Another important structural condition was the fact that most propertyless women, regardless of their socioeconomic status and level of education were, for all practical purposes, servants in their own homes.* This, in combination with the other factors listed above, was a powerful determinant of the positive acclaim with which Betty Friedan's *The Feminine Mystique* (1963) was received. This is a book that captured the discontent of white, affluent, and educated middle class women with the narrowness of their lives as domestic workers secluded in their suburban, appliances/filled homes. This book, which has been called "the single inspiration of the movement" (Mitchell 1971, 52) could not have experienced the success it did if it had not reflected the experiences of millions of women; furthermore, it could not have been written if the material conditions for the "problem that had no name" not only existed but were widespread. In other words, it would not have been successful if the vast majority of relatively affluent middle class housewives had had access to permanent domestic help on the scale it is available to the upper classes in core countries and to vast sectors of the population in periphery countries.

The other side of the "industrialization of housework," which enables women to do what would have required the help of husbands, children, and/or servants in the past, is the demise of domestic servants as regular, expected members of middle class and even working class households. This has entailed the structural and functional transformation of *all* propertyless women, except the most affluent, into domestic servants themselves; that is, they are transformed—for all practical purposes—into servants in their own households, servants who, as feminists have pointed out, are not only on call twenty-four hours a day but are also unpaid, engaged in invisible and seemingly valueless labor. Sociologically, one could refer to this process as one of functional integration in which—among the "middle classes,"—two roles, the role of servant (primarily engaged in tasks of physical reproduction) and the role of "lady of the house" (primarily engaged in management and tasks of social reproduction) became fused into one single role, the housewife. It is, on the other hand, obvious that the vast masses of working class women never played the role of "lady of the house," while many poor immigrant and non-white women (especially black women) were forced into the servant role.[3]

The ideological construction of domestic labor emphasizes the tasks of social reproduction and minimizes those of physical reproduction. This, and the fact that feminist analysis tends to focus on the oppression of women "as women," minimizing class differences, has resulted in an analysis of domestic labor that neglects the differential impact upon women's consciousness and political interests of the fact that the tasks of physical and social reproduction do not constitute a monolithic unit oppressing all women. It neglects the variation—within the propertyless class—in the degree of differentiation of such tasks, i.e., the extent to which some housewives must do both or can concentrate mainly on social reproduction, while women from the less privileged strata of the propertyless class must earn a living working for low wages or for other women, neglecting, to some extent, their need to use their labor for their own households.

The structural and functional differentiation between the servant rate and the wife role is permanent in the households of the capitalist class and the most affluent strata. Among the propertyless, it varies according to levels of income and education. In capitalist and very affluent households, domestic labor engaged in the tasks of physical reproduction is paid labor; that which deals with social reproduction is partially paid labor. Among most propertyless households, domestic labor is unwaged. As socioeconomic status increases, households are more likely to substitute paid labor for their unwaged domestic labor in the less pleasant tasks of physical reproduction. The ability of working women, particularly of career and professional women, to work and have families, depends more on their ability to purchase domestic labor than on a radical reorganization of the household division of labor (see, for example, Holmstrom 1972). Most working class women, however, have managed with little or no extra help, to the detriment of the quality of working class life. While the *need* for childcare services, for example, was always there, the *demand* (backed with money) became visible and grew as middle and upper-middle class women entered the labor force.

The impact of *The Feminine Mystique*, the appeal of the women's movement among white collar workers and professional women, and the feminist demand for nurseries and childcare services that could allow women to have careers and families at the same time, all reflect the realities of the structure of domestic work in the core capitalist countries. The demand for childcare itself reflects the options open to a society in which an ideological commitment to political equality makes the call for more and affordable servants a political impossibility, at least at the level of public utterance. But practice tends to differ from theory, and in practice those who can afford it hire domestic labor in the quantity and quality they can afford. In fact, the "liberation" of professional and career women and the ability of vast numbers of working women to work is predicated on the labor of other women, a large proportion of which are immigrant and non-white women.

One of the topics that has occupied a central place in the context of feminist writing, both theoretical and political, has been the domestic conflict emanating from men's resistance to do their fair share in domestic work. The material basis of this conflict (i.e., the fact that most property-less households rely primarily in the unpaid domestic labor of wives and daughters) is absent from households where most of the tasks of physical reproduction are done by servants or by the waged workers employed by companies providing cleaning and childcare services for a fee. To make the point differently, to the extent feminism in the periphery may be limited to the left or to the scholarly concern of a few—generally foreign-educated—women, this may reflect the widespread availability of domestic servants who work for full-time housewives as well as for working women. In fact, from the standpoint of the average middle class or professional woman from the periphery, the lot of their U.S. counterparts leaves much to be desired, to the extent that they lack permanent domestic help. These remarks, tentative as they are, should highlight the complexity of the structural determinants of the oppression of propertyless women in core and periphery countries while placing at their center the dialectics between waged and unwaged labor.

## Conclusion

This essay has focused on the changing relationship between paid and unpaid labor, and on the significance of the latter for capital accumulation, household survival, and the oppression of propertyless, especially working class women. Unwaged labor—as a quantity of labor that benefits capital by cheapening the value of labor power and undermining the relative power of the working class—takes place in a variety of settings. At the *level of circulation* of commodities, it is embodied in the vast amount of time consumers spend in self-service activities of all kinds. At the *level of production*, unpaid labor takes place at home; it is labor primarily, but not exclusively, executed by men in the process of assembling and finishing goods. At the *level of physical and social reproduction* (daily and generationally) of different social classes and strata within classes, I also examined the usefulness of unwaged domestic labor for the economic survival of households. I argued that the intense proletarianization that has taken place in the United States, as a core country, indicates that a conceptualization of working class households as wage-dependent units would be more useful than the notion of income-pooling units. Proletarianization and universalization of commodity production in the United States have abolished the conditions that would, theoretically, allow households to use domestic labor for market oriented production. Wage-labor is the condition for the usefulness of unwaged labor and, paradoxically, the higher the wage or salary, the greater the contribution of types *b* and *c* of unwaged labor to a household's quality of life. On the other hand, the lower the wage, the greater the economic importance of type *a* unwaged domestic labor, particularly in families with two adults where only one works outside the home. In dual-earner households (currently the most numerous in the United States), the quantity of type *a* unwaged domestic labor actually declines. The decline in real wages, the fact that women's jobs are generally low-paid, and the lack of affordable childcare force many single mothers to become wards of the state. Their situation highlights the problems created when the price of unskilled labor falls below the cost of its daily and generational reproduction. Under those conditions, given the socially necessary nature of domestic labor, women become full-time domestic workers paid by the state and, in that sense, unwaged domestic labor becomes, for all practical purposes, exceedingly low-paid waged labor.

I have linked the dialectics of waged and unwaged labor to the oppression of women through the analysis of the relationship between the capitalist structuring of the relations of physical and social reproduction between the sexes, and the eventual demise of the servant strata. If domestic servants had continued to be available on a permanent basis for vast sectors of the propertyless class, the women's movement—had it emerged at the time it did—might have taken a different direction, and the content of its ideology and theories might not have been the same. It is not a collusion between men, either individually or collectively, which placed propertyless women into the location of domestic unwaged workers, but the structural effects of the laws of capital accumulation, the secular trends towards a relative decline in the demand for labor combined with the universalization of commodity production and proletarianization, mediated by the material conditions of physical and social reproduction. Finally, I have shown the theoretical importance of examining class differences and intra-class differences, not only in the relative ability of households to use unwaged domestic labor for their benefit, but also in the extent to which the tasks of physical and social reproduction become structurally and functionally differentiated or integrated.

*Integration* entails the oppression of women as full-time domestic servants in their own households. Theoretically, this could be ameliorated by men agreeing to shoulder part of the burden (becoming part-time servants themselves), with help from friends and relatives, or with inexpensive paid full- or part-time domestic servants. I use the word ''servant'' not pejoratively, but to call attention to the fact that most of the tasks of physical reproduction are menial work, something that tends to be obscured when euphemisms such as ''housekeeper'' are used. While people in the core countries may treat their domestic help in ways far more democratic than in periphery countries, the social differences and the differences in social and economic power between those who hire and those who do the work do not disappear.

*Differentiation,* on the other hand, increases with level of wages and socioeconomic status, resulting in substitution of unwaged for paid domestic labor within the sphere of physical reproduction, while householders reserve for themselves the more pleasurable aspects of social and physical reproduction. While within the propertyless class differentiation fluctuates according to many factors impossible to examine in this essay (e.g., the level of education of women, age, stage in the life cycle, etc.), it is institutionalized within the capitalist class and the top layers of the petty bourgeoisie and socioeconomic stratification: here, domestic labor in charge of physical reproduction is always paid labor, while the tasks of social reproduction are shared in ways likely to vary with age, number of children, level of education, social expectations, and so forth.

Given the fact that the socialization of housework and childcare is unlikely to become a reality in the near future, the conflict between waged and unwaged labor as it exists today could theoretically be resolved, in the absence of widespread affordable quality childcare and provision of reliable and inexpensive housecleaning services, by the development of a new servant class, this time composed of immigrants whose willingness to work for low wages, or even for board and room, might make them accessible to working class households. Women's rate of labor force participation of over 50 percent in the United States is high if compared with past rates, but relatively low if compared to some western and eastern European countries; in 1980 it had reached 54 percent in Austria and the United Kingdom, 56 percent in Denmark, 60 percent in Finland, 71 percent in the U.S.S.R., and 69 percent in eastern Europe (Sivard 1985, 39–40). Using 1982 data on women's labor force participation, it has been estimated that childcare facilities would considerably increase those rates (e.g., from 47 percent to 59 percent among white women and from 56 percent to 79 percent among black women (O'Connell and Bloom 1987, 8). Hypothetically, similar increases could be expected to the extent affordable immigrant domestic servants were available. While the percentage of black domestic servants has considerably declined, their place is being taken by immigrant women, especially from the Caribbean and Latin America (Rollins 1985, 56–57). The extent to which the increased labor force participation of U.S. women, especially at the upper echelons of the occupational structure, is *already grounded* in the use of domestic servants (many of them immigrant and, perhaps, undocumented) has yet to be empirically established. Their number, however, is likely to be considerable. The uncertain immigration status of many domestic servants renders them vulnerable to exploitation and makes it difficult to find out their numbers and location. This is not pure speculation. Dill (1987) alerts us to these possibilities by suggesting that the self-interest of middle class women who want to work could lend support to proposals similar to that made by Anne Colamosca in *The New Republic,* which would seek to increase the availability of household help "with a government training program for unemployed alien women to help them become 'good household workers'" (cited in Dill 1987, 212). Clearly, the dialectics of waged and unwaged labor place the issue of domestic servants at the heart of "the woman question," highlighting the presence of social class contradictions and status antagonisms among women which are generally unacknowledged in the literature. This should call our attention to trends already in the making which reflect, in unexpected ways, the effects of the operation of the world-system upon both core and periphery countries through processes which might reproduce, in the future, periphery patterns in the core (i.e., the widespread use of domestic servants) while undermining them in the periphery, through proletarianization and political changes placing domestic servants beyond the reach of the average housewife.

# Part II

# THE SOCIAL RELATIONS OF
# UNWAGED WORK

*The articles included in this section examine the ways in which unwaged labor is structured in several contexts, and all represent an attempt to apply a socially and historically grounded Marxist analysis to forms of unwaged work. While each article attempts a rigorous specification of the articulation between unwaged work and labor and commodity markets, each is also attentive to the various non-market relations that are essential to the reproduction of the enterprises involved. Each documents the non-market mechanisms for the mobilization of labor, the informal sources of credit, and the understandings about work and the division of labor that support these arrangements.*

*Gavin Smith compares livelihood strategies and domestic politics among petty commodity producers in Huasicancha, central Peru, with those of their counterparts in the Pais Valenciano in the southeast of Spain. His concern is with the dynamic relationships between forms of waged and unwaged work. Not only do wage labor and markets provide imperatives to the self-provisioning sphere, he argues, but the developmental logic of the latter also modifies processes of wage labor and commodity production. The two cases he presents both demonstrate the erratic nature of the monetary economy and the way that this requires maintenance of the land and social networks that make unwaged work possible. It was the erosion of landholdings, as a result of the expansion of a large hacienda, that initially drove Huasicanchinos into petty commodity production. It was, in turn, the uncertainties associated with that form of production that reemphasized to them the need for a secure subsistence base and led to their struggle for more land. In the Pais Valenciano, Smith describes the ways that families allocate labor among self-provisioning, wage labor and a variety of forms of "putting-out" work. In both cases, he is concerned with how individuals actively manipulate networks surrounding kinship, community, and neighborhood.*

47

*Susana Narotzky describes women's work and the ideologies that support it in the region of Les Garrigues, Catalonia, Spain. The women she describes formerly worked on an unpaid basis for the household or* casa, *both in agriculture and in domestic tasks. Today, they are more and more drawn into the underground manufacture of clothing (in combination with domestic tasks), while mechanization has tended to separate them from most agricultural work. This process has gone hand-in-hand with a growing emphasis on the western-style nuclear family, at the expense of previous ideologies of the* casa. *Women are pressured by male family members to pursue the income derived from home clothing manufacture, in order to free the profits of the farm from the expenses of reproducing the household. The responsibility for household reproduction thus shifts from the domestic group as a whole to women in particular. At the same time, clothing contractors seek (and find) women workers because the ideology of family ensures their availability and willingness to work for a lower (supplementary) wage. The new ideology of family thus articulates—through its implications for women's work—the needs of the increasingly mechanized small farm enterprise and the demands of certain sectors of capital for low-cost manufactured goods.*

*Scott Cook describes women's production of petty commodities (mainly woven and embroidered goods and grass mats) in peasant-artisan households of Oaxaca, Mexico, and the way that shifts in productive relationships affect the cultural construction of gender and class. He begins by positing the following hypothesis: that when women become more involved in commodity production, this will generate conflicts in the allocation of their labor within the household. What he found was that women involved in petty commodity production work a "double day" in which they combine production for use, production for exchange, and childcare; and that, despite the economic return from their production, with few exceptions they referred to it as a hobby or pastime, or a way of helping out for awhile. Cook finds a greater consciousness of the value of what they produce, however, among women who are involved in putting-out work. He provides extensive transcriptions of the women's own statements about their work, its value, and the relation of commodity production to the domains of housekeeping and child care.*

*Dale Tomich addresses the issues of the articulation of self-provisioning with dominant production relations in an historical context. He examines the apparently widespread practice (at least in the nineteenth century Car-*

*ibbean) of granting slaves the use of parcels of marginal land on which to cultivate food for use or sale. The paper demonstrates the organic interdependence between slave self-provisioning and the export commodity production of the estates. It describes the changing historical relations between these forms of productive activity and the simultaneously complementary and conflicting interests they entailed. Tomich concludes by addressing the implications of slave self-provisioning for post-emancipation society.*

*Beyond their consideration of the interrelationships between dominant social relations and the non-market relations that structure unwaged work, all of the articles are attentive to struggles over the control of unwaged work, to the implications of unwaged activities for class relationships, and to the contradictions that arise—in lived experience—between waged and unwaged work regimes. Narotzky and Cook are able to demonstrate, through their presentation of the words of unwaged workers, the integral relationship between the work process, the social relations that structure it, and the workers' understanding of it. Gavin Smith, Narotzky, and Tomich present historical material that allows us to see that changes in unwaged work are neither unilaterally imposed nor the result of individualistic "survival strategies," but rather are the result of conflict and negotiation between the classes involved. The cases presented should do much to undermine the notion that unwaged production is "traditional," a "survival" of past practices, or an enclave of production isolated from the larger society. Each demonstrates clearly the dynamic relationship between world economy and local practices, and the conditions under which new forms of unwaged labor come into being.*

*Jane L. Collins*

# Chapter 3

## Negotiating Neighbors:
## Livelihood and Domestic Politics
## in Central Peru and the Pais Valenciano (Spain)

### Gavin Smith

> The bourgeois economist, whose limited mentality is unable to separate the form of appearance from the thing which appears within that form, shuts his eyes to the fact that even at the present time the labour-fund only crops up *exceptionally* on the face of the globe in the form of capital. . . .
>
> Entirely leaving aside all accumulation, the mere continuity of the production process, in other words simple reproduction, sooner or later, and necessarily, converts all capital into accumulated capital, or capitalized surplus value. Even if that capital was, on its entry into the process of production, the personal property of the man who employs it, and was originally acquired by his own labour, it sooner or later becomes value appropriated without an equivalent, *the unpaid labour of others materialized in the money form or in some other way.* [Emphases mine]
>
> —Marx, *Capital*

In these passages, Marx draws attention to the ubiquity throughout the world of production relations of a not strictly capitalist nature, on the one hand, and to the dynamic effects on social reproduction of surplus-extraction relations, on the other.[1] In Marx's day it was only in the minority of cases that the extraction of surplus took the form of the wage relationship and while that relationship is the most significant in our own day, it is probably still less widespread than other forms. On the other hand, Marx suggests that once capitalized surplus-value becomes an essential element in the reproduction of an enterprise, a certain iron logic sets in. The combination of these two observations gives rise to a quite complex set of possibilities, for two distinctions are alluded to: a distinction between commodified and non-commodified social relations, and a distinction between a *real* capital relationship and a merely formal one.

For social relations to be expressed through the medium of commodities, those relationships must appear to have an exchangeable value generalized throughout society (usually expressed in monetary form). The most obvious such relationship would be that of the wage, but it is important to note too that, when goods are exchanged as commodities, this simply means that the social relationships which went into their making are being given a value as well. Marx suggested that when commodities insert themselves between social relationships in this way, they reduce the particularistic and qualitative features of more direct and immediate personal ties. Commodities as concrete tokens of the relationships they embody can be stored over time and transported over space. The sociological effects are that, removed thus in time and space, the original relationships become alienated the one from the other, such that eventually the notion of the commodity as embodiment of the social relationships which created it becomes lost: the commodity itself becomes fetishized.

Marx's interst in the formal subsumption of labor is not entirely unconnected to the distinction between commodified and non-commodified relationships. He wanted merely to remark that often all the characteristics of the capital/labor relationship may superficially appear to be in place, while the real essence of capitalism was lacking. Driven to increase production, the "real capitalist" invests in more sophisticated machinery, rationalizes the organization of production, and so on. In the merely formal situation, we find capital and labor but, faced with competition, this capitalist resorts only to increasing the amount and intensity of the work the laborers do, using threats, inducements, and any other ideological devices at his or her disposal. In this case then, the demand for increased production does not focus attention on the (commodified) machine, but on the social relationships themselves and the terms which express those social relationships.

What concerns us here are the implications for domestic politics which arise when people's livelihoods span across these two sets of distinctions proposed by Marx, for in the majority of such production relations there is room for negotiation, which is another way of saying that every relationship is the outcome of struggle and every social category the subject of manipulation. This is especially important when we remember that subsistence is not the reflection of some kind of biological bedrock so much as it is "socially prescribed." The amount of labor in a production unit available for self-provisioning (or what is often referred to in a rather general way as "subsistence") is not not just necessary labor, but *socially* necessary labor. And social prescription doesn't just happen in some natural balance of functionally arrived-at consensus; rather, it is the outcome of the balance of forces, struggle and negotiation.[2] Market exchange is thus not inconsistent with subsistence production; through comparative advantage, market participation (in a variety of kinds of market) may offer a means of increasing the efficiency of labor within the overall subsistence sphere. According to this frame of reference, the relevant poles on a continuum are not those of sub-sistence and cash-cropping, but self-provisioning and surplus-appropriation. Since this understanding differs from some conventional notions of subsis-tence, I have used quotation marks around the term.

## Self-Provisioning and Domestic Activities

In this paper I want to use material from central Peru and southeast Spain to show how the social relations within the sphere of self-provisioning can-not be understood in isolation, but must be understood in terms of a strug-gle over appropriation—appropriation which occurs both through non-commodified relationships and through the commodified relationships we associate with petty commodity production and the sale of wage labor on the market. The issue is made more complex, moreover, by the fact that these two kinds of social relationships have distinct reproductive logics.

In the contemporary economies of Latin American and southwestern Europe, the dominant struggle in the countryside over the sphere of self-provisioning has shifted from one directed against appropriation through rents toward a dialectical interplay between the social relations of self-provisioning on the one hand and the social relations of fully commodified markets for labor or goods on the other. As a result, the social relations of self-provisioning cannot be isolated from the imperatives of those markets. It is not just that domestic relations, for example, cannot be understood outside the context of wage-labor imperatives, but also that the kinds of developmental logics referred to by Marx for simple reproduction (see also Bernstein 1979; Friedmann 1980; Kahn 1980; Chevalier 1982), are them-selves modified by the possibilities and limitations deriving from the sphere of self-provisioning, a characteristic referred to by Friedmann (1980) as "double specification."

In both of the cases examined here, enterprises are not only involved in agriculture but in a range of different sectors of the economy. Their multi-occupational nature and the heterogeneity of their form suggests that it may be less helpful to see the household as an agricultural concern linked to a family unit than to characterize it as a *livelihood-seeking enterprise* whose corporateness varies, whose memership is subject to manipulation, and whose members' rights and duties, while culturally prescribed, are not dis-tributed uniformly through the different types of enterprise. The terms the participants themselves use, therefore, to decribe crucial institutions and relationships—what Raymond Williams (1976) would call "keywords"—are therefore subject to distortions. These distortions derive simultaneously from the fact that enterprises have historically been located on the cusp between two different reproductive imperatives which effectively place different values on essential relationships, and at the same time from the ability this gives people to manipulate meanings.

Mingione (1983, 1986) has studied differential responses to economic recession (in Italy) by envisioning the household as pursuing its reproduction needs through three potential sources: monetary pursuits, "domestic activities,"[3] and "extraordinary domestic activities." The last refers to activities—such as clothes-making, chicken-rearing, or allotment cultivation—which might initially cater only to immediate family needs, but can be extended to serve a larger clientele. For the material to be discussed here, it is useful to see the linkage between these three sources as being the subject of struggle and negotiation *within* households (and communities), just as I have suggested for the struggle which occurs *beyond* the households over self-provisioning versus surplus-appropriation. Households in both cases are multi-occupational, seeking out livelihood by combining activities which give them access—directly or indirectly—to a cash income with others that provide subsistence needs. Differences between various enterprises can therefore be seen in terms of the way in which each allocates resources to meet these needs, combining monetary sources of income with the possibilities of saving on consumption costs through self-provisioning.

Mingione points out that the degree to which households can expand the proportion of total labor put aside for domestic activities toward "extraordinary domestic activities" is tied to the history of the way household members have been inserted into the structure of capitalism. Where demand for female wage labor has been high over a reasonably long period, normal domestic activities can be reduced by investment in domestic appliances, the purchase of services such as laundries and food processing, and use of public childcare facilities. The circuit of reproduction for such a household will clearly differ from one in a context where the demand for wage labor is low and erratic. In this case, the well-being of the household will have less to do with increasing the cash income than with reducing monetary costs by expanding domestic activities. Mingione himself is concerned with the effects of the restructuring of capital on households, and he points out that the social and political consequences of recession in the two hypothetical cases just described can be quite different. In the first case, domestic activities and the various networks associated with them have been so thoroughly eroded that the possibility of their future expansion toward "extraordinary domestic activities" is unlikely. It is more likely that such households will turn to increased political pressure for the provision of more extensive welfare services, and so forth. Mingione suggests that

come, it is noteworthy that agriculture too was pre-eminently cash-oriented, producing hemp, cotton, olives, almonds, and grain crops. An inadequate income from agriculture—be it in the form of share-cropping, day labor, or small-holding—was offset by a variety of non-agricultural pursuits, none of which could properly be described as proletarianized labor in the sense of large-scale capitalist factories.

While households in this region have a long history of combining agriculture with non-agricultural forms of income, this took a new turn—first with the expansion of the northwestern European economies (France, Germany, and the Benelux countries) and their demand for migrant labor—and then with "the Spanish miracle" after 1959. Prior to this period there had been a practice of men and women going to France to work in the grape harvest. By the late 1950s men began to take up industrial jobs. Whenever possible, their wives and children joined them. At the same time, small factories employing from one to two hundred workers sprang up in southern Pais Valenciano—chiefly making shoes, carpets, clothing, and toys. While men were most likely to find work in these factories, women and often adolescent children worked in the smaller workshops that did contracted outpiece work. Meanwhile in the homes, women's artisanal activities gave way to subcontracted home work, connected to shoe, clothing, and toy manufacture.

The growth in demand for non-agricultural labor took place within the context of small, highly competitive and often under-capitalized companies. In the shoe industry, for example, which was the largest source of employment for the people studied, firms were initially family-run and relied on a small number of major contracts from western Europe or the United States. Apart from a core of stonger firms, the rate of bankruptcy and turnover in ownership was very high, making employment extremely unreliable. In the agricultural sector meanwhile, improved irrigation and heightened demand led to the expansion of intensive crops, such as melons and artichokes, and the extension of the area devoted to orange and lemon orchards.

By the late 1970s and early 1980s the period of high demand began to slacken off, leading to a gradual restructuring of the non-agricultural sector. Generally this implied an increase in small, often illegal workshops and an attempt to replace factory workers with home workers. Meanwhile, a large irrigation scheme drawing water from the area's hinterland and supplying it to an area to the south lowered the water table for the old irrigation system of this area, making intensive agriculture and fruit production more difficult.

As with the Peruvian case then, households did not confine themselves to agricultural pursuits, but rather were multi-occupational in character. In both cases, too, monetary and non-agricultural sources of income were characterized by instability, uncertainty, and often geographical separation between those family members engaged in petty commodity production, or wage labor, and those working "at home." What the two cases serve to emphasize is that the erratic nature of this monetary income put pressure on the non-commodified self-provisioning domestic sphere, forcing its expansion toward what Mingione calls extraordinary domestic activities. But the possibilities provided in the social environment for expanding the non-commodified sphere were distinctive, resulting in development of different social relations and different forms of political expression.

*Peru*

Social relations were thoroughly modified for the Huasicanchinos during the late 1950s and early 1960s. This was a period in which migration was characterised by risk and uncertainty, and was institutionalised around linkages between colonies of migrants involved in petty trade and production on the one hand and the domestic enterprises of village residents on the other.

These arrangements can best be understood by reference to two elements in Huasicanchino social relations prior to this period. In the first place a household unit composed of an elderly mother or father, a married couple, and their unmarried children was frequently linked to a number of other households who had access to arable plots in slightly different ecological zones than their own (see Lehmann 1982), as well as to households with pastoral *estancias* in which they dispersed their livestock. The complex arrangements through which farming and pastoral activities were undertaken were such that the term "household" must be used with caution: children were moved from household to household according to labor and consumption requirements; arable plots were farmed for convenience by one household while pastoral activities were carried out by another. Reproduction was dependent upon these complex and extensive relationships (Smith 1979, 1989).

In the second place, the success of these arrangements was dependent upon adequate arable and pastoral land, yet from the latter part of the nineteenth century the expansion of neighboring haciendas eroded the community land base. The effect was that tasks initially done complementary to agriculture by many of households were taken on by a few households who began to provide a service for others. This included muleteering, petty trading, carpentry, pottery, weaving, and so on.

By 1972–73, when the major fieldwork was conducted, this past history had combined with contemporary economic conditions to generate a variety of domestic enterprises which for our purposes can be placed into three groups:[5]

(1) In the first place, there were migrant household enterprises which had come into existence—in the early 1950s—through the sale of livestock in Huasicancha. Such households would use the proceeds from their livestock operations to set up small trading and production operations in the provincial capital or Lima. A husband would transport fruit from the wholesale market to retail sellers at points throughout the city and sell fruit from a tricycle during the day. The wife would sell fruit from a fixed stall in the shantytown where they lived, take in washing, and do some child-minding. A son would take over the operation of the tricycle in the afternoon, freeing up his father to sell ornamental plants in middle class suburbs, the product of his wife's small garden in the shantytown.

These households not only began with livestock but, because pastoralism had tied them into a wide network of contacts, they also possessed broad personal networks, deriving from institutions having some continuity into the past. These networks have facilitated the establishment of domestic enterprises strategically located in Lima, in the provincial capital, in the mining centers, and in the village, where they are still engaged in livestock farming to some degree. This is accomplished, as in earlier periods, through joint ownership of livestock. That is, the village households involved in these networks—themselves engaged in a variety of different occupations—herd the livestock of migrant households with whom they have reciprocal links.

(2) A second type of migrant enterprise emerged from households where livestock husbandry was less important. A greater proportion of these families' resources (at the time of migration) derived from petty trading or artisan activities. These households had less-developed networks of personal ties and less capital resources in the form of livestock, and their migration experience took longer to become institutionalised. For these reasons they have found it more difficult to develop extended domestic enterprises of the kind described above. They have been more inclined to seek out skills which give them access to low-skilled jobs or to concentrate their resources in one trading operation.

In Lima this strategy takes an especially visible form in their concentration in ambulant strawberry-selling. This is a risky undertaking in which prices are volatile and spoilage great. Nevertheless, these people have formed a *sindicato,* or union of sellers, which acts as a source of mutual help, credit, labor exchange, and so on (as well as providing some protection against unbridled competition).

Because risks and uncertainty are a major characteristic of these operations, it is hardly surprising that these people too have invested heavily in livestock to offset such risks. Lacking the networks of the previous group, this was done originally by splitting the household, with women and young children caring for the farm in Huasicancha, while their husbands worked in Lima. Over the years, however, some of these households have managed to build up linkages with others in different sectors as in the previous type. Here, however, rather than being built on the old herding linkages, they emerge from friendship ties made in the work centers during the migration experience itself.

In both these two types of household then, the hazards of an erratic economy are offset by the multi-occupational activities of interlinked networks of households, and in this they differ from the third type to be discussed next. They also offset the hazards of petty commodity activity by investing in livestock back in the village. This propensity they share with the next type of household.

(3) This third type of enterprise is made up of migrants returned to the village, who have begun to herd livestock by supplementing their domestic labor with wage labor from the village. They have few linkages of the kind described for either of the two previous groups. This can be illustrated by reference to credit arrangements. An enterprise in one of the previous groups, in need of credit, would have first recourse to a member of its own network of friends and kin. Cash would be lent without interest, although it would be assumed that the creditor now held "shares" in whatever the cash was used for. Should the enterprise fail to raise cash in this way, however, it might go to one of these latter people. Here the enterprise would borrow money for interest and would be expected to put up collateral.

Such enterprises are in the process of systematically accumulating livestock and are engaged in a number of relationships which I would call "commodified." Even so, there are many benefits accruing to these enterprises which derive specifically from their membership in the community of Huasicancha, not the least of which is the political protection which has played such an important role in the past.[6] For this reason there are limits to the extent to which such enterprises can entirely remove themselves from the sets of "claims" described in the quote I made earlier from Gerald Sider (page 000).

In all these cases the self-provisioning sector has played a major role in the way in which people became inserted into the capitalist economy. But the extent to which these enterprises had available to them institutional arrangements to support this sector was quite different in each case. In Mingione's terms, it is clear that in all cases the "extraordinary domestic activities" were a precondition for the survival of the monetary activities. This was the case both where the male adult in a domestic unit migrated, leaving the wife, the old, and the young behind engaged in food production, and also where a household migrated while entering into arrangements with another in the village such that it could continue in food production.

Even so, non-commodified relationships were not uniformly available to all members of the community. People in the second category were constantly attempting to erect the kind of edifice used by the ex-pastoralists in the first category, but the resources in their immediate social environment were often not available. People in the first category continually voiced the desire to erect more distinct lines between their own domestic enterprise and those of others, as had those in the third category. It is notable, though, that even these latter enterprises—so close to being straightforward petty commodity producers—maintained their viability precisely by manipulating the non-commodified sphere not just of the labor of the immediate family, but of the community as a whole. In fact, it was these systematic accumulators who were the most vociferous spokespersons for the maintenance of the community's institutions.

So the survival of a broad area of non-commodified social relationships gives plasticity to the notion of the domestic. If in our own society commodified relationships seem to begin where our domestic family ends (see Harris 1982), this is not the case for the Huasicanchinos. Needless to say, this in turn affects gender relations within the immediate family. The pressure put on self-provisioning by an erratic petty commodity economy falls especially heavily on women in the latter two categories, but less so in the first because the "subsistence" activity of herding and crop production is distributed among a number of partner *households* in a confederation of households, rather than on individuals left behind in a fragmented household. It is also because these confederations depend on the maintenance of networks, many of which are sustained through the use of livestock inherited equally by both partners in a marriage. The more removed from such networks a household becomes, the more extensions into the area of unpaid labor—to increase the monetary end of the enterprise through greater self-provisioning—must be found from within the unit. This tends to increase the use of the labor of children, adult women, and older people.

## Spain

I have suggested for the Peruvian case that it was largely the need for a secure self-provisioning base that created pressure to regain the land on whch this base depended. In the Spanish case, taken from the area around Catral, in southern Valencia, people's struggle in the face of an erratic economy has taken a different form in line with the different social context within which households operate.

Throughout the 1970s young married and unmarried men found work in the nearby shoe factories around the local town of Elche. The work involved a low base pay with geometrically increasing piece-rates once a certain quantity of goods had been produced. On first working in the factory, many were surprised to find how difficult it was to reach even the base quantity of goods. In order to improve their output, men began to take unfinished goods home, where they left them with their wives who worked on them during the day. The operative then returned with them the following morning and thus acquired the higher piece-rates.

It soon became possible for a man with a position at the factory to subcontract his place at the machine to another and work full-time distributing work. Virtually all work-distributors in the area followed this career trajectory. Initially the pressure was on the wife to produce as many items as possible, with inadequate tools, and then to find friends and relatives who would also be interested in doing this kind of work. Once the husband moved into full-time distributing, however, he was able to provide home-based machinery to the women, through a variety of financing schemes.

The major problems faced by work-distributors were quality control on the one hand, and locating a series of subcontract workshops on the other. The speed at which women were required to work in home work led to erratic quality in the product, and inspecting the goods at the point of pick-up, or returning them thereafter, proved less practical than simply upgrading faulty items at home. The wives of work-distributors therefore had the twofold job of maintaining a network of home working women and upgrading items at home during the day. Apart from finding factories with batches available to be processed and then delivering them, often across widely dispersed areas, to the home workers, the husband had other tasks. One way of bidding for a batch was to offer to have two phases rather than one phase of the operation completed. Factory owners, wary of dealing with clandestine operations directly, were often happy to pass on this phase to work-distributors who then had to search out the often semi-legal smaller workshops where the next stage of the job was to be done.

Out-work of this kind took place within the context of a complex agrarian structure. In terms of agricultural enterprises, the area around Catral is made up of a few large farms, a greater number of farms worked directly by family labor supplemented by occasional paid labor, and then a majority of the population who own insufficient (or no) land to support the family and are dependent upon the sale of their labor. The labor available to an enterprise takes four forms: family labor, day labor, share-cropping, or reciprocal labor from one or more neighbors.

Day labor is extremely erratic and, until very recently, workers tried to offset uncertainty by cultivating the patronage of one or two farmers in regular need of labor. With the ending of the Franco regime, however, virtually all male day laborers belong to the PSOE (the Socialist Workers' Party of Spain) and its union and conditions of work and daily wages have been fixed. Among women, day labor is only taken on by older people and is restricted to crops requiring fluctuating seasonal demand for labor.

Share-croppers must be prepared to accept verbal contracts which tie them and their families into draconian working conditions. The attraction to a household head, however, is not just the flexibility share-cropping gives him in the exploitation of his own labor and that of his wife and children, generally it is also more secure than day labor, though this depends, since most agreements are only for the life of a specific crop (a few months for melons, a year for cotton, or a number of years of artichokes).

To these two forms of labor must be added a third: labor-pooling, in which three to five small farmers pool their labor and equipment. This often begins as an arrangement in which the crops each farmer plants depend on the proportions planted by the others, and so on. After one or two years of this practice, however, first one and then another partner tends to find work off the farm, until only one or two of the original partners are left farming on a contract basis for their "partners." (This is a practice to which orange and lemon production is especially well-suited.)

Any one farm entrprise will in fact combine many of these practices. A household with a small plot of its own land may also share-crop land belonging to another. Throughout the year, the husband may seek out day labor opportunities, and in certain seasons the wife will do so too. It is in households such as these that, traditionally, various artisan jobs took place and today women—wives and unmarried daughters—are engaged in home work. As a home-worker the woman accepts a certain amount of work from a distributor, which she processes on a machine she either hire-purchases or rents on financing arranged through the distributor.

The demands for work on the family's own farm are erratic—the husband/father, for example, may get a day's work and, finding a task on the farm left incomplete, will put pressure on his wife or daughter to put aside the home work in favor of the farm. In such circumstances a woman relies on being able to off-load work which she has already spoken for to a neighbor. Work-distributors, anxious to minimize the amount of traveling and contacting they have to do, moreover, encourage women to take large batches by paying geometrically higher rates up to the last item completed. To acquire these rates, home working women, already under pressure from their farming husbands, may speak for excessive batch sizes with a view to off-loading some to a neighbor. Even where this is not the case, the reputation for reliability, which is so crucial for women who wish to remain high-up on the distributor's list, depends on their ability to maintain a small but "friendly" network of neighbors who will "help out in a squeeze." Parallel to this network another, comprised largely of older female relatives—mothers, mothers-in-law, and aunts—is called upon to provide domestic services, such as childcare, washing, shopping, and occasional cooking, which are encroached upon by the heavy demands of home work and/or work on the farm.

This then is one form of multi-occupationality. But in a situation where no one source of income is reliable, there is a continual tendency for capital-spread: the head of a farm sufficient to support a family invests in a small canning operation, a transport firm, or a retail outlet. As he increasingly draws upon domestic labor for the operation of these new enterprises, he finds that he must denude the farm of such labors, and hence the farm cannot be properly run. In such a case, the need for close supervision and management decisions makes the use of day labor unattractive. An informal share-cropping agreement is therefore struck.

Another solution, however, would be to turn to one of those farmers who stayed back to work the combined units of their partners who took up off-farm work. Such people have begun to contract themselves out, with the partnership's equipment, to work other farms on a fee-per-hour basis. To take equipment away from their own partnership for this purpose, however, they must substitute it with the manual labor of their wife and unmarried sons and daughters, thus reproducing a pattern originally found in the share-cropping family.

This very complex set of social relationships is a direct consequence of a long history of erratic economic conditions. This area has not seen a continuous and enduring concentration of capital, proletarianization, and separation of agricultural from non-agricultural occupations, as was the case, for example, in Engels' Manchester. The response to recession therefore is not one which sees a radical change in these relationships, so much as their reformation to deal with the new conditions.

In the 1980s far less work is to be found on factory floors. At the same time, water supplies to the irrigation system have become so expensive and unreliable that market-gardening and fruit-growing are becoming unviable for all but the most geographically well-located plots. In many cases, moreover, the move to less water-reliant crops is also a move to less labor-intensive ones, and the demand for day labor has declined.[7] These are ideal conditions for an increase in putting-out work, as households, faced with unemployment and poor farm incomes, take on any work available. Clandestine workshops make up a far greater proportion of the overall production of both shoes and toys than hitherto. Small-hold plots continue to be used for the production of cash crops, but small areas are now devoted to household vegetables, chickens, and other items for self-provisioning. In the absence of opportunities for off-farm income the farming partnerships have collapsed, as the off-farm partners have returned. On the other hand, the problems facing agriculture have led to the efflorescence of a multitude of small service and manufacturing ventures, while a number of farmers have let out their buildings to the operators of workshops servicing the shoe industry in nearby Elche.

Faced with a long experience of an erratic economy, how then have Spanish enterprises sought to improve their viability through what Mingione refers to as "extraordinary domestic activities?" A much longer and more thoroughgoing insertion into the capitalist economy than was the case for the Huasicanchinos has eroded the organic links between households, replacing them with the increasing atomization commonly associated with simple commodity production. As a result, there are far greater limits on the availability of unpaid sources of labor beyond the family than we have seen in our previous case.

The first point of pressure to improve viability through maximizing the use of unpaid labor, therefore, is within the home. But when a point of saturation has been reached, this process is pushed out to another household through networking. Thus a work-distributor, already maximizing the use of his wife's domestic labor, may buy a plot of land and give it over to a share-cropper. The conditions of the share-cropping agreement, in turn, are such that the tenant will maximize the use of unpaid labor in *his* household. And the share-cropper's wife or daughter, thus put upon, extends work to yet another household, allowing herself a small margin deriving from the high quality of work she has accepted.

In fact, very little of this work has anything to do with self-provisioning—in the sense of "subsistence"—nor is it, properly speaking, unpaid. But it is an invasion of the domestic sphere. In addition, when the possibilities for improving overall household income are constrained by declining agricultural income and a loss of wage work, the number of *commodities* needed for domestic consumption make subcontracted out-work under appalling conditions a better alternative than expanding domestic activities for direct self-provisioning. In the Peruvian case, supposedly self-provisioning pastoral production is in fact used to acquire market items not producible locally: fleeces and meat are sold, and woven goods are traded. Expanding self-provisioning in Catral for this kind of barter purpose—to sell extra eggs to acquire a needed commodity—is far more limited, partly because the range of market goods the people of Catral have come to depend on is so great, and partly because similar strategies by others in the neighborhood quickly saturates demand for locally producible goods (see Mingione 1983).

While self-provisioning to retain the viability of the household takes on a very different form to that found in Peru then, it is nevertheless true that the Spanish households reveal much greater plasticity in social relations in the face of crisis than do the more thoroughly proletarianized urban households in Mingione's mode. It is quite possible that this occupational flexibility is a result of an historical context where economic insecurity has been combined with political oppression. Under such conditions there are few institutions powerful enough to bring pressure on the state, either to provide stability through subsidies, price supports, etc., or security through state institutions (see Harding 1984; for a useful comparison from southern France, see Lem 1988).

## Conclusion

In the absence of powerful political pressure then, being at the bottom end of an erratic monetary economy encourages the maintenance of flexible self-provisioning resources and institutions. In both the Peruvian and Spanish cases, a lengthy experience of this predicament has created such resources and institutions.

Of most relevance to us are the implications this has for the conventional distinctions between "domestic labor" (in the household) and "social labor" (outside it), for we can see from these examples that the manipulation of these two spheres is an essential feature of all enterprises. But I have referred not just to domestic labor, but to any labor which is "unpaid and ideologically predisposed to this conditiion." We have seen that both households within the local social context and people within those households face different possibilities of access to these two spheres. As a result, a person's position within a domestic unit, as well as that domestic unit's position within the overall social context, condition the effective meaning of even—perhaps especially—the most intimate of terms, such as "my kin" *(mis parientes)*, "my friends" *(mis compadres y mis amigos)* and "the community" *(la comunidad)*.

The constitution of this sphere of non-commodified labor is the product of past historical resistance—for example, between self-provisioning communities and appropriating landlords, between domestic units and merchants, and within domestic units themselves—and this provides the conditions within which the boundaries between these two spheres can be manipulated. Clearly these were somewhat different for the Peruvian and Spanish cases.

Because the line between claims on the domestic sphere and claims on the community sphere are less clear in the Peruvian case, there is a broader field within which participants can constitute and reconstitute the arena of non-commodified labor. By contrast, in the Spanish case the sphere of non-commodified social relations appears to be less extensive and has less institutionalized visibility—people from Catral cannot, for example, make appeals to "community sentiment and responsibility" as do their Huasican-chino counterparts. For the Spanish, therefore, the erratic nature of a variety of forms of cash income and the payment of labor below reproduction costs (itself the result of a long history of Franco's repression) has put great pressure precisely on the domestic sphere, because a more extensive general sphere of non-commodified social relations is not present in the immediate environment. Therefore, the tendency is to increase unpaid labor in the home to saturation point and only then to use extended kin and neighbors.[8]

But this latter strategy requires a suitable social environment: some network of "those whom I can count on and those who count on me" has to be in place. In the Spanish case, the past history of erratic economic conditions and of artisan work meant that these networks were endemic so that they coud be called into existence in the face of adversity. In the Peruvian case, the social context took a different form: confederations built up among households inserted into diverse economic sectors and geographical locations were a reformulation of interhousehold networks from a previous period.

But the interaction between a household's coping strategies and the historically-given social context affects women and men differentially. Thus, in Peru, for the majority, linkages between households were multiplex, serving a variety of purposes, and they were activated as much by men as by women. In Spain the pre-existing networks had been activated by women in the performance of domestic tasks or as a function of their artisan activities—so the nearest thing in Catral to the Huasicanchinos' non-commodified community sphere, beyond the domestic unit, is the interhousehold networks. In Huasicancha that sphere was differentially available to the various kinds of enterprises depending on their past human resource base. In Catral, too, the non-commodified sphere is not uniformly available to all; it is pre-eminently available to women, and not just any women, but those with an historical background of production relations that made networks endemic.

The fact that these relationships among friends have provided an essential component in the maintenance of (quasi-commodified) out-work, just as subsistence networks were crucial in effecting the insertion of Huasicanchinos' petty commodity production into the market, draws attention once more to the relationship between self-provisioning on the one hand, and the production and sale of labor and commodities on the other. The Huasicanchinos use interhousehold links in the subsistence sector to shore up their activities in the petty commodity sector, and the Catraleñas use interhousehold networks to handle domestic activities, the better to concentrate on contract work. But this should not blind us to the fact that the Huasicanchinos also use links within the community for raising capital and finding labor for their petty commodity activities, and the women of Catral use their networks—though often not the same ones—not just as a means to extend their "extraordinary domestic activities", but also as part and parcel of their subcontracting work.

The point then about "subsistence production" is that it should be seen in terms of an alternative in the struggle over a variety of forms of appropriation. A person released from one such form, say rent, may—immediately or gradually—become entrapped in another. Thus, in Peru, once the local hacienda had expanded to occupy most of the available pasture, some Huasicanchinos began to migrate, substituting precarious petty commodity activity for labor service on the hacienda. Others tried to shun the hacienda and engage in "subsistence production" on what was left of the community land. In either case it was the reproduction of the domestic enterprise which was at stake, not retreat from the market for its own sake. If a less exploitative situation could be achieved through market linkages of one form or another, this was entirely consistent with the goal of subsistence as I have defined it. If, over a period of time, this leads to dependence on yet another appropriation relationship, then a further form of struggle is likely to occur.

In the Catral case, it is necessary to deal simultaneously with a variety of sets of relationships—between capital and labor, between one household and another, and within households—each of which contains its potential for struggle over dependence/independence and appropriation/self-provisioning, *but in each case vis-á-vis some other specific relationship*. It thus becomes especially clear that a person is released from one such relationship only to be entrapped, over time, in another. Subcontracted home work, for example, reduces the household's dependence on the share-cropping relationship. And for the women it mitigates against the particularly autocratic patriarchal relations associated with share-cropping. Yet in another direction—for the household as a whole and for the woman so employed—it increases dependence on the capital-labor relationship. Then, as the imperatives of the putting-out firm to extract absolute surplus-value through increasing the hours of work (rather than investing in means of production) take hold, so the home worker finds herself increasing her dependence on networks beyond the household—either to lessen her domestic tasks or to take on part of her home work.[9] The extent to which these latter relationships are entirely non-commodied, moreover, is subject to negotiation, thus providing the different parameters for the struggle over the respective spheres to those suggested for the Peruvian case.

Generally speaking, however, the *boundaries* of the domestic are not as available for manipulation in the Spanish case as they are for the Peruvian—though the claims which can properly be made on kin, friends, neighbors, partners, and union colleagues most certainly are. This means that the ideological point of contention is likely to arise less on the shifting horizon of the domestic sphere than on social relationships *within* that sphere. In the case study itself artisan production, family farming, petty commodity production, a variety of forms of subcontracting and wage labor occur. Each of these requires greater or less organic interlinkage within the domestic unit for the process of its reproduction to occur. This in turn gives rise to the particular form domestic politics takes in Catral.

The purpose of juxtaposing these two cases has been to examine the complex possibilities thrown up for political agency in situations where the process of commodification has been uneven and where the subsumption of capital to labor has been more formal than real. Axiomatic has been my initial suggestion that the analysis should focus less on the degree to which social relationships are expressed in the commodity form than on ascertaining just where those relationships are occurring. In both the cases discussed, enterprises are at most only partial simple commodity producers, and the political implications this has depended on the particular historical conjunctures experienced in the two cases.

For the Huasicanchinos the maintenance of a sphere in which claims and deferences are operative cannot be unproblematically limited to the domestic sphere, for a history of political survival in which struggle against expanding haciendas and the ravages of the local merchant class have required united effort and hence have impressed upon them the necessity of the community. Potential simply commodity producing enterprises, in short, cannot dispense with the community and hence cannot establish the unquestionable hegemony of the domestic over community claims. Where non-commodified social relations cover a wide circuit, the bounds of the (privatized) domestic sphere becomes hard to maintain, without the threat of losing the benfits deriving from participation in that wider circuit. The character of Huasicancha politics revolves around different formulations of this issue.

In the Spanish case, the partial character of simple commodity production takes on a different form. It has been the historical role of artisanal production which has provided the basis for the emergence of petty commodity production and partial proletarianization. As Lenin (1964, 337) points out, "Of course, it is not always easy to distinguish the village artisan from the small commodity producer or from the wage-worker." And this difficulty of distinction has played a significant part in Catral's insertion into the larger economy. Where, as in the case of the artisan, customer and producer come into contact prior to production—materials are advanced, tools too sometimes, and even specific designs are "bespoke"— artisanal production can almost accidentally shift, unnoticed, into the formally more capitalistic relationship of work-distributor and home worker. All these features characterise the social relations in the Spanish case with the growth of local industry and the resulting haphazard wage labor and subcontracting. The extent to which such historical precedents make it possible for local work-distributors (and more especially their wives) to categorize their relationship to home workers as only quasi-commodified, suggests a similar phenomenon to that found in Peru: that partial commodification is not so much a transitional stage as an essential ongoing characteristic for social reproduction in both cases. Both kinds of operation derive a special advantage from retaining their position on the watershed between strictly contractual relations and those of a more personal kind. And though history has provided quite different social environments, it is precisely the maneuvering of participants and the negotiation of essential meanings that this allows which give domestic politics its particular form in each case.

# Chapter 4

## "Not to Be a Burden": Ideologies of the Domestic Group and Women's Work in Rural Catalonia

### Susana Narotzky

This study argues that a double ideology is important to the exploitation of women's work in an underground economy. Its object is to understand how a specific segment of the work force is ideologically defined and how the abstract work it provides is devalued.

The fieldwork on which this study is based was conducted in the region of Les Garrigues, in the interior of Catalonia (Spain). This is a zone of dry farming where olive oil is produced on small- and medium-sized farms of five to thirty hectares. In this zone and surrounding areas, a strong ideology of "household" (*casa*) is recognized (Assier-Andrieu 1984; Iszaevitch 1981; Terradas 1984; Bestard 1986; 121–147; Harding 1984; 99–110). The household (*casa*) ideology serves to integrate aspects of both production and reproduction, including the division of labor, transfer of property, matrimonial alliances, etc.—although its transformations have yet to be carefully studied. The growing participation of women from this zone in underground clothing manufacture for national and international markets demonstrates the degree to which some family members are incorporated into the capitalist labor market. It is important to articulate their situation with the small farm production also conducted by the domestic group and to study them as a single process instead of a distinct series of sectoral transformations.

The analysis that follows is organized around a key concept: that of the *casa* or household. The transformation of its meaning in a changing context from 1900 to 1987 is the focus of this study. This does not assume this concept was either static or "traditional" before 1900, but simply delimits the scope of the work conducted.

If we begin by defining a domestic group as a set of individuals related by kinship ("real" or "assumed") that crystalizes around access to certain resources, we find that the household concept does not distinguish between the spheres of production and reproduction. All the members of the domestic group perceive themselves as working "for the household" and are implicated in some way in the production-reproduction of the farm that forms its nucleus and its relations of production. With the introduction of the capitalist concept of "family"—that is to say, the domestic group devoted exclusively to reproduction while production is relegated to an explicitly different and exterior sphere—a clear distinction emerges between work tied to the production of commodities on the farm and work tied to reproduction of the labor force.

At the same time, growing mechanization since 1960 has separated women—except during the period of the olive harvest—from agricultural work, thus provoking an exclusive identification of men with the farm and with the material benefits derived from it. The superimposition of the capitalist ideology of family (perceived to be exclusively reproductive) upon that of the household (a group centered around farm production) has led to the exclusive association of the household with the farm and men's work. Women increasingly see their work as tied to the normative capitalist family (i.e., reproduction); this occurs despite the fact that the ideology of household continues to define a common project and justifies a differentiation in the domestic group according to the lines of sex.

Detailed analysis of the source of the domestic group's income and its use reveals that income from men's agricultural labor is held separately and invested primarily in farm improvements. Income derived from female labor in underground clothing manufacture is kept aside, under the control of the women, and is used for expenses related to the maintenance and reproduction of the family. From the point of view of household ideology, however, income from work accomplished outside of the family farm—which permits individual control of profits—remains devalued and relegated to the domain of "money squandered" (*malgastos*) on "luxuries, leisure, and extras." It is contrasted directly with labor invested in the family farm by the domestic group in its productive-reproductive endeavor. In this way, the superimposition of the ideology of the capitalist family upon that of the household constructs a segregated although common project. Domestic groups become increasingly constituted as families but, at the same time, maintain the cohesive nucleus that defines each as a household. Some of the individuals from domestic groups, however, come to be differently assigned to production or to reproduction. It is within this context, and in relation to the international division of labor in sectors of intensive production—sectors in which there are large seasonal changes, rapid product obsolescence, and the technical possibility of decentralization of production—that a specific form of exploitation of the female work force emerges.

## Case Study

Seventy-five percent of the women who work in the context of Spain's underground economy work at home. Of these, 93.2 percent are employed in clothing manufacture. In this sector, the percentage of women workers according to their age is as follows: less than sixteen years old, 0.5 percent; from sixteen to twenty-nine years old, 17.6 percent; from thirty to fifty-four years old, 61.1 percent; fifty-five years and older, 20.8 percent. Finally, 76.8 percent are classified as "housewives" as compared to 11.8 percent as "daughters." These data were compiled by the Ministry of the Economy and Treasury for a national survey in 1983 (MEH 1986). They provide an idea of the magnitude of the female work force in the underground sector of clothing manufacture, specifically in the category of home work. The results of the survey also form a broad typology of these female workers in which there are two outstanding characteristics: most of the women are older than thirty and "housewives" (compare Sanchis 1984).

The village in the district of Les Garrigues (province of Lerida) where this study was conducted has fewer than 1,000 inhabitants and is situated in a dry land zone where the principle crop is the olive and the secondary one the almond. There are also half a dozen poultry-breeding and rabbit farms. The most important activity is agriculture, followed (distantly) by construction and small business. A majority of the domestic groups in the region receive most of their income from the cultivation of their own land, in spite of the fact that various family members customarily accrue smaller sums from other sources. A large number of adult women manufacture clothing at home, while younger, single women, who still live at home with their families, work in underground clothing workshops.

### Ideologies: The Household and the Family

As argued elsewhere (Narotzky 1988), "household" and "family" are basically distinct concepts. As analytical tools, their different nuances are indispensible for understanding the organization of peasant domestic groups. The household as a concept reflects an ideology structured around production, inasmuch as the gathering together of persons under the same roof is made possible, modified, and perpetuated according to access to resources and farming of the land. Various studies (Berkner 1972, 1973, 1976; Mitterauer and Sieder 1979; Terradas 1984; Segalen 1980; Iszaevitch 1981) provide support for this hypothesis. From the perspective of the household, the primary goal of the co-residents (whether kin or not) is production within the context of an agrarian economy of small- and medium-sized farms where production and reproduction are two sides of the same coin, and probably not conceived of as distinct. From the point of view of the individuals who constitute the household, the situation is one of "working for the household," understood as a fluid group of members whose composition varies according to how ongoing tensions between the labor needs of the farm and alternative employment possibilities are resolved.

The family, as currently conceptualized, manifests itself as an ideology centered around the physical and social reproduction of the work force in a system where production itself is set apart from the rest of the social relations and adopts, as its objective, its own expansion. Progressively, since the Industrial Revolution, reproduction has grown to be the axis around which the new concept of family turns. At the same time, labor productive of commodities remains identified with a space distinct from that of the household. This emphasis on reproduction (primarily biological, but also social reproduction) privileges the mother-child relationship. The biological component of this relationship contributes to the sense of "naturalness," so that little by little, with the amplification of socialization as part of the process, this naturalness comes to encompass all of the activities related to the reproduction of the domestic unit. The fluid concept of household is separated from that of family—if we take as our starting point the eighteenth century definitions (Flandrin 1979; Covarrubias 1984; Berkner 1972)—by conceptualizing the latter as an isolated and closed nucleus separated from the outsdie world, whose "natural" function is its reproduction. This distinction, which represents a sharp division between an exterior, public world of production and an interior, private world of reproduction, is one of the distinctive features in the constitution of a capitalist ideology of work. To support this unit of reproduction which the family ideally represents, an internal sexual division of labor is created: the father as provider of the material means of subsistence, the mother as biological and social reproducer (and thus as the daily supporter of the members of the family). With respect to this division of labor, the woman has, as her primary commitment, the physical and psychological constitution of individuals, while the man provides the raw materials that allow this reproduction. The ideology of family as something separate and distant from the process of production or, alternatively, of reproduction as the primordial objective of every group—even if productive—that takes the form of a family, has filtered into the analytic use of these concepts (this has often been the case of the Chayanovian "peasant" domestic group). Nevertheless, it is important to bear in mind that while the ideologies associated with concepts of household and family both reflect and tend to maintain different organizations of production, they also contribute to the manipulation of the social relations of production and to the transformation of the socioeconomic reality they represent.

The case presented here represents a first step in the effort to clarify these types of problems. Peasant domestic groups are simultaneously presented in two ways: as agricultural production units—in their appearance as households; and as groups of biologically close relatives clustered around a conjugal couple with the objective of reproduction (procreation, maintenance, and socialization)—in their appearance as family. The farm is inserted into the logic of the market and the explicit objective of those in control is an increase in profitabililty. On the other hand, the domestic group as family assumes responsibility for the maintenance and reproduction of a work force basically through commodity consumption, which requires income.

This does not imply that these two functions of the domestic group appear complementary in the eyes of its members. What seems to occur is an ambivalence in interpretation that explains the activities of the members of the group in one way or another, depending on whether the context is seen as that of household or family. What is of interest here is how this ambivalence allows contractors or intermediaries in the underground manufacturing sector to use the labor of women who are members of these domestic groups.

## The Progressive Division of Spheres

From interviews carried out with various women between the ages of twenty-seven and eighty-four, it can be inferred that until about twenty-five years ago women actively participated in farm work throughout the whole agricultural cycle. Besides harvesting olives and almonds (work that most still perform), they collected branches during pruning season, looked after the vegetable garden, participated in the harvesting of grains (there was much more land devoted to these crops then than at the present time), gathered and bound crops into sheaves, threshed, etc. They worked not only on their own land, but also as day laborers on property belonging to others. Nowadays, the participation of women in farm work varies according to individual circumstances but is always limited to the harvesting of one's own crops—principally olives and almonds. On the other hand, according to informants older than forty, domestic work has increased considerably in the last twenty years, above all in "cleaning." Nevertheless, other work priorities continue to exist for women: the olive harvest and the manufacture of clothing. During the harvest, housework "piles up," and when there are no clothes to make, women say that they make good use of the extra time by cleaning. This seems to indicate that when much work is available in clothing manufacture, this takes precedence over cleaning. All the same, the task of harvesting continues to have first priority, and many women will put aside clothing manufacture to gather olives at harvest time. Other domestic tasks, such as shopping, cooking, and making beds, do not seem to be discretionary and also take priority over clothing manufacture. That is to say, when there is an abundance of work making clothes, certain domestic tasks will be put aside, but not others. This can be interpreted both as an ideological distinction in the value of certain types of domestic work and as an economic calculation of the comparative profitability of women's labor invested in various tasks.

In summary, women have seen their participation in farm work progressively reduced and their domestic tasks increased over the past few years. Similarly, in the past fifteen years home clothing manufacture has been added to the total work carried out within the material limits of the home.

On the other hand, the household's farm work has been reconfigured more and more as men's work, from which they obtain some income. That is to say, women's lesser rates of direct participation in agricultural production lend themselves to the identification of agricultural income as exclusively male. Although farm production is tied to the interests of all members of the domestic group through the ideology of household, it has been increasingly transformed into an exclusively "productive" sphere where the men in the family work. This has led to a progressive division between a sphere of production (farm work and its profits) and a sphere of reproduction (the family and the maintenance of its members). At the same time, the diminishing participation of women in agricultural production has given these spheres a distinct sexual identity. But, above all, this process implies that farm labor performed by men—which was previously conceptualized as their individual contribution to the communal productive/reproductive enterprise of the household—is being converted into "men's work" that produces the family's "principal income." This last process is made possible by the masculinization of the agricultural sector. The profits obtained through farming are therefore perceived as a direct result of male labor and as more or less equivalent to the "family income."

## The Sexual Division of Labor

If we analyze the sexual division of labor within the domestic group, the evaluation of female activities seems to differ depending on whether one adopts the point of view of "household" or "family". The perception of work changes according to whether it is considered a contribution to the household, that is, to the collective economic project of the domestic group on the farm, or as a contribution to the maintenance of the family. In the context of the household, the responsibility of its members is to contribute a *jornal* (day's work); the woman considers her domestic labor to constitute such a contribution, and it is valued as such in purely economic terms. If she considers that her domestic work constitutes a *jornal*—her fundamental economic contribution to the household—this is not because it is her principal responsibility according to a sexual division of labor that "naturally" designates reproductive and domestic tasks as feminine, but because it represents the greatest economic benefit for the household. This is one informants' reasoning:[1]

> I think that what a woman does at home is more important because, you see, if they would have to get some other woman to do the work here, if I weren't here, they would have to hire someone, and the woman might charge, I don't know. . . . If she charges 300 or 400 [pesetas] an hour, I cannot earn 300 pesetas an hour making clothing, you understand, because the pay from making clothing is so small. And in order to earn what you earn at home you have to work night and day, and even then you would not earn it.

Work in clothing manufacture is also considered from the point of view of the household and is defined as a second *jornal* that the woman carries out in addition to the first:

> Economically, it [making clothing] provides a small contribution that, for example, I always put aside. What can I tell you . . . ? Forty or fifty thousand pesetas that I would have in case the washing machine breaks down, then it doesn't hurt if I have to call a repairman. If it was going to cost thirteen thousand pesetas, well, I would pay for it. And, it is as if I would find it [the money to pay for such expenses]—because I do it in addition to housework. It's that it is an additional burden, that is, it's not possible to do two day's work—but a woman does. It is as I said before, a man will do a day's work related to agriculture and that's all, but a woman does more than just the housework. Naturally, some will have it [the house] more sparkling, cleaner, but if one does what's important, what's fundamental for giving life and rhythm to these people. . . . And to this one adds another job, a job that enables one to bring in a small or large income or what have you. This is the equivalent of two day's work from my point of view. Because by taking care of my husband and my children, I have already

earned a day's wages. It is as I said to you, if we got a maid, they would have to pay her salary out of their pockets. That is to say, it would already be a deficit. . . . But I have not done it this way. I have contributed here [in the house] as I have said, and in addition, I have earned a bit of income, whether large or small. But I have covered many expenses with all of this.

A difference is noted between those women who work in the underground workshops, and thus do not perform domestic chores, and their mothers or other persons on whom these tasks fall. The distinction is communicated in this way:

The person who goes out to farm the land has only one task to do. The person who sews and has someone else to do the housework has only a single thing to do. While women who work. . . .

The *jornal* seems to refer directly to the labor invested in an activity regardless of whether this is translated into monetary income. In fact, women's domestic labor is counted as a kind of ''savings''—an opportunity to forego certain expenditures—that benefits men, the farm, and the household (these three elements remain closely associated because, among other things, the head of the household remains in charge of the farm's fiscal responsibilities and because of the growing masculinization of the agrarian sector). This type of ''negative calculation'' is not foreign to a peasant farm economy; in fact, it is similar to the sorts of calculations used to appraise all of the daily work that members of the domestic group contribute to working the household's land. Nevertheless, one difference that probably has been accentuated by the masculinization of agriculture is the fact that daily work invested in farm labor is translated, in the long run, into monetary income, while daily domestic labor is not. With the growing separation of women from the farm, the concept of women receiving a wage for agricultural work is disappearing. As a result of this situation, the woman's *jornal* is not translated into a monetary benefit, thus rendering it less visible. On the other hand, the fact that a monetary value is not attached to the *jornal* contributed by women, together with the increasing identity of the household with the farm and the sphere of production, renders difficult their access to farm income for use in meeting domestic expenses. Finally, from the point of view of the common economic project of the household, some expenses appear to be ''squandered money;'' that is, they appear to be peripheral to the common objectives of the farm in the two facets of production and reproduction. That is to say, these expenses do not appear to contribute directly either to the reproduction of the work force (the domestic facet of the household) or to the production of commodities (the agricultural-business facet of the farm). These peripheral expenses are identified with the individual interests of distinct members of the domestic group; they seem always to have been met, in the memory of the informants, by income obtained by individual labor outside of the farm.[2]

With respect to the sexual division of labor from the perspective of the household, the difference between a day's work and a day's wage discloses the difference between the male farm manager and the woman who does domestic work. The former has access to farm income, which is justified by his work in this sector and by his responsibility to administer production in the most profitable way. The woman's domestic work, while it is an essential part of production, does not directly yield an income that she could administer.[3]

This situation directs women toward off-farm sources of income—such as clothing manufacture—but this strategy is confused both ideologically and in fact with the notion of meeting "personal" expenses:

We have always kept it [the money from making clothes], it must be said. We have made a small nest egg, a small savings . . . , more than anything for my daughter because, you see, "now I want to buy myself some shoes, now a coat, now I'm going to the discotheque." Well, it is not necessary to ask anybody for anything; that is, we are able to take care of ourselves, because, you see, there are many household expenses and in order not to be a burden on them—not that we have been. . . .

—In order not to be a burden on the men?

—On the men, because they already have expenses such as tractors and all the other farm machinery. Well, then, we [women] have tried to have something [money] . . . because, for example, the sewing machine, well, we couldn't have bought it, we would have had to wait until they could have paid. . . . And we got it on our own when we worked [making clothes]. The machine is still here and the possibility that there will be more work to do. I don't know how to express it, but it has always been this way—that we have been able to have some money, that although it is all from the same household, it is always used for those expenses that the young ones might have, for example, when they were in military service, if something needs to be repaired, such as the washing machine, I no longer have to ask for it, or the refrigerator, or some other household item, that we may have a little something so that it's not necessary to take from elsewhere.

The preoccupation of "not being a burden on them" shows a clear differentiation between consumption that is related to production and to reproduction, and it confirms the masculinization of the separate productive sphere: "they already have expenses such as tractors and other types of machinery. . . . " However, and this is one of the most important characteristics of the ideology of the household, it is believed that all members of the domestic group work with the same objective in mind—that is, "to improve the household"—and nowadays this means obtaining the maximum profit from production. This leads to the appearance of a contradiction between the "household" as a collective social and economic enterprise of the domestic group as a whole, and the "household" as the embodiment of masculine farm labor.[4] This double aspect of the household makes it possible to consider that one can contribute to its improvement either by increasing production profits or by preventing the diversion of income to other spheres, such a reproduction and leisure (that is to say, by not "being a burden") and thus permitting agricultural earnings to be reinvested back into that sector with the goal of modernizing the enterprise and increasing its profitability. This also explains, to some extent, how the agricultural benefits derived from the collaboration of all the members of the domestic group come to be identified with masculine income.

Seen from the perspective of the ideology of family, the domestic group is turned inward. Its goal is seen as the reproduction of its members, and this reproduction is accomplished, in part, by means of the consumption permitted by cash income. This income symbolizes the material support of the father of the family, and it is the raw material that the mother must transform. It is by means of income and of consumption that the autonomous cell that is assumed to be the "family" connects with the exterior world of production. It is in these two points of contact that a whole series of emotional and spiritual values are transformed into economic values.

If we consider income within the context of the ideology of the family, the sexual division of labor can be redefined as follows: the husband/father contributes the income and the wife/mother administers it, transforms it, and, in a certain sense, "consumes" it. All of the income that does not come through the normative route of the father is relegated to a secondary position; it is considered to be circumstantial or temporary, a "complementary" income, or a "help." Nevertheless, the family ideology implies that the objective of the various members is singular and shared, and thus the income from various sources will ultimately end up in a common fund that expresses the identity and homogeneity of family interests. In the cases we have studied, nevertheless, almost all of the members of the domestic group—grandparents, parents, children—obtain some income, and this income does not become part of a common fund; rather, it is customarily maintained apart and its consumption is governed by the distinct interests of family members.[5] Curiously, the husband/father's farm income hardly ever becomes the family income, but is maintained as business profit and reinvested. This means that income for reproduction must come from other sources: petty commerce conducted by women, old age and disability pensions, construction work, service, or underground clothing manufacture. In spite of the fact that it does not provide for domestic reproduction, the principal family income is considered to be that provided by the land (and therefore by men).

In any case, income from clothing manufacture is used largely to cover reproductive costs (maintenance and social reproduction), such as repairs of household appliances and furnishings, girls' trousseaus, packages to sons in the military, communion gifts, etc. It is considered to be a "small help" for "those expenses that you don't have everyday" because "from this [income from clothing manufacture] one cannot live." Although these are domestic expenses that reproduce the family, they correspond to women in the sexual division of labor from the perspective of the family. The "complementarity" of female contributions to reproduction is questionable if one considers that the masculine contribution appears sporadically and is tied to prestige expenses (house repairs) more than to the maintenance of the work force.

Ironically, these "peasant families" do not live from the land. In fact, agricultural production absorbs a work force that is reproduced with income derived mostly from other sectors of production. Not only is the amount of labor invested in agriculture not accounted for, but neither does agriculture contribute in a regular way to the maintenance of this work force. To the contrary, the income that actually contributes to the maintenance of the work force is carried out in a context that obscures its role in maintaining the family.

## Women's Work

Women's work can be divided into two groups: work that generates income and work that does not. The first group includes the manufacture of clothing at home or in a workshop, petty commerce, and domestic service. In the second group is domestic work and work on one's own land. The two groups have in common, however, the fact that the work carried out is valued in negative terms: the first, because it makes it possible not to spend the proceeds from agricultural work; the second, because it is labor that is not charged against the farm's capital resources. In both cases, the result is the same: the women's work always appears referred to other work—work that ultimately turns out to be masculine farm labor. It almost seems that this "non-work" is the objective; women's labor makes it possible to "save" labor invested in the farm, as well as to save the cost of reproduction of the work force.

On the other hand, in spite of this negative valuation of work that "reduces" expenses rather than "producing" income or benefits, these women have a clear notion of how their labor contributes to capital formation; this explains, for example, the purchase of industrial or semi-industrial sewing machines. What this seems to indicate is that they have a clear awareness of the economic processes insofar as individual strategies are concerned. There also exists, on the part of these women, a desire to increase the profitability of their labor. Although the income they obtain is perceived as a saving of other income, its growth is directly tied to their personal autonomy as women since this wealth can be administered without giving explanations to other members of the domestic group. We have seen that this income largely covers the cost of reproducing the work force; one important element of this is daughters' clothing. This clothing is used to enhance a daughter's appearance at the same time that it plays a role as an enticement in the marriage market. It is clothing that not only heightens the physical appearance of a person, but it also, within a household system that assumes these expenses will be met by means of personal effort, expresses a young woman's capacity to work. Nevertheless, moderation in one's dress is also important since it communicates that income spent on oneself is but the tip of an iceberg, the vast majority of which reverts to the household.

Without doubt, the increase in women's income results in personal benefits, whether because they can lighten their domestic chores with household appliances or can dress better; and in the case of young women, they can perhaps find better matches in marriage so their future lives might be easier. In any case, these are benefits that are intimately attached to the social reproduction of the system through a process that tends to reduce to a minimum the burden of reproduction upon the sphere of production.

## Life Cycle and Work Discipline

Up to this point we considered the work of making clothes as being very much the same for the informant as well as her daughter. Nevertheless, an important distinction exists, namely, that the daughter works eight hours a day in an underground shop while the mother makes her clothing at home. This entails considerable differences with respect to income, the flexibility of schedules, the intensity of work, and productivity. Labor involved in home clothing manufacture yields less because it is constantly interrupted by the requirements of housework, but it does allow for the two tasks to be carried out at the same time. Nevertheless, the total work carried out by women who make clothes at home is considered to be more (two *jornales*) than that of women who labor only in workshops ("you have only one thing to do"). The amount of work done by women making clothes at home is thought to be exceeded only by women who labor in workshops and also take care of domestic chores at home afterward. (There was no such case in the village studied.) This point of view exists in spite of the fact that women who work at shops earn larger incomes. It is also interesting to point out that the "flexibility" attributed to home clothing manufacture by the contractors (MEH 1986, 67) is perceived by the informant as a factor that scatters energies and is bad for health:

> What happens is that I can't do everything, and this is what makes me nervous, of course. When I'm sewing, I remember that upstairs the beds are still unmade. And, alas, there's this huge amount of clothing that must be mended. That is to say, I accumulate a huge amount of things in my head. When I go to bed, I think of all the things I will have to do the following day. It's such a tremendous struggle, that sometimes I think that if I don't have a heart attack, it is because God doesn't wish it because I do everything necessary [to put myself at risk]. That is to say, because practically my body never rests and my mind even less. . . .

It would appear for the most part that working in a shop is preferable to working at home. But this possibility depends on whether or not the daily domestic labor could be assumed by another woman in the domestic group; as we have seen, the unpaid performance of housework is considered to be the best use of womens' labor for the household. In general, this seems to be the case: "the person who sews and, at home, has another person who takes care of the house . . . ". And this situation is tightly bound to the life cycle of women and their position in the reproductive cycle of the family. From the perspective of household, however, the emphasis on domestic work is of an exclusively economic order, calculated as income "not spent," while from the ideology of family, the emphasis on domestic work continues to be bound to the natural relegation of all reproductive tasks to females. This perception of family is clearly not the dominant one in the informants' reasoning about domestic labor. The few times a reference is made to an "obligation" of a woman or mother to carry out these tasks, it is presented to a certain extent as a misunderstanding on the part of the rest of the members of the family (including daughters). In the case of women, it ceases when they take on domestic labor and they come to think of it not as an obligation, but as a "sacrifice." It is this concept of sacrifice, laden with the idea of voluntariness and not naturalness, that comes to be seen as constitutive of a woman's role and as defining her relation to domestic work.[6] It is a sacrifice, among other things, because from a capitalist vision of labor, only the sale of labor-power and labor which produces commodities and income are valued. Work in a shop remains, then, reserved for young women. It appears tied not only to separation from domestic labor, but also to the objective of increasing productivity at a stage in the life cycle when young women are at the maximum physical potential:

> Making clothing, be what it may, one must have nimble fingers and not be on the moon. Of course, one person is always cleverer than another, . . . has more agile hands, fingers. When one is young, then, one is alert and puts more into everything. One doesn't have to redo things or whatever. . . .

But this physical potential has to be controlled by a rigid discipline of work so that it is not lost. This is what the framework of the workshop provides. For the older women who work at home, this discipline (in the form of well organized work) is already acquired:

> Besides, when you work at home, it seems as if you don't work as many hours. And you don't work as many hours, right? Because you are more distracted. I, no, I don't get distracted because if I do, it's to do other chores. But my daughter, well, yes [she does], because, now she's watching TV or listening to music for a little while. It is very different. Whereas, if they go there [to the workshop], they know they have to work eight hours. They spend the eight hours that I mentioned before. And they don't move from the chair. They work. Eight hours are spent at the machine.

Therefore, the labor power of the women in the informant's domestic group is used to the maximum in all cases, although its use varies depending on the stage in the life cycle. In the first stage, productivity in the manufacture of commodities is maximized, while in a second stage this objective is superceded by that of reproducing the labor force, although the subsidiary production of commodities continues to be profitable at minimal expense. The preceding perspective emanates from considering the elements of this study within the context of the capitalist system as a whole.

### Justification for Home Work in Clothing Manufacture

Women who work in home clothing manufacture and who accept working conditions that entail the lowest salaries, no social security, and bearing the costs of production (purchase and maintenance of machinery, electricity), do it because there are no other work alternatives in the village. They also do it because their labor-power has been placed by ideology outside the category of socially necessary labor. They are caught between two distinct ideologies that contribute to the devaluation of home work at the same time that they drive women toward it.

The ideology of household shows, in the first place, the lack of differentiation of production and reproduction in a context where the labor-power of the different members of the domestic group is occupied in various tasks. The objective of these tasks is the profitability of the farm, which necessarily entails the maintenance and reproduction of the work force. In this situation, each individual—as long as, within the set of available opportunities, he or she chooses to do so—collaborates with his or her day's work in this common enterprise. Daily labor is the contribution of labor-power to the cultivation of the land, and in the case of at least one of the women of the domestic group, to the domestic tasks of reproduction. On the other hand, the needs of individuals in the domestic group which are not considered necessary for production/reproduction of the household are covered by means of the income each receives from working on someone else's land or in other remunerated activities. Work appears, then, in two forms: negative work for the household that materializes in the farm's agricultural produce and the monetary benefits (fruits of a collective effort) that it brings, and work that yields a direct income over which each individual has greater control and which is destined at least partially to cover individual expenses. From the perspective of this ideology of household, the daily work that a woman contributes to the household is that of her domestic labor and her occasional work in the harvest; at the same time, the daily labor contributed by the man is his work in agricultural cultivation.

Nevertheless, to the extent that a division between the spheres of production and reproduction has taken place, as expressed in the progressive separation of women from agricultural work and the increase in domestic labor, the household has come to identify itself more and more with the farm and its production. This distinction is pertinent because, as long as reproduction is no longer part of the objectives of the "household-agricultural enterprise" and women remain separated from agricultural production, their access to farm profits is considerably weakened. Their daily work for the household is no longer valued as a positive contribution to production of commodities or labor-power itself; rather, it appears as savings on reproductive expenses. However, women's role in the collective enterprise is still considered in terms of the ideology of the household as a productive/reproductive unit, and this tempers the use that men, as agricultural entrepreneurs, are able to make of women as reproducers of the work force.

Women's work in clothing manufacture, seen from this double perspective of the household, appears on the one hand as work detached from the collective interests of the domestic group that produces income for individual expenses. On the other hand, it appears as a savings for the household to the extent that it is used for uncommon expenses of reproduction. It is a savings, however, that is to some extent secondary—that is, it is added to the principal savings accrued from housework. The type of consumption that is carried out with this income—maintained in a separate purse—expresses the character of the work.

But if the division of the spheres relegates production to the household, reproduction remains relegated to the family. From the perspective of the normative western family that is constituted as a "natural" unit, whose destiny is reproduction, appears a sexual division of labor that is also laden with "naturalness." Men contribute income to the family from their work in the sphere of production, and women contribute their work directly in the domestic sphere of reproduction. In the cases in which masculine income does not suffice in meeting domestic needs, it is acceptable for a woman to work in order to "complement" this income. Her contribution, however, will be considered secondary to the principal domestic responsibilities of women in the family.

In spite of the fact that this normative ideology of the family seems to be present in the cases studied, it is peripheral and not dominant. It is said that men must support the family, but the men find themselves in a contradictory situation: as heads of families, their duty is to contribute income that allows reproduction; but as managers of a farm, their duty is to maximize profitability—a goal that assumes increasing productivity by investing in machinery and reducing costs, especially those of labor-power. In the context of this dilemma, the ideology of the household remains dominant and privileges the reinvestment of profits on the farm. For this reason, the "principal" masculine income derived from the farm and destined for the family is minimized. "Complementary" income becomes necessary to cover most family expenses. From the perspective of the ideology of family, the work of making clothes is secondary because it is not "naturally" women's work, and because it complements a masculine income that is insufficient to reproduce the family. The growing ideological pressure on women to assume domestic reproductive responsibilities is—together with the need not to be a burden for the household-farm—what pushes them to look for other income to cover the costs of reproduction. The return of women to the sphere of production as a worker in the underground clothing economy co-incides with a greater emphasis on their reproductive responsibilities. Re-production, in this case, has become distinct from a commitment to the household (production/reproduction) and more closely tied to a commitment to the family. This is important because it minimizes the perception of pro-duction—the manufacture of a commodity—and of the relations of produc-tion, while it maximizes the work-family income nexus. And this in spite of the fact that, from another perspective, this income appears individual and personal since it does not become part of a common fund.

## Consequences for the Labor Market

At the crossroad of the two ideologies of household and family, these women are driven to home clothing manufacture because in this way they can contribute to the household group in a local situation where there are no other alternatives for work. In such a context, the contribution of a woman to the household group takes the form of "not spending" income that could otherwise be used for production. As mother of the family, she has the responsibility to cover the expenses of reproduction.

There exists, then, a devaluation of women's labor, specifically tied to the context of these small- and medium-sized family farms, that operates through the ideology of household. Although they seek and accept paid work in order to improve the situation of the family and the profitability of the farm, the income obtained by women is maintained in a sphere of per-sonal control (separate purse) destined for personal interests.

These women appear in the labor market with their labor power doubly devalued by perceptions that originate from the ideologies of the family and household—each with its distinct reasoning. The ideological conditioning that we have seen operates such that—given the priority placed on farm production and profitability, and given the growing separation of spheres—virtually all women can be counted as a potential labor supply, which fur-ther reduces the value of their labor-power.

On the other hand, the arguments of labor contractors who employ women in home work (according to a study by the Ministry of the Economy and Treasury for the footware sector in Alicante) deny that home employ-ment implies unfair competition, since all companies resort to this and

A second characteristic of work done at home, cited in defense of the lack of regulation, is that the majority of these workers are women, and they accept the activity in order to supplement family income. This fact is interpreted by the contractors in the sense that, on the one hand, home workers do not really need the social benefits derived from work since they can secure them through other workers, and on the other hand, in contracting laborers who work at home it is supposed that work is being given to a sector of the population that would otherwise not have any other opportunity to work. The contractors are aware of the advantages, to those who work at home, of having the ability to work part time or with flexible schedules. . . . (MEH 1986, 67; translation my own)

For the contractors, who create the demand for labor, the ideology that allows them to identify a particular segment of the work force as specifically apt for underground home work is based in part on the family and in part on a business ethic according to which what is truly reprehensible is "unfair competition."

## Conclusion

In order for there to be a market, supply and demand is necessary. In the case of the black market for labor in home clothing manufacture, we observe that there are similarities—but not an identity between ideologies that constitute supply and those that justify demand.

Women's acceptance of the conditions of labor in this sector is not the only possible expression of these ideologies, but it is the only viable one since there are no other alternatives for paid work in the village. On the other hand, it is interesting to remember the economic emphasis that these women place on their activities as a result of the household ideology that still continues to be dominant: if the principal day's labor is housework and agricultural labor (during harvest time), it is because, economically, this represents a greater value of labor-power, not because it is the most important social contribution that women can make to the domestic group. Paradoxically, it is this attitude that justifies women's irregular work participation, and the devaluation of their labor power in the market. It is likely, in any case, that a more extensive offer of work, with better pay, would change the work priorities of these women since, among other things, it would contribute to freeing more capital for the farm.

Contractors without exception seem to justify the underground employment of women by reference to the ideology of family. Nevertheless, it would be interesting to ascertain whether they differentiate between the urban and rural supply of this type of worker when they are seeking labor in the black market.

The labor market is not divided in two segments, one that belongs to the formal economy and another relegated to the informal or underground economy; this is simply a fiscal criterion that defines the control of the state over production. The labor market is fragmented into a multitude of segments whose power of negotiation is circumscribed by the ideological characterization of the value of its labor power. In order to understand why the exploitation of specific segments of the work force is accepted and how it is justified, the study of these ideologies is necessary. If women accept the miserable labor conditions of home clothing manufacture, it is in large part because the interests of the farm, represented—within the domestic group—by the husband, pressure them to free the profits of farm work from the expenses of reproduction. On the other hand, if the clothing contractors seek women workers, it is in large part also because the ideology of the family confirms the reduction of the costs of reproduction of the work force—in addition to reducing the costs of fixed capital—and thus allows them to minimize the costs of labor-power in a labor-intensive industry at a time when the internationalization of the labor market threatens to destroy the competitiveness of many industries.

We see, then, in this case, how the pressure from one sector of production (agricultural) can benefit another sector of production (industrial) through a complex array of ideological propositions. In the case studied, all indications are that a growing separation between the spheres of production and reproduction tends to limit responsibility for reproduction of the work force, not to the domestic group, but to women exclusively. In this way, womens' work can be used not only for reproduction of the labor force but also for the production at low cost of manufactured goods. It is significant that the circumstances that make both possible are ideologically articulated.

# Chapter 5

# Female Labor, Commodity Production, and Ideology in Mexican Peasant-Artisan Households

## Scott Cook

This paper examines the role of peasant-artisan women in rural industrial commodity production in the Oaxaca valley located about 350 miles south of Mexico City. A number of previous publications resulting from the analysis of data collected during an extended period of fieldwork have treated problems of structure and process in the rural social economy of the Oaxaca valley, with a focus upon the relationship between petty commodity production and petty capitalism in various rural industries (Cook 1978, 1982, 1984a, 1984b, 1984c, 1985; Cook and Binford 1986; Binford and Cook 1986). In this paper the nature and implications of female labor in commodity production will be more specifically addressed.[1]

A preliminary analysis (see Cook 1984a, 167–172) suggested that, when peasant-artisan women in the Oaxaca valley became more directly involved in wage labor or in independent commodity production, their household status changed. The reasoning was that female (especially housewives') involvement in commodity production (whether in male-dominated industries or not) created scheduling conflicts in household allocation of labor for domestic own-use production. Accordingly, the importance of the domestic own-use sphere would be highlighted—especially because of its crucial role in the short- and long-term reproduction of labor-power (Bene-ría and Sen 1981, 291–93). This would have practical as well as ideological repercussions. It would begin to subvert the rigid stereotyping of sex roles in the regional division of labor by dramatically demonstrating women's capacity for hard, remunerative work in the sphere of commodity production on a level commensurate with that of men, and also by emphasizing the importance of domestic use-value production traditionally dominated by women (Cook 1984a, 173).

Given the absence of a control population (i.e., women whose labor time is not involved in commodity production or exchange), I cannot critically evaluate the validity of the foregoing speculative, preliminary analysis against the project's empirical record. What I can do, however, is examine the nature and implications of increasing pressure upon women to extend the amount and intensity of labor in commodity production, compare their participation in different branches of petty commodity production, and, finally, compare their participation in petty commodity production with that in capitalist piecework.

It is precisely under circumstances of increasing pressure to extend labor-time commitment to cash-raising activity that it becomes most appropriate to conceptualize women's involvement in commodity production as engendering the strain and conflict of the "double day" (Young 1978, 146). However, it is logical to assume that the attendant "strains and conflicts" are not uniform across the gamut of different labor processes and social relations of production. One important goal of this paper, then, is to examine the sources and implications of differential strains and conflicts.

Prior analysis of the Oaxaca data (Cook 1984a, 173) has provided the basis for framing one specific proposition for critical evaluation, namely, that peasant-artisan housewives who are directly remunerated only for labor they expend in petty commodity production generally have lower degrees of gender or class consciousness than housewives whose "double day" includes the performance of ancillary, detail labor (perhaps unpaid) or outwork (paid according to piece-rate) in peasant capitalist industries like treadle loom weaving or brick making, or in merchant capitalist industries like embroidery. An analysis of interview and case study data from palm plaiters and backstrap loom weavers who independently produce and market their commodities, and from independent petty producers and out-workers in embroidery who deal with buying-up and/or putting-out merchants will be used in this paper to evaluate this proposition.

It can be noted at the outset that there are four ways in which women contribute to rural economy in the Oaxaca valley:

(1) As principal decision-makers in those households which are not headed by men (about 8 percent of our total sample of 1,008).

(2) As domestic workers who prepare food, wash clothes, care for children, and perform other unpaid tasks which are critical to the long-term reproduction of households.

(3) As unpaid laborers within domestic petty commodity-producing enterprises wherein they carry out specific tasks in a labor process for which the male household head is the sole recipient of cash remuneration.

(4) As income-earning commodity producers (either self-employed or as piece-rate out-workers), directly remunerated, whose contribution to household income is therefore overt rather than being concealed behind the control which men exercise over production in other circumstances.

It will come as no surprise that rural Oaxaca valley women, with a few exceptions, are found in lower-paying craft occupations than are men. Many petty commodity enterprises are exclusively household undertakings which involve the coordinated participation of both sexes in production; there are also a number of industries with a strong component of sexual segregation in which household income is generated by a male agriculturalist and female domestic worker/craft producer. The predominantly female industries are characterized by the lowest rates of return. In the remainder of this paper I analyze the participation of female workers in three branches of rural industrial commodity production—palm plaiting, backstrap loom weaving, and embroidery—and discuss some broader economic and ideological implications of their participation.

## The Palm Plaiters[2]

Palm plaiting is a predominantly female activity transmitted intergenerationally through matrilines. Most native-born women in the Albarradas villages fully participate in the industry by the time they reach their early teens and continue to do so in their old age. Mothers, grandmothers, and aunts teach daughters, granddaughters, and nieces the craft, and it is quite common to find female representatives of at least two generations working side by side during the day or evening in village homesteads. A majority of twenty informants attributed their involvement in palm plaiting essentially to the fact that it is their village's traditionally accepted occupation through which females contribute to household budgets, either through cash earnings or wage goods acquired in exchange for mats with village buyers-up/grocers (i.e., the *empleadoras*).[3] The only partial exception to this is in the case of one male informant (a bachelor and the only male who regularly plaited palm) who, however, took up the craft when he was nineteen following an incapacitating accident. Nevertheless, as is the case with the female informants, he viewed his participation as a consequence of a lack of viable employment alternatives which, for him, was summed up in the saying "When need obliges, one loses even his freedom of choice."

In the case of this unique male plaiter, as for all of the females, the fact that plaiting is done in the confines of the home gives it an added attraction since it can be conveniently interspersed with household work. In the words of a female informant: "Working palm permits me to be at home and at the same time tend the animals and do my chores." The male plaiter's statement of the problem is also representative: "First, I make my tortillas and prepare my meals, then I begin working palm for short periods (*por ratos*)." Indeed, Albarradas women's participation in this branch of commodity production is taken for granted, just as is their participation in householding duties. As one informant expressed it matter-of-factly: "One cooks in order to eat, and one plaits *petates* in order to earn a few cents." However, the widespread pragmatic acceptance of this double workload is not accompanied by a uniform fondness for the craft. Another informant expressed the view, shared by many of her companions, that, "If we could find another occupation, we would stop weaving *petates* since it is a lot of work, is poorly paid, and one gets fed up with it."

It is also the case that the acceptance of the double workload is not accompanied by a single strategy for performing it—even though large family size suggests that it is. One notable consequence of the relatively high number of offspring per housewife-plaiter is the availability of daughters who help ease the burden of work on their mothers. Only two of our thirteen married informants had no daughters, seven had one daughter each, and the rest had from two to four daughters each. Moreover, all of our informants who were either widows or unmarried lived in households with other females of working age. This is not coincidental; it is a demographic consequence of the high demands placed on female labor in these peasant-artisan households. Only in those households with more than one female worker can mat production posssibly begin to approach the status of a full-time activity. Even so, it is typically described as a "for a little while" (*por ratos*) activity; household tasks are assigned highest priority, even to the extreme that women often say they turn to plaiting when they are "not occupied" ("When one is not busy—*desocupada*—one makes a *petate*" or "One has to do her chores first and then when she's not busy—*luego que se desocupa una*—she has to make a *petate*"). The following responses to a question as to how the informant managed to combine household tasks with mat plaiting are illustrative:

(1) First I do the household chores, and then I grab the *petate*. My daughter helps me make tortillas before she goes to school. When she comes home from school she helps me to plait.

(2) In the morning after one prepares the meal, one begins plaiting a *petate*. Afterwards, when it is mealtime again, one stops plaiting. My daughter helps me to haul water and to make tortillas. Daily we spend about two hours plaiting.

(3) When I finish making tortillas, and after caring for the children, I plait a little. For short periods only. To sit down and plait all day long is not possible.

(4) I do all the household chores: the tortillas, to wash dishes, to prepare meals, to make the beds. Then I sit down to plait a *petate*, if only for a little while.

(5) First we go to the mill; afterwards we make tortillas by hand; then we prepare the meals. First the chores, then the plaiting. We sit down for short periods.

(6) When one finishes with the kitchen chores, one starts making a *petate*. When my daughters are here the work is divided. When they are here I plait more because they make the tortillas and the meals, and I earn. But alone, you do what you can.

These statements underline the importance of the sexual division of tasks within peasant-artisan households and, more specifically, highlight the extent to which the household mix of production for own-use and commodity production requires collective and cooperative female labor, usually involving representatives of two generations.

The fact that one-quarter of our informants reported that they had left their villages for periods of time ranging from less than one year to eleven years to work as domestic servants in Mexico City exposes another cash-earning strategy involving the deployment of female labor which is widely employed by rural Oaxaca households in lieu of or to supplement craft production. Typically, young women (through a family-kinship network) find jobs in Mexico City as "live-in" domestic workers (cooking, washing, cleaning) and send regular cash remittances back to their village households until such time as they resume their status as resident members or, in other cases, set up independent households (either in the village or in Mexico City).

While this involvement of rural females in urban domestic labor markets in Mexico is well-documented, less well-documented is their return to the sending villages and their re-integration into the peasant-artisan household division of labor. There has been a tendency to view rural-to-urban female labor migration as a one-way route to urbanization or modernization, whereas our data lead us to view it as a circulatory process linking rural and urban branches of what has been characterized as an "informal sector" (Portes 1983) in the Mexican economy. Or, alternatively, it can be said that village household economy is partially reproduced through cash inputs derived from the urban informal sector without necessarily entailing the eventual permanent loss (through urbanization) of its female wage-earners. The most striking case illustrating this is that of a sixty-year-old informant, Rosa, who grew up as a palm plaiter in Santo Domingo, left as a young woman for a twenty-six-year career in domestic service in Oaxaca City and Mexico City (where she spent eleven years as the cook for a well-known and wealthy popular songstress), and returned to the village to reside with her niece and resume palm plaiting in her "retirement."

The case of Rosa is especially significant because it provides a graphic illustration of the comparatively low remuneration received by female labor of "peasant-Indian" origin in both the urban domestic service and rural craft sectors of the Mexican economy. Her twenty-six years of work in domestic service did not generate adequate savings to support her retirement, thus obliging her to take up palm plaiting, which she had not practiced since her youth. Admitting that she liked it better in the village because she was with her family, and emphasizing that it is sad when one has to leave one's village and family because of need, she nevertheless would have preferred after her return to the village to have taken up an occupation other than palm plaiting which she said tired her out. The theme of "obliging need" is evoked by her explanation of the rationale for having to plait palm: "One tires out sometimes. When one is tired, one does not want to plait. Sometimes one stops plaiting for two or three days. Afterwards one says to oneself: 'Where is the money?' So, one is obliged to plait."

There are variations and complexities in the perception of differences, their significance and sources, among the palm plaiters. On one plane most informants would agree with the generalization that, "One spends a lot of time making a mat and earns a few cents" but, on another plane, there is widespread recognition of differential household productivity and earnings (e.g., "There are people who work more, and some who earn more"). Also, it is recognized that there are differences in the quality of plaiting which are associated with differential earnings (e.g., "There are persons who know how to plait really well, and others who plait more simply; buyers take note and pay accordingly"). Differential productivity is understood to result from either self-exploitation (e.g., "Some plait a lot, others a little; the ones who have time work all day; the ones who don't leave work for the next day") or from reciprocal joint work arrangements referred to in the mountain Zapotec villages as *golaneche* (e.g., "Some earn more because they sit down with two persons to one *petate*, and if they sit down early they can finish it in one day," or "There are households that plait a little more because they plait together," or "One advances more working with another; one *petate* is plaited between two persons so the work is not so punishing; working together has no other advantage").[4]

Regarding value and price, a majority of informants considered that they confronted a buyers' market in which the village intermediaries set prices. They recognized the possibility of bargaining for better prices in the extra-village marketplace, but rejected this as unrealistic given the need to quickly convert mats into cash or wage goods in the village. One informant stated the dilemma well in the context of her answer to the question of whether she would like to have another kind of employment:

If there was other work here, even to earn five pesos a day, we would do it. Then we would stop plaiting. Since we plait *petates* for short periods over three days—what do we do about the cash that we need daily? Well, if there isn't any during those three days that I plait a *petate* then I ask for a loan. When I finish the *petate* I have to pay off the loan. Well I'm back where I started; there is no progress. For that reason I am telling you that if there was other work where I could earn five pesos a day, well it would be good for me.

In other words, the daily need for cash would incline her toward work in which daily earnings were possible. Only in households with more than one plaiter is it possible to earn daily from plaiting mats (it is possible to do so from plaiting fans or small baskets, although the *empleadoras* prefer to buy mats). Households, like this informant's which have only one plaiter, are obliged to meet their daily cash needs through credit extended by *empleadoras* in return for a claim on future mat output.

The following statement by an *empleadora* who operates a small store in one room of her house outlines the kind of transactions she habitually has with palm plaiters: "Women come here to buy on credit and say to me, 'Well, give me credit and later I'll bring you a *petate*.' That's how I do business." In reply to a question as to whether she liked to transact business in this fashion, she stated: "Yes. The women need something and don't have the money to pay for it, so I give it to them on credit and they pay me later with *petates*." A more established *empleadora* storeowner claimed, however, that although she continues to make cash advances to plaiters, she no longer exchanges inventory in her store for palm products because the practice lost her money. She prefers to conduct her transactions strictly on a cash basis—a preference which can readily lead to a drop in customers in a perennially cash-scarce economy.

Relatively few households build up an inventory of their own palm products for periodic sale in the extra-village marketplace, although such a strategy is recognized as desirable for those households with the resources to support it simply because mats or baskets can be sold for higher prices there than in the village. The following statements by palm plaiters regarding their sales preferences provide a representative cross-section of what they think about the two basic marketing alternatives available to them:

(1) If we need a few cents we sell here. If not, we store *petates* and then take them to the marketplace where we sell them to buyers who use them.

(2) I have never sold *petates* to resellers. I keep them and then take them to the Tlacolula marketplace. There I sit down and sell them by haggling with clients.

(3) I don't go to the marketplace—it comes out better here. One has to lose a lot of time and abandon one's home to go to the marketplace. That's why I don't go.

(4) When one needs cash for daily expenses, one makes a *petate* and sells it right here. When we have food on hand, then we keep our *petates* and later take them to the marketplace.

A common theme in these and other statements is a use-value oriented pragmatism which places short-term consumer needs above any possibility of longer-term profits. The plaiters tend to sell in the village as a matter of expediency and need. They are first and foremost producers of commodities to compensate for deficiencies in their capacity to produce for own use, that is, they are unable to produce themselves everything they consume, so must enter the market economy to acquire commodities and services necessary to their way of life. As one woman expressed it, "We earn from our craft, but we consume what we earn for the household."

When products are taken to extra-village marketplaces, some plaiters express a preference to sell to clients who buy for their own use; this seems to reflect a homespun quasi-Thomistic bias against profit-oriented resellers (e.g., "I prefer to sell to people who will use *petates* rather to resellers who only do business with them"). The majority, however, simply express a desire to sell to whomever will buy at a price which is subject to negotiation but which they see as hovering around a going price that no single seller can control. Also, their view is that resellers have a right to whatever profit the market will bear, although this is counterbalanced by a grudging (and, perhaps, envious) recognition that what is for them a craft pursued for subsistence is for the resellers a business pursued for profit.

The palm plaiters do not subject cash returns from mat (or basket) sales to any sort of accounting procedure which would include a summation of costs in terms of labor or raw materials to arrive at a profit estimate. This is consistent with their image of palm plaiting as a non-business which yields cash but not profits (*ganancias*). One informant who rarely goes to an extra-village marketplace with her products expressed it this way, "We make petates, but we don't account for the days that we spend making them. I get twenty-five or thirty pesos for a *petate,* that's all, so I sell them because I have to. We don't account for anything." Another informant who does regularly travel to the marketplace expressed a similar view with a different emphasis:

> Upon arrival in the marketplace to sell, buyers come to look over the *petates* and ask how much, and one quotes a price. Then one haggles until she sells it. I don't take into account hours worked since it's only a matter of short periods (*ratos*)—one hour here, a half hour there. I don't take work time into account.

The discontinuous nature of mat production, which this informant alluded to, also confuses labor accounting even in the case of our lone male informant who periodically works as a hired hand (day wage) in agr ture. This is apparent from the following statement:

> This year I went to work in Tlacolula since they paid sixty pesos with meals. But one can't calculate this way with *petates*. One can't finish a *petate* in a day, so as to be able to say that he's going to sell it for sixty pesos because that's what my day is worth. It takes two days to plait a *petate*. So one earns thirty pesos a day and has to provide his own meals.

This informant is aware of the opportunity cost of allocating his labor to plaiting mats in the village (as opposed to working in agriculture outside the village) but accepts that cost as a necessary trade-off for the convenience of working at home. He is, in effect, in the same situation as the women whose limited cash-earning opportunities preclude their use of "opportunity cost" logic to valorize their labor.

With regard to broader questions of social inequality, a majority of the palm plaiters considered that the households in their villages were divided into relatively better-off and poor strata, and explained this generally as reflective of differential work performance. The better-off households were said to work harder or to have more available workers or fewer dependents. Interestingly, a few informants directly linked palm plaiting to poverty (e.g., "The poor do not have jobs, only the poor woman with her *petates;* that's why they are backwards") and, in one case, the reselling of palm products by *empleadoras* was associated with relative wealth as follows:

> They are poor because of the family, since they have a lot of children who can't help them. The men go to work elsewhere because here in the village they can earn only fifty pesos daily. Where there is family, that's not enough. Then there's the mother with her *petates* and *tenates;* she sells them to the *empleadora*. To store *petates* one must have money. If not, one can't do it. Some people here have money and they begin to buy and store *petates*.

That's how their money keeps growing. They sell *petates* in the marketplace and bring back other things to sell; that's where the money is.

In corresponding fashion, the possibility of material progress from a condition of poverty was seen by several informants as realizable only through hard work and saving, though others viewed it either as unrealizable in the village context (e.g., "In this village a poor family cannot become rich—leaving the village, perhaps") or requiring luck (e.g., "If a fortune falls in his lap") or divine intervention ("God decides" or "If God so wills it").

Without exception, the palm plaiters asserted that men earned more than women. Many agreed that this was the case because men worked harder than women, and also noted that men were customarily paid by the day and often worked outside the village. There was no expression of antagonism regarding differential pay. Nor was the fact that palm plaiters were paid by the piece, whereas most men's work was paid by the day, cause for lament. In fact, the differential earnings and payment forms between men and women were not described as being unjust; they were apparently accepted uncritically as expressions of the way things were. Indeed, if any tendency exists in their responses, it is for women to belittle the contribution their plaiting makes to the household economy by dismissing it simply as "passing the day." There was only one reported case of disagreement between a palm plaiter and her husband regarding work, and her account of it serves as an appropriate summing-up of the role of this occupation in the village economy:

He says that I am entertaining myself with the *petate,* nothing more. But I tell him that there are times when the children ask for snacks or things like school supplies and that I pay for them with the *petate.* I tell him that if he alone works there is not enough money. It's just a way of helping out a little.

Time and time again the empirical record shows that female craftwork is hardly a hobby or pastime, but an activity critical to the survival of peasant households in a cash economy.

## The Backstrap Loom Weavers

Like palm plaiting, backstrap loom weaving is customarily associated in popular and scientific culture with the female domain in the rural Mesoamerican sexual division of labor (compare Villanueva 1985, 19). Nevertheless, it is by no means an exclusively female occupation in the villages we surveyed. Indeed, in the Jalieza area of Ocotlán district there is a striking contrast between Santo Tomás, where 71 percent of the weavers in our random sample of half its households were female, and the neighboring villages of Santo Domingo, Santa Cecilia, and San Pedro where the percentage of female weavers was significantly less (10 percent, 17 percent, and 53 percent respectively). In other words, if backstrap loom weaving was once an exclusively or predominantly female industry in the Oaxaca valley, it clearly is not one today.[5]

Before examining these contrasts within the sexual division of labor more closely and, particularly, before attempting to explain the partial defeminization of the labor force in weaving, it is necessary to present some background information regarding the Jalieza villages and the weaving industry. Santo Tomás, while not the largest of the Jalieza villages in terms of population (110 households versus 138 in Santo Domingo, 84 in San Pedro, and 60 in Santa Cecilia), is the head village politically—probably because of its strategic location on the valley floor near the highway linking Oaxaca City to the district town of Ocotlán de Morelos. Santo Tomás, curently the Oaxaca valley leader in backstrap loom weaving, generally produces a wider variety and better quality of products than its neighbors. Its pioneering and leading role in this industry, together with its proximity to the highway, has made Santo Tomás a favorite stop on the tourist circuit (especially on Fridays, which is market day in Ocotlan, an event which attracts tourists from Oaxaca City). The Santo Tomás weavers display their products on Fridays in a site adjoining the municipal plaza and garden. This activity is organized by a marketing cooperative which has operated in the village since 1963 and which, despite the fact that it has never had a majority of weavers in its membership, has had considerable impact upon the craft (Bertocci 1964).[6]

By contrast, in the other Jalieza weaving villages, which are linked only by a dirt road to the highway and are essentially inaccessible to the tourist trade (especially Santo Domingo and Santa Cecilia, which are located in the mountains several miles from the highway), there are fewer weavers, no formal weavers' organization, and products are sold on an individual basis to intermediaries or to tourist shop owners in Oaxaca City. Their product line is limited to sashes (*fajas*) and bags (*bolsas*) of generally poor quality in comparison with those from Santo Tomás. This is probably not unrelated to the fact that backstrap loom weaving in these villages has been recently adopted from Santo Tomás, where it has been practiced continuously since the prehispanic period.

Given Santo Tomás' position of prominence in backstrap loom weaving, it is likely that the entrance of male labor into the industry occurred first there and then spread to the other Jalieza villages. Several male weavers in Santo Domingo reported that they learned to weave by a friend or acquaintance in Santo Tomás, whereas most of the others reported that they learned from neighbors or on their own. It is not clear under what conditions Santo Tomás weavers taught the Santo Domingans, but we have no evidence of any employment relationship between them. Probably the serious entry of Santo Tomás (and other Jalieza area) males into weaving occurred in response to their search for ways to compensate for a shortage of good quality arable land and, consequently, low yields in agriculture, as well as to the growing demand for woven goods which created unprecedented cash-raising opportunities. In other words, in opportunity cost terms there is a material advantage to Santo Tomás (and the other Jalieza area) households to allocate male labor to weaving rather than to other cash-earning activities.

The average age of the male weavers in our Santo Tomás sample (N = 22) is thirty-four (range from twelve to fifty-nine); fifteen are household heads. They weave for an average of thirty-five hours weekly with most reporting that they did so on a permanent year-round basis—although those with arable land worked fewer hours per week during the agricultural season. These male informants, at the time they were interviewed in 1978, reported that they had been weaving for an average of 8.5 years; the longest that any of them had been weaving was twenty-three years, and only six others had been weaving for more than ten years (all between eleven and fifteen years). This explains why a 1964 (Bertocci) study of weaving in Santo Tomás correctly characterized it as a female industry and made no mention whatsoever of male participation (which our data indicate was minimal). The fact that all of these male informants were taught to weave by females, more than half of them by their wives, provides convincing support for the proposition that a defemenization of labor in the industry occurred during our informants' lifetime—probably not much before 1955 (assuming that the informant in our sample with 23 years as a weaver told the truth and was among the pioneering male weavers, a not unreasonable assumption to make considering our random sampling procedure).

Even though males now comprise almost one-third of the labor force in backstrap loom weaving in Santo Tomás, they have taken it up largely to supplement rather than to replace females. What appears to have happened after 1963, probably as a result of the establishment of the cooperative which rationalized production and marketing in ways which diversified the product line and improved quality—thus stimulating sales (see Bertocci

1964)—is a village-wide increase in the weaving population. This, in turn, led to an increase in the family labor force and/or an intensification of work at the household level.

More specifically, our survey data point to an elaboration of the household division of labor with task and/or product specialization by gender. For example, adult males tend to be associated with the weaving of newer products such as tapestries, which often require wider looms, or the making of belts, which requires leatherwork in addition to weaving (which is done by males and females), whereas women are increasingly associated with weaving smaller or finer products and in operating sewing machines to assemble newly introduced clothing products such as vests (*chalecos*), slipover shawls (*cotorinas*), and bags (*bolsas* or *morrales*).

More male weavers (70 percent) than females (50 percent) in Santo Tomás tend to sell their products weekly; males also earn larger average sales receipts than do the females (median = 690 pesos versus 270 pesos). This may reflect the greater productiveness of male weavers, which perhaps derives either from their greater time commitment to weaving (because of fewer competing demands for their labor, especially in land-poor households) or higher productivity per hour worked. The earnings differential may also reflect a further gender division in marketing patterns since a somewhat higher percentage of males than females reported that they sold their products in Oaxaca City; the data also show that men were more likely to sell their products to resellers instead of to buyers for own use. Since the latter are generally agreed to pay higher prices than resellers for the same products, this practice would be materially advantageous only if another pattern suggested (but not confirmed) by our data is true, namely, that women (with some exceptions) tend to specialize in finer, higher-quality products which are relatively underpriced, whereas men tend to specialize in standard quality, higher-volume products which range from fairly priced to overpriced. More conclusive answers to the comparative performance of men and women in the Jalieza weaving industry will be forthcoming only as a result of further research.

The average age of the female weavers (N = 13) who were selected for post-survey interviews conducted in 1980 is forty; all were either married or widowed (average age at marriage was eighteen; range thirteen to twenty-eight) and, with the exception of two who were childless, each had an average of 4.6 children. The average age at which these women began to weave was twelve (range seven to fifteen) and, at the time they were interviewed, they had been weaving for an average of twenty-eight years each (versus twenty for the whole sample). As might be expected, most of them learned to weave from their mothers, grandmothers, or mothers' sisters (although, somewhat surprisingly, in the total sample the same percentage reported having learned with their mothers as with a non-relative). Only four women stated that they had worked in family agricultural activities prior to marriage, and all of them helped with various domestic chores from a young age. One index of the importance to the household economy of their weaving is the fact that only two of them had extra-village work experience (as domestic servants, one in Mexico City and the other in Oaxaca City)—which, incidentally, is a much lower percentage than for the palm plaiters from the more remote Albarradas villages.

It is somewhat surprising that only five of these thirteen female weavers considered that their life was better now than it was when they were growing up, a judgement which belies any simplistic assumption that everyone has benefitted equally from the apparent increase in weaving business or that benefits have been enduring. That neither of these conditions has been achieved is suggested by a wide variation in per capita income and in the living conditions index among weaving households in Santo Tomás.[7] Accordingly, their explanations as to why they weave reinforce the "obliging need" theme: weaving is the most viable cash-earning activity available to them in the village, and the need for cash income to meet daily household expenses is constant.

Despite a nearly universal insistence that they weave because they want to (*lo hago porque quiero*), many female weavers also admitted paradoxically that weaving is the work the village provides for them ("That is our work" or "That is the work for a person from here" or "That is the only occupation there is here"). Many also volunteered that they were not obliged to weave by their husbands. Several, however, expressed the beliefs that there is a mutual obligation between husband and wife to help each other out ("It is an obligation for one of us to help out the other") and that their household cannot survive only on their husband's earnings ("I do it because I have an obligation to work as does my husband . . . with the children we can't make it on what my husband earns"). We are reminded of the material urgency of their situation by one informant's statement: "With the sashes that I weave I buy food for my children."

As was the case with the palm plaiters, these same themes emerged repeatedly in informant responses to the question as to whether or not they would like to withdraw from their occupation. Even though a majority of them reported paltry, if variable, earnings and complained of steadily rising costs of materials (thread, dyes, etc.) and that the work was tiring (especially hard on the back and knees), they argued unanimously that they would not consider quitting, simply because there was no other convenient or acceptable way to earn cash ("Why would I give up weaving? How else am I going to earn a few cents?'') either for a housewife with dependent children (''Only here can I earn something . . . since I'm in the house and can't leave to look for outside work; I weave daily; with that I maintain my children'') or for a widow (''From that work come the cents to keep me going''). In short, backstrap weaving is a tiring activity with limited rewards in most cases, but it is the only one available to many women (''When it no longer is worthwhile I'll stop doing it; but otherwise what would I do? I would just be seated, nothing more; it's better to keep it up'').

There was widespread agreement among these informants that differences existed within the industry related to the quantity, quality, and value of work performed by weavers representing different households—a perception which is supported by our research. The following answers to a question as to whether or not the informant felt there were differences among the weavers are representative:

(1) There are others who earn more. There are persons that make things of more value—for example, wide sashes—and there they earn more. Not all of us do the same weaving.

(2) There are those who weave more, they weave bags, and they earn more.

(3) When there are large families in which everyone weaves they get better results. Where the family works a lot they earn more.

The sources of differential productivity in weaving mentioned in these statements—family size, more work, product mix—were all confirmed by our research to be associated with socioeconomic differences between households.

However, when asked specifically about the sources of wealth and poverty in the village, most informants emphasized the importance of landholdings and especially of inheritance as the principal means for acquiring them. The attitude linking relative wealth and proverty of village households to the land situation (the less land the more poverty) was prevalent, as was the notion that the more households are dependent upon weaving rather than agriculture for their livelihood, the worse off they will be. As one informant expressed it:

One-third of the village is in difficult circumstances, but others go to the fields and don't bother with weaving; they have land. They don't suffer much. Those who weave are the only ones that find things more difficult. We don't have land and we dedicate ourselves to weaving. If we had land we would stop weaving.

Among other things, this statement reminds us once again that the ideology which portrays (accurately in some cases, less so in others) rural industry as the handmaiden of agriculture is espoused by carriers as well as by students of peasant culture.

Regarding the scheduling of work and task management, what was reported for the palm plaiters is essentially applicable to the backstrap weavers. Most women prefer to get up early and complete domestic chores so as to free up a block of time for weaving ("One does household chores early, and when one finishes she begins to weave; we begin at 1:00 p.m. and work for about five hours"), whereas others intersperse chores with weaving throughout the day ("A little while making tortillas and a little while weaving"). They spend an average of between two and five hours daily at weaving (average approximately 3.5 hours), seven days a week—weaving time varies daily ("There are days that I can weave longer and other days that I can't"), but only three informants said that there were days when they could not find time to weave. Seven of the thirteen informants stated that they did household chores unassisted; however, most had help from other household members in weaving. Only one informant said that she paid to have tortillas prepared for her family—and on occasion would buy prepared food in the village marketplace—so that she could devote more time daily to weaving. Two weavers alluded to a strategy of self-exploitation as a means of coping with scheduling ("One hurries up so as to earn some cents to be able to eat" and "I do my chores in a hurry and then I begin to weave").

Compared with the palm plaiters, the marketing of products by the Santo Tomás weavers is more diversified. In addition to selling in the village plaza to tourists, about one-third of the weaving households surveyed also sold periodically in Oaxaca City or outside the state (e.g., Mexico City). Sales are to buyers for their own use as well as to intermediaries. Probably proportionally fewer sales of woven products are to intermediaries than is the case with palm products, but the woven products business, dependent as it is on the tourist and export trade, is considerably more lucrative. Given this situation, it is not surprising that all of our informants cited the intermediaries to whom they sell in response to the question as to whether or not others earned money from the weavers. A high percentage of them expressed a clear understanding of the marketing and profit strategies of the intermediaries (e.g., to buy cheap and sell dear), and a few expressed veiled resentment against intermediary practices as the following statement illustrates:

> The buyers-up pay cheap. They earn more than those who work. Since I don't agree with this I don't work very much. The

buyers-up are together regarding prices and they are bothered if one asks them to increase prices. They say that they can't. They take advantage of us.

Again, as is invariably the case with craft producers in the Oaxaca valley, most of the backstrap loom weavers agreed that intermediaries were entitled to their profits. However, there were two notable exceptions which deserve quotation here since they express genuine awareness of exploitation in the relationship between petty commodity producers and merchant capitalists:

(1) The one who does all the work is the one who ought to earn. The buyers-up buy a product and sell in a little while, and the one who spent two days to make it earns a little. The buyers-up from one day to another have their money.

(2) The buyer-up earns but the weaver who did the work doesn't share the earnings. The buyer-up wants to enrich himself with the sweat of the weaver.

It is precisely through expressions such as these by producers themselves that the idea that petty commodity production contains the wage-labor/ capital relation (Gibbon and Neocosmos 1985) assumes credibility as something other than a logical construct and merits more systematic empirical inquiry.

**The Embroiderers**

It is, however, when merchant capital relates to peasant-artisan producers not merely to buy up their products but also to put out their raw materials that social relations more closely resembling those of industrial capitalism are established. Whether the context be the East Anglian textile industry beginning in the fourteenth century (and subsequently in much of England [Goody 1982, 12–21]), the nineteenth century lace industry in the Moscow Gubernia of Russia (Lenin 1964, 362–369), or the present-day needlework industry in the Ocotlán district of Oaxaca, Mexico, when merchant capital penetrates industrial commodity production, either from outside or inside the ranks of direct producers, it has a contradictory impact upon the household economy.

In the case of the Ocotlán district embroidery industry, one such impact is expressed through the recruitment of commodity producers with little or no previous experience in wage labor but whose petty commodity background has instilled in them a double-sided familiarity with merchant capital—one side which perceives it as opportunistic profiteering, and the other which perceives it as a career model to emulate. So the small-scale rural putting-out merchant must come to grips with the fact that each new out-worker or commission agent recruited is a potential future competitor. Given the dispersal of out-workers in their separate villages and homesteads, organization is difficult even when they work for the same merchant. Accordingly, a prevalent out-worker strategy for increasing earnings—aside from producing more by working harder or for longer hours—is to go independent, enlist the cooperation of family workers, and if sufficient capital is eventually accumulated to establish a small buying-up and/or putting-out business.

Although the needlework industry can be said to be dominated by merchant capital through dispersed mass production on a buying-up and putting-out basis, the independent petty commodity producer is by no means absent. Indeed, given the internal horizontal complexity of the division of labor which opens up space for independent units with specialized skills and a marketing network which provides a variety of sales opportunities, not to mention the prevailing accumulation strategy mentioned above, self-employed producers are unlikely to disappear any time soon. There are, however, signs that self-employed producers will become inceasingly dependent upon buyers-up who extend cash advances (*adelantos*) so as to establish liens on future output.

One interesting feature of the needlework industry is the variation between and within villages regarding the status and role of household enterprises. Most needlework households in several villages (e.g., Santa Cecilia and Santo Domingo Jalieza, Magdalena Ocotlán, San Baltazar Chichicapam, and Santa Lucia Ocotlán) are out-worker units for absentee merchants; the out-workers pick up a pre-patterned unassembled set of pieces for one garment (with or without the necessary thread) from a merchant in the regional marketplace or from a village commission agent, embroider the separate pieces at home (often with different household members being allocated a particular piece within the set), and then turn in the completed set (pieces embroidered but not assembled) to the merchant (or commission agent) for a lump-sum payment.

In some villages (e.g., San Juan Chilateca and San Pedro Mártir), side by side with out-worker households of the type just described there are other households which independently cut, design, embroider, crochet, and assemble the garment by machine-sewing (usually a blouse or dress). These self-employed units may or may not have dependent out-workers; if they do, they will distribute various tasks in the production process to out-workers and specialize in assembly and other selected tasks themselves.

Consequently, there are different levels of skill, task assignments, and piece-rate remuneration within the out-worker population. Some specialize in embroidering intricately designed figures on the pleated front of blouses below the neck (referred to appropriately as *hazme si puedes* or "make me if you can"), whereas others specialize in simpler embroidery, crocheting, or designing and cutting garment sets. It is worth reiterating that there is evidence to suggest that these self-employed embroiderers are becoming increasingly dependent upon buyers-up through cash advances (*adelantos*) or special order (*encargo*) relationships.

Data from San Pedro Mártir, one of the Ocotlán villages where there is an interhousehold specialization of tasks in the embroidery industry, show that out of thirty-four women surveyed, three specialized in designing and cutting for an average wage of ninety pesos weekly, eleven did the intricate embroidering of figures on pleated blouse fronts and earned an average of eighty-seven pesos weekly, and five did crocheting for an average wage of sixty-eight pesos weekly. Women who did simpler needlework earned substantially less. The average payment by piece was ten pesos for designing and cutting, eleven pesos for intricate figure embroidery, and nine pesos for crocheting. Our data show that the women who specialize in these tasks earn higher weekly incomes than non-specialists, but that they also work longer hours.

Another interesting feature of the needlework industry parallels one in backstrap loom weaving, namely, the entry of males into a craft which has traditionally been a female domain. I still recall my surprise one morning in 1979, upon first visiting San Isidro Zegache, where I found male heads of household seated on chairs, either on their porches (*corredores*) or under the shade of trees on their house lots (*solares*), diligently embroidering floral designs on blouses or dresses. These were the first male embroiderers I had seen in the Oaxaca valley. As it turned out, only four of the eleven villagers with embroidery households had no male embroiderers. San Isidro, with 35 percent of its embroiderers being males, was far and away the industry leader in that regard, although nearly 15 percent of the embroiderers in San Jacinto Chilateca and 10 percent in Santa Cecilia Jalieza were also males. Overall, however, the embroidery population surveyed is predominantly female (92.7 percent of 450 embroiderers), and there is no reason to believe that a process of extensive defeminization of the embroidery labor force is underway.

Some clues as to the structure of the needlework industry can be ascertained by considering what the four villages without male embroiderers have in common and, especially, by looking at them in comparison with the three villages with the highest incidence of male embroiderers. The first common feature is that three of the four villages without male embroiderers (Santa Lucia Ocotlán, San Baltazar Chichicapam, and San Dionisio Ocotlán) are peripheral latecomers to the industry. They have a low percentage of household participation in embroidery and have major occupational involvements in other areas. For example, for historical reasons both Santa Lucia and San Dionisio have a large number of men employed in highway maintenance and construction jobs, whereas San Baltazar is an important agricultural village, has several mescal distilleries, and a thread-spinning industry which is the largest employer of women. San Juan Chilateca is a prosperous agricultural and commercial community with a small sugar industry and with many households having members with salaried jobs in the public and private sector of the modern economy.

By contrast, San Isidro Zegache is a newly established, land-poor agrarian reform community of *mestizo* ex-ranch hands, many of whom practice modern horticulture on small private plots or work as hired hands or share-croppers in neighboring villages (especially San Antonino). In other words, the men of San Isidro took up embroidery as a cash-earning supplement to *minifundio* horticulture and agricultural wage labor or share-cropping. This was the only village in which all of the embroidery households (with one exception) were independent petty commodity producers (two of which had a few out-workers). It was also the only village which participated in just one branch of craft production.

One-third of the embroiderers are between ten and nineteen years of age; 46 percent are equally divided between the twenty-twenty-nine and thirty-thirty-nine age categories. Participation in embroidery steadily declines in subsequent age categories to a low of 2.4 percent among women over sixty. Two factors are probably involved in this decline: (1) in many villages embroidery has only been recently introduced and is usually learned in school or is self-taught rather than being transmitted through the family structure, and (2) failing eyesight. These same two factors no doubt have a bearing on the high participation rate of girls between ten and nineteen, together with the fact that they are either in their prime as dependent family workers or are new housewives in the initial stages of the independent household cycle without heavy domestic chore obligations. Although female participation in embroidery diminishes as the independent household cycle progresses (from stage 1 to stages 2 and 3), it is significant that it declines by only about ten percentage points and that it remains steady among women between twenty and thirty-nine. This is possible because embroidery is perfectly suited to the "for a little while" pattern of work necessitated by the daily regime of domestic chores which is most demanding during these years.

Of 265 embroidery households distributed among eleven Ocotlán villages in our sample, eighteen households in two villages, Santa Cecilia

Jalieza and San Jacinto Chilateca, were selected for follow-up interviewing. The average age of these informants (all females) at the time they were interviewed was thirty-eight (range from sixteen to fifty-seven); only two were unmarried, and the fifteen women with children had an average of four each. Work histories of these two groups of women are different. Most of the San Jacinto women grew up as weavers (most as family workers, others as out-workers for Santo Tomás weavers) but abandoned it for embroidery after they were married. The major reasons cited for the change-over were the steadily rising cost of yarn, sluggish and erratic sales, and low earnings. Since rising costs and low earnings also characterize embroidery, it is more likely that the key to the abandonment of weaving in San Jacinto is attributable to marketing difficulties which were probably an outgrowth of the market dominance of weavers in the neighboring village of Santo Tomas Jalieza. In any case, not a single informant expressed regrets about switching from weaving to embroidery. Even those who were unhappy with embroidery did not want to take up weaving again:

> Embroidery no longer pays. I like weaving better because it was the work of my childhood. I have wanted to quit embroidery because I earn so little. If I had a place to deliver what I produced where they paid a good price it would be different. But right now one earns nothing. I want to quit. I don't want to take up weaving again because my lungs are too weak. (A common complaint of the weavers is that weaving damages their lungs.)

And:

> I don't like to embroider but I don't want to work in weaving again. Weaving tires you out more than embroidery.

One thirty-eight-year-old informant who was taught to weave when she was seven years old by her mother (who later died in childbirth) and who was a pieceworker for a Santo Tomás weaver, took up embroidery, in addition to weaving, after she married because of her husband's poverty (they are landless and must buy all of their food). This is the only case among our informants of a continuing involvement in both weaving and embroidery. Why has this informant chosen to pursue both? In her words, "I weave and I embroider because I have to do both to earn enough for food and to help with the children's expenses" (she has five children ranging from three to fourteen years of age). How does she manage household chores and schedule her craft work? She spends five-six hours daily, mostly in the afternoon and evening, embroidering. She weaves for about four hours once a week or spends more time weaving and less time embroidering when she needs money quickly. As she expressed it: "The sash can be woven more rapidly, I make one when I need to raise quick cash. Embroidery pays better but it takes longer."

It is clear that the viability of embroidering independently rather than as a out-worker—once the embroiderer has sufficient experience and knowledge of the labor process—hinges on the ability to earn enough cash to cover production costs (e.g., cloth and thread) plus a net income. One informant who alternately does out-work and works on her own account commented on the difference as follows:

> When I finish my own shirt I am going to embroider one for another since I have run out of cloth. I deliver a dress every two weeks. They pay me 150 pesos. It is someone else's dress. When it is mine I sell it for 300 pesos. It doesn't pay much but it helps to buy food for the children.

An embroidered dress which sells for 300 pesos requires four meters of cloth at thirty pesos per meter and thirty-five pesos worth of thread—a total cost of 155 pesos (1979 values, 1 dollar = 22.50 pesos). Thus, an out-worker presumably earns about the same per dress as she would be buying the raw materials and selling it herself. Our data suggest, however, that successful independent embroiderers either sell their dresses for higher prices or pay out-workers less per dress than the above figures indicate. For example, one informant who told us that she sells her dresses for 300 pesos each to a merchant from the Zona Rosa in Mexico City said that she had five out-workers whom she pays only 100 pesos per dress. (Incidentally, the Zona Rosa merchant resold these 300-peso dresses for 800 to 1000 pesos, a common level of mark-up).

The difficulties faced by these women in dealing with costs, prices, and earnings emerge clearly in the following statements:

> I don't know how much it costs. The people who buy it say how much it's worth—well-embroidered 350 in pieces, but if it's poorly done only 250. The buyer says, "That's all I'll give you. If you don't want to sell it, keep it, go and find another buyer who'll pay you more." With luck another buyer will pay ten pesos more. They no longer want to pay. The buyers-up do our accounting (*nos sacan las cuentas*). I don't do it because I don't know how to read. What am I going to do? Sometimes when I buy cloth I earn a little for each meter but, at times, there are no earnings.

And:

> One figures her accounts, but one is obliged to sell even
> though she realizes that she's losing. One takes into account so
> much for the cloth, so much for the thread—and if she takes her
> work into account—it doesn't come out. One realizes how much
> she lost but it doesn't matter. What can we do? No one pays more.
> Prices are the same everywhere.

And:

> We don't figure our accounts with a pencil and paper, but we
> do make an accounting in our heads of the cloth and the thread. It
> figures out to be a gift. There are no earnings. Our work is given
> as a gift.

To the extent that these embroiderers (most of whom are illiterate) keep
accounts, they do so only in their heads. But all of them recognize that their
work is grossly underpaid. None of them, however, calculates exactly the
returns on her labor. In this industry the primitive system of payment by
results neatly circumvents labor-time accounting. Petty merchant and producer alike think only in terms of lump-sums—the former of cost per piece
and net earnings per sale, the latter only of gross income per piece. In some
general sense Lenin's assertion (1964, 363) that "production for sale
teaches that time is money" may be true, but petty producers' understanding
of the lesson does not so easily lead to labor-time accounting in production,
much less to a strategy for securing just compensation for labor expended.

The Santa Cecilia women began to embroider during the 1970s; some
of our younger informants had been doing so for less than one year at the
time we interviewed them. Several of them were participating in a program
sponsored by FONART (*Fondo Nacional para el Fomento de las Artesanias*), which included instruction in design, cutting, embroidery techniques,
and machine sewing. FONART was helping to finance and supply the in-
structor, the sewing machines, the cloth and thread, and was buying up the
finished garments (discounting cost of cloth and thread). Although the program seemed to be functioning reasonably well, several informants stated
that they could make more money by making tortillas for sale in Oaxaca
City and that they also found tortilla making less tiring. As one of them
expressed it:

> I prefer to make tortilas for sale because the earnings are better.
> Embroidery is slow work; it tires out one's brain. I don't see well.
> But with tortillas, even when I fill up my bucket with dough, noth-
> ing happens to me.

This same informant said that it took her two days to make one hundred tortillas, which she sold for one peso each in a Oaxaca City marketplace. Working on her embroidery for two or three hours daily, it took her approximately one month to finish embroidering a dress for which she was paid 110 pesos. Clearly, the material incentive would seem to favor tortilla making and discourage embroidery—except, of course, that tortillas require corn as well as a prolonged stretch of labor time.[8]

The reason why most of these women embroider mostly during spare time intervals ("For short periods, when there is time") is clear from the following description by this thirty-three year-old woman with four small children:

> When I finish making tortillas and preparing *tejate*, then I grab my embroidery. Later the children cry, I nurse them and I have to stop embroidering. When the children fall asleep I grab the embroidery again.

Another informant described how her first work priority daily is food preparation and how friction with her husband arises when embroidery interferes with this:

> Women don't just embroider. The husband is always asking for his *tejate*. One prepares meals, one hurries up more in preparing meals than with the embroidery. The husband will say, "Give me some food; stop that work. I go out to work so that we have money. Stop it. First give me something to eat and then you can continue to embroider."

In Santa Cecilia, women's involvement in commodity production is completely subordinated to domestic provisioning. Both tortilla making and embroidery are undertaken strictly as necessary cash-raising activities. "One's life is poor," one informant lamented. "Hunger itself obliges us to embroider."

Although the embroidery women are poorly educated and functionally illiterate, and in the case of the Santa Cecilians relatively recent direct participants in commodity production, their experience has taught them that direct producers earn little, resellers earn more, and that the best route to increase cash income is to combine production for sale with putting-out and/or buying-up for resale. Despite the fact that half of the embroiderers rejected the proposition that the poor can successfully escape poverty through hard work and enterprise, they would agree with their out-working colleague (who did accept it) that, "I work and the owner takes the cents." In other words, regardless of their position in the embroidery industry, producer for own-account or out-worker, our informants shared the judgment that intermediaries were the biggest earners in the industry and that this condition obtains because they pay low wages (or prices) and sell dear. This was succinctly summed up by a Santa Cecilia informant who said, "The buyer-up earns, and the ones who do the work don't."

## Conclusions

What I have documented in this article are some contradictory organizational and ideological aspects of the evolution and functioning of various commodity-production forms in the household economies of contemporary peasant-artisan communities which have long produced and trafficked in commodities. We know enough about the evolution, structure, and functioning of the political economy of Mesoamerica to be certain that in the complex tributary economies of the late prehispanic and colonial periods, there was considerable pressure on women in the peasant household economy to produce tributary craft commodities (see Villanueva 1985). It is unclear whether the Oaxaca valley had anything comparable to the *repartimiento de hilazos* (the distribution of thread) that operated in the Guatemalan highlands to the end of the colonial period in which Spanish officials put out raw cotton to peasant-Indian women of highland Maya towns to be spun into thread for token or no payment (Bossen 1984, 324–325), an arrangement quite similar to that which binds today's urban merchants to peasant-artisan women in the embroidery industry.

In any case, it is untenable to argue that the "double day" or the "segmented labor market" are twentieth century capitalist innovations in the Oaxaca valley social economy. This is especially true when we consider the fact that household craft production was important not only as a source of tributary commodities but also of market commodities which have been essential to the material reproduction of peasant-artisan households and communities in Mesoamerica for centuries (Taylor 1971, 1972; Cook and Diskin, eds., 1976; Blanton et. al. 1981; Blanton and Kowalewski 1981; Kowalewski and Finsten 1983). In other words, the labor of peasant-artisan women in the Oaxaca valley has long been subject to the stresses and strains of the double burden of production for use and for exchange.

It must be emphasized, however, that in today's multi-tiered political economy the process of commoditization is more advanced than ever before; to an unprecedented degree, capitalist accumulation has become both a pervasive and an integrative force. Without making comparisons with the situations of their forerunners in past centuries (which may be impossible in terms which measure up to standards of discourse about present-day realities), this imposes a heavy burden on today's peasant-artisan women. It requires their participation in household production for own-use and in commodity production, both of which are essential to the short-term reproduction of labor-power; and in childbearing and childcare which are essential to the long-run reproduction of labor-power (compare Beneria and Sen 1981, 291–293; Young 1978).

Among the Oaxaca valley peasantry, women's work in the domestic sphere of mothering and household chores tends to be ideologically separated from men's work. Petty commodity production by women has traditionally been viewed as an extension of their householding activities and has not been perceived as "work" (trabajo) but rather as "helping out" (ayuda) (compare Deere and Leon de Leal 1981, 349; and Cook 1984a, 169). With some exceptions, such ideological segregation continues to be present in those cases in which women particpate as petty commodity producers in industries where buying-up merchants are prominent (if not dominant) but where capital accumulation potential is low, such as palm plaiting, and even in those petty capitalist industries like treadle loom weaving and brick making where women are engaged as unpaid pieceworkers' assistants or are family workers in petty capitalist enterprises run by men (Cook and Binford 1986). In all of these situations, the ideological mystification of women's roles belies their real contribution to household subsistence and capital accumulation.

There is evidence from several cases of seamstresses in the treadle loom weaving industry and of at least one woman pieceworker in the brickyards (Cook 1984a, 163–167), that women experiencing direct proletarianization begin to reject the traditional view of women's work. In other words, they no longer refer to their work as "helping out" and develop clearer understandings of the proposition that exploitation is a relationship of production rather than of exchange. Similarly, the increasing subordination of women's labor by merchant putting-out capital in industries like embroidery seems to be accompanied by inchoate but empirically demonstrable changes in consciousness of exploitation.

However, most of the housewife out-workers still view their embroidery work as "helping out" and as a "for a while" adjunct to householding. Like their petty commodity producing sisters, they practice self-exploitation but begin to recognize that their failure to earn more income has to do with their market relationships rather than with themselves. These "market relationships" are personified by "buyers-up," or by "putters-out"—both of whom are referred to as "intermediaries" ("regatones" or "comerciantes"). Some out-workers, however, have begun to view their employers (or the buyers of their labor power and the owners of the raw materials they work with) as unjustly depriving them of a portion of the fruits of their labor by, in essence, paying them less than their labor is due. Outworkers reject the idea, so common among the petty commodity producers, that even though the merchants' *modus operandi* is to buy cheap and sell dear, they are entitled to whatever the market returns to them for their haggling prowess or luck.

# Chapter 6

## Caribbean Slavery and the Struggle over Reproduction

### *Dale Tomich*

The practice of granting slaves the use of parcels of marginal land in order to cultivate food crops either for subsistence or for sale on the local market appears to have occurred to varying degrees throughout the slave colonies of the Americas, but the discussion of its significance has been particularly active with regard to Caribbean slavery. It is a central feature of processes that have been variously described as the formation of a "proto-peasantry" and as a "peasant breach" in the slave system. Sidney Mintz uses the term "proto-peasantry" to characterize those activities which allowed the subsequent adaptation of a peasant life-style worked out by people while they were still enslaved. According to Mintz, (1974) the cultivation and marketing of crops, and the acquisition of agricultural skills and craft techniques entailed in this practice, became basic to establishing the freedman's independence from the plantation after emanicipation. For Tadeusz Lepkowski (1968), the slave parcels formed "a variegated slave-peasant mosaic alongside the indubitably dominant compact mass of land belonging to the master, in which the slave was an agriculture or industrial worker forming part of a great productive organism." In Lepkowski's view, the "peasant breach" demonstrates "an intent toward another alternative for agrarian development of the country, a contradiction to the economy of the latifundia based on the exploitation of the slave." In both cases, the emphasis on the (at least relative) independence of slave activity, its actual or potential opposition to the domination of the slave system, and the consequences of these for post-emancipation social organization have deepened our understanding of slavery and its historical evolution. In this paper, I would like to examine the phenomenon of autonomous cultivation and marketing by slaves more closely. I propose that the possibility of this type of peasant-like activity was engendered by the nature of slave social relations themselves and expresses the contradictory character of commodity production and the reproduction of the labor force (and social reproduction more broadly) within slavery. This form of non-wage commodity production, instead of appropriating the direct producers from the means of subsistence, gave them access to the means of producing a livelihood and thus provided them with the means to resist the domination of capital both during slavery and after.

The possibility of self-organized subsistence production emerges from the contradictory nature of the slave relation itself. The same social relation that shaped labor as a mass, disciplined, cooperative force also created the possibility for autonomous individual subsistance production and marketing by the slaves. The commodification of the person of the laborer compressed these two kinds of labor—commodity production and the reproduction of the labor force—into the same social space and defined the relation between them. Slavery thus made possible, and in some respects even required, the development of provision crop cultivation by the slaves as a means of reducing or avoiding market expenditures for their maintenance. But this labor of reproduction developed within the antagonistic relation between master and slave. For the master, the provision ground was the means to guarantee the cheapness of labor. For slaves, it was the means to elaborate an autonomous style of life. From these conflicting perspectives evolved a struggle over the conditions of material and social reproduction in which the slaves were able to appropriate aspects of these activities and develop them around their own interests and needs.

This paper seeks to examine the inner connection between self-provisioning, slave commodity production, the world market, and the development of world capitalism as an historical social economy. Slave self-provisioning is seen in organic interdependence with and changing historical relation to export commodity production within a complex of inter-related processes of production and exchange. From this perspective, the focus of historical analysis is on the interrelation and mutual conditioning of these two forms of productive activity. The slave relation itself is the nexus that links these practices conceptually and practically, and establishes the inner coherence between them as aspects of a unified, structured, contradictory historical relation.

Slavery was a relation of force and direct domination which imposed the commodity form on the *person* of the laborer and the *product* of his labor. The slave had no relation to the means of production, but was himself an instrument of production as is an ox or a mule. He represented an investment in constant capital no different from that in machinery or livestock. The price of a slave was based upon his capacity to produce and was subject to depreciation as the slave was "consumed." But this capital was separate from the capital laid out to exploit him in the production process itself. Legal title to the slave was not identical with the expenditure of his labor, but rather was its prior condition. The price of labor, whether purchased on the market or "produced" on the estate, was a deduction from the capital available for production. Only with the investment of additional capital was the slaveowner able to exploit the labor of the slave. If the slave was lost for one reason or another, the capital invested in him was lost and had to be replaced with a new outlay of capital (Marx 1966: 809).

However, under slavery, the *activity* of labor or the slave's *capacity* to labor does not take the form of a commodity and cannot thereby be distinguished from his physical being. Thus, the category labor-power cannot appear as a social relation independent of the person of the laborer. The production and appropriation of a surplus is organized not through the "free exchange of equivalent values" between capital and labor, but through the direct and explicit domination of the slaveowner. *In principle,* the slave as chattel property has no voice in determining the conditions of his life and labor. Through the property relation, the slave's control over his person, the labor process, and the whole product of his labor are directly alienated and appropriated by the slaveholder without exchange.

The appropriation of the person of the laborer compelled the coincidence of commodity production and the social reproduction of the slave population within the same social and spatial unit. The slave plantation was at once an economic enterprise and a human community. As the property of the master, the subject population was incorporated into the plantation for life, both as workers and as residents. The production activities of the body of slaves as well as their reproduction, both as a labor force and as a social group, were formally organized through the immediate personal domination of the slaveowner. The slave was regarded as an instrument of production whose purpose was to produce wealth and bring a return on the capital invested. By means of compulsion, the activities and conditions of existence of the slave population were subordinated to the interests of commodity production. Production and reproduction were thereby constituted as separate spheres of activity, and the relation between them was established and maintained by the explicit control of the master. The cost of slave subsistence was thus reduced and commodity production increased. However, the efficiency of the plantation as a productive unit and its value as a capital investment were dependent upon the well-being of its slave population, *both* as workers and as social group. The master had to balance his interests as controller of the slave's working activity against his interests as proprietor of the slave's person.

Because labor-power is not a commodity and has no value distinct from the value of the laborer, the labor necessary to reproduce the laborer and surplus labor are manifested differently in slave-labor production and wage-labor production. The activity of laboring does not possess exchange value and is not a cost of production under slavery. Instead, the value of labor is subsumed under the value of the slave, and all of the slave's labor appears as surplus labor expended without compensation and independent of the value of the slave. The slaveowner has to bear the costs of reproducing the laborer, but what is renewed is the person of the slave which remains separate from the activity of labor. These costs must be paid whether the slave works or not, or the investment in his person will be lost. Even that portion of the slave's labor which reproduces his physical existence, whether indirectly through the market or directly on the estate, does not appear as the reproduction of his labor-power, but as the renewal of the stock of constant capital and is equivalent to the cost of maintenance, fuel, or parts for machines. The cost of labor does not appear directly as the price of labor-power, but takes the form of a series of investments in constant capital (housing, food, clothing, the purchase of new slaves, etc.) Thus, there is no distinction between the costs of the enterprise and the cost of maintaining the slave population. The slave's reproduction remains separate from his work. It appears determined only by the needs of his physical existence, and has no direct and necessary relation to the expenditure of labor in the production of commodities. The property relation and the labor process presuppose one another as given, external conditions, but there is no economic relation mediating between the two of them. Slave price, the cost of slave maintenance, and the activity of labor remain independent of one another. The slaveowner can compare monetary expenses to the revenue from the sale of the product, but the activity of labor remains outside of this calculation and cannot be organized through it (Marx 1976a: 680,1031–1034; 1976b: 554–555; Weber 1978: 87–100).

Under these conditions, to allow slaves time off to produce for their own subsistence on marginal land is not a deduction from the production of a surplus. Rather, by reducing monetary expenses—i.e., the purchase of consumption goods for the slaves—it increases the money profit of the estate. The slaveowner must therefore calculate whether it is more economical to devote land and labor to the cultivation of food crops for the estate or export commodities; that is, whether or not the income derived from the increased amount of sugar, cotton, or coffee is greater than the expense of provisions that would have to be purchased on the market if they were not produced on the estate. In practice, of course, this was by no means a simple calculation, and there are many intervening factors that complicate it. But to judge from the extent of provision ground cultivation in virtually all of the slave colonies of the Caribbean throughout their history, it would appear that complete reliance on the market for slave subsistence goods was the exception rather than the rule. Imported consumption goods were always expensive, and at times their supply was irregular, while an increment in income from the sale of the commercial crop was not simply a function of putting more slaves on more land. On the other hand, however, land and labor for the cultivation of provisions were already at hand. "Free" time for the slaves and marginal lands for provisions emerged from the natural and technical conditions of the cultivation of the commercial crop. For example, during the so-called "dead season" on sugar plantations, the master's concern was to keep the slaves occupied while there was little to do with sugar.

Thus, the "proto-peasant" activities emerged almost naturally in the interstices of the slave plantation. They were interstitial not just in the sense that final authority over the use of land and the disposition of time resided with the master, but also in that the time and space for such activities arose out of the rhythm of plantation life and labor. These are not activities and relations separate from the plantation system. They are intertwined in its logic and develop within and are dependent upon its temporal and spatial constraints. Slave provision ground cultivation is thus intimately linked to the organization of export commodity production and develops in close association with it. What can be seen is the formation of stable small-holdings within the plantation cultivated by slaves without supervision. The common pattern in the Caribbean was to have a small plot next to the slave cabin where fruit trees and vegetables were planted, and where occasionally chickens or even a pig or goat were kept, and a larger plot on the margins of the estate where manioc, bananas, potatoes, yams, and other staples of the slave diet were grown. Generally, the slaves were given all of half of Saturday off to work on these parcels, although they also worked on them during their mid-day break and in the evening after work on the plantation was done. The slaves were allowed to dispose of the entire product of these plots, including selling it on the market. Evidence indicates that the amount and variety of food produced went beyond the needs of direct consumption and was oriented to sale on the local markets. The slaves provided not only a substantial portion of their own subsistence needs, but a large part of that of the free population as well. To give some idea of the scale these activities could attain, the Sunday market at Cap François in Saint Domingue regularly attracted 15,000 slaves, while Lamentin in Martinique drew several thousand slaves from all parts of the island to trade in a wide variety of goods. It must also be pointed out that for most of the history of slavery these activities took place despite the attempts of metropolitan authorities to suppress them (Mintz 1974, 1978; Debien 1974: 178–183, 207–209).

There "proto-peasant" practices reveal the contradictory nature of the master-slave relation, and their development both modified the character of slavery and provided the means of securing the transition to a post-slavery society. On the one hand, these activities clearly served the interests of the slaveholders by reducing the costs of the plantation and by integrating the slaves into the system. The planters did all they could to encourage these activities and regarded them as the mark of a good slave. But, at the same time, these activities had a different meaning for the slaves and subverted the slave regime even as the activities reinforced it. For the slaves, the activities represented the opportunity to:

(1) Improve the material conditions of life by increasing the amount and variety of food and clothing, to acquire goods, and accumulate wealth in various forms (including money and slaves).

(2) To organize their own activity without supervision. Slaves had an avenue to exercise decision-making and demonstrate self-worth otherwise closed off by slavery. Perhaps more importantly, these activities allowed collective self-expression and form what Roger Bastide describes as a "niche" within slavery where Afro-American culture could develop (Bastide 1978: 58). The "little Guineas," as the provision grounds have been described, were important for aspects of slave life as diverse as kinship, cuisine, and healing practices. Conversely, this autonomous cultural activity was important in organizing the use of these parcels and their product.

(3) Marketing put the slaves in touch with the wider world outside of the plantation and allowed them to form independent associations and networks for economic, social, cultural, and at times even political purposes.

Outside of these simultaneously complementary and conflicting interests, the slaves were able to appropriate aspects of these processes and establish a degree of control over their own subsistence and reproduction. They claimed rights to property and disposition over time and labor that the masters were forced to recognize, and they were able to resist infringements upon them. For example, parcels of land, fruit trees, animals, and other slave property were passed from generation to generation, and slaves successfully demanded compensation either in time or money if the master required their free time. These practices were at times contrary to the wishes of the master or to the detriment of the estate crop. By the nineteenth century, these customary claims increasingly acquired the force of law in the French, British, and later, Spanish Caribbean. The assertion of these rights and the exercise of autonomy by the slaves reduced their dependence on the master and undermined his authority. They restricted his capacity to exploit land and labor, and presented a fixed obstacle to surplus production. The very process of the successful integration of the enslaved into slavery transformed a system based on coercion and absolute authority into one were compromise and negotiation had to be recognized. This opened new spaces for the slaves to contest the regime and resulted in subtle and complex changes within the prevailing relations of slavery that were an element of its dissolution and the means to establish new forms of social and economic organization.

Rather than the formation of an independent peasantry, the focal point of the development of these autonomous cultivation and marketing activities is the struggle between master and slave over the conditions of labor and of social and material life within slavery. Beyond the formal juridical distinction between free and unfree labor, these activities indicate the substantive complexity of slave labor which combined both "proletarian" labor in the canefields, mill, and boiling house, and the "peasant labor" of the provision ground. This "peasant" dimension of slave labor emerges within its "proletarian" dimension and forms a counterpoint to it. While provision ground cultivation arose from the planter's attempts to reduce costs and create an interest for the slave in the well-being of the estate, its further elaboration depended upon the assertation by the slaves of their own individual and collective needs within and against the predominant slave relation. The condition of the development of autonomous provision ground cultivation and marketing was the appropriation of a portion of the labor time of the estate by the slaves. This struggle for "free" time entailed and was reinforced and conditioned by struggles to appropriate physical space and the right to property and disposition over their own activity. In turn, the consolidation of slave autonomy in provision ground cultivation provided leverage for more struggles over the conditions of staple crop production. These interrelated practices transform and subvert the organization of labor within slavery as they reinforce it (Rodney 1981; Mintz 1982).

This process reveals both the contradictoriness and historically developing character of the master-slave relation. As the assertion of slave autonomy continually pushes, at least tendentially, "beyond" the limits of the slave relation, the master is compelled to try to recapture and rationalize labor under these changing conditions. Thus, for example, task work may be seen as an attempt to create a new, more effective form of labor discipline, whose *premise* is autonomous slave self-interest. Industrial discipline here depends on the existence of provision grounds and adequate material incentives recognized by both parties, though meaning something different to each. Slave struggles for autonomy and planter efforts to contain them within the bounds of the prevailing relations of production developed the slave relation to its fullest extent and created both the embryo of post-emancipation class structure within slavery and the conditions for the transition to "free labor." See from this perspective, the reconstruction of the post-emancipation plantation system was not simply a unilateral and functional shift to a more adequate and rational "capitalist" form of organization. Rather, it was a process whose outcome was problematic, requiring violence and compulsion to recapture labor in the face of material and social resources acquired by the laboring population while still enslaved. The struggle over conditions of labor and of social and material life continues in a new historical context.

## Conclusion

Let me conclude by suggesting the importance of these activities for post-emancipation economy and society. The ability to elaborate autonomous provision ground cultivation and marketing within slavery provided the slaves with an alternative to plantation labor after emancipation and allowed them to resist its re-imposition. The very activities that the planters had encouraged during slavery now incurred their wrath. Carlyle scorned Quashee and his pumpkin, but far from representing the "lazy Negro" it is a testimony to the capacity of the Afro-Caribbean population to learn, adapt, create, and articulate an alternative conception of their needs despite the harshness of slavery. Probably few could escape the plantation entirely after emancipation, but for the great majority of the freed slaves the existence of provision ground cultivation and marketing networks enabled them to struggle effectively over the conditions of their labor. Jamaican historian Douglas Hall suggests that, upon emancipation, the freed slaves sought to separate their place of residence from their place of work. Where planters tried to compel a resident labor force, the workers left to establish free villages on lands off the plantations. In either case, the skills, resources, and associations formed through "proto-peasant" activities during slavery were of decisive importance in enabling the free population to secure control over their own conditions of reproduction and establish an independent bargaining position vis-à-vis the planters (Mintz    ; Hall 1978).

The immediate consequence of emancipation throughout the French and British Caribbean was the withdrawal of labor, particularly the labor of women and children, from the plantation sector, and struggles with the planters over time, wages, and conditions of work in which the laboring population was able to assert a great deal of independence and initiative. It represented, in Walter Rodney's expression, an attempt to impose the rhythm of the village on the plantation. The successful separation of work and residence forced a new relation of production and reproduction on the plantation system itself as the planters attempted to recapture the labor of the emancipated population or find a substitute for it under conditions that guaranteed profitability. This resulted in the formation of new coercive forms of labor extraction in which the laboring population maintained control over subsistence activities and petty commodity production to one degree or another. This transformation of the plantation system, and the transition from one form of coerced labor to another, was not the inevitable result of unfolding capitalist rationality, but rather is best understood as the product of the contradictory relation between production and social reproduction within the relations of slavery and of the struggle between masters and slaves over alternative purposes, conceptions of needs, and modes of organization of social and material life (Rodney 1981).

# Part III

# CAPITALIST CRISES AND
# UNWAGED WORK

*The last section of the book deals explicitly with the effects of the global restructuring of capital on the patterning and intensity of unwaged work. As in the previous section, the contributions are unusual in their ability to link large-scale changes to the lives of individuals and families. The analysis in this section is somewhat more macroscopic in focus, however, examining changes in work patterns across regions and classes in the United States and the linkages between changes in work regimes and consumption patterns in the industrial nations and the developing world.*

*Joan Smith's article describes the ways in which the actions taken by industry to recover from the recession of the 1930s have forced the restructuring of consumption and labor practices in U.S. households, and how these actions create contradictory conditions for unwaged labor. She examines such trends as the growth in consumer spending, the increase in the debt burden of households, changes in welfare payments, and the growing participation of wives and mothers in the paid work force. She argues that these new arrangements preclude further downward pressure on wages and will, in fact, force workers to struggle for increased wage packages in the near future. Further downward pressure is precluded, in part, because female labor is as fully employed as possible (in a combination of waged and unwaged activities), and thus unwaged labor cannot be further expanded to supplement or extend the wage. Smith's documentation of the way in which labor is invested as a condition of consumption of many products currently being used within the home is particularly striking.*

*Nona Glazer's contribution to the volume addresses the question of how the domestic labor of women is affected by changes in the manufacture and marketing of commodities. She describes the emergence of "involuntary unwaged work" in retail sales—in particular, the emergence and growth of self-service retailing strategies. The paper details the shift from heavily ser-*

*viced, small family-owned specialty shops and diversified "general" stores to supermarkets and giant chain-store organizations. Glazer also describes the assumptions about women's work (and women's "personalities") that underlie the marketing of self-service operations to females, and the way in which retailers have pitted male and female employees against one another in competition for jobs and have encouraged both to perceive their interests as antithetical to those of the consumer (who often shares their class background). She notes that the increase in self-service in retailing does not necessarily imply consumer dissatisfaction—in fact, careful marketing strategies help to insure that consumers perceive it as a benefit. But she argues that such perceptions are irrelevant to the fact that the cost to industry is reduced by self-service and that the labor burden placed on consumers (mainly women) is increased.*

*The paper by McGuire and Woodsong describes variation in the labor force participation of women and children in this century and consequent shifts in the intensity and patterning of unwaged labor. Perhaps the most interesting feature of the paper is their demonstration that the "family wage" has been little more than an ideal for most working class families in one northeastern U.S. city for several generations. They document the tremendously diverse and creative strategies by which households in Binghamton, New York, "pieced together" a living in the 1930s, the 1950s, and the 1970s. In the 1930s, unwaged activities were proportionately more important than they are today, and mothers held authority over children and extended family members residing in the household in organizing their waged and unwaged work. In contrast, by the 1950s, a combination of rising wages (for men) and a desire to keep children in school for longer periods led to a decrease in the number of women in the paid work force and a decrease in children's work generally, while women assumed more or less full responsibility for housework. By the 1970s, more adolescents were involved in waged work (but to meet their own needs for things like stereos and clothes), and women's participation in the work force had increased again due to declining real incomes. Men's work remained more or less constant through this period. While women had worked a number of hours roughly equivalent to that worked by men in the 1930s, by 1980 they were working 20 percent more.*

*Harriet Friedmann's paper explores the ways in which new agro-food industries link production and consumption practices in the industrialized and developing nations. She examines the complex linkages between the es-*

*tablishment of the world economy in food grains, mass production in North American industry, and the mechanization of North American agriculture, as well as between the extension of commodity relations into more and more aspects of daily life in both first and third worlds and the concomitant reorganization of domestic relationships. Friedmann draws on a new variety of regulation theory, which focuses on the ways that particular patterns of consumption are linked to regimes of accumulation. She focuses on the effects of the emergence of a regime of intensive accumulation in the industrialized countries between 1947 and 1973—a period in which living standards increased and mass consumption became crucial to profits for the first time. Friedmann traces the implications of mass consumption (and the practices of the industries that fuel it) for the lives of ordinary people in first and third worlds, dealing most explicitly with the integral link between the nature and intensity of unpaid domestic labor in North American farms and that paid and unpaid labor in the third world that buys and consumes its products. She concludes by suggesting a potential solution to the "impasses of grain surpluses, farm crises, expensive public subsidies, ecological and aesthetic simplification of the countryside, and chemically dangerous foods."*

*Like earlier chapters, these contributions avoid reifying unwaged work or locating its root in the past. In the words of J. Smith, "Unwaged household labor is one of the* results *of capitalist production and as such is guaranteed by capitalist relationships and not by some precapitalist social form." They reveal the ways in which capital has tried to re-integrate the "free time" obtained through workers' struggles into its processes of accumulation. They also demonstrate how frequently unwaged labor can be seen to be the integral link between restructured consumption patterns and new forms of production.*

*Jane L. Collins*

# Chapter 7

## All Crises Are Not the Same:
## Households in the United States during Two Crises

### *Joan Smith*

There is little question that the capitalist world has entered a period of contraction. Following on the heels of a long boom, the world economy in general, and that of the United States in particular, is now experiencing a general period of economic stagnation.[1] In 1985 we witnessed only a 2 percent rise in gross national product; U.S. unemployment remains extraordinarily high by normal standards—though both the media and the Republican Party are attempting to establish an alternative standard by which current unemployment figures will appear more acceptable. Inflation has been reduced, but the principal ingredient in the reduction are goods and services that are more discretionary than necessary. Housing costs continue to rise astronomically, as do the costs of medical care, childcare, and education.[2]

Yet, as bad as it is, the economic downturn of the 1970s and 1980s has not left nearly the detritus of the 1930s. Although real incomes have fallen perceptibly over the course of the last decade, household expenditures remain at an all time high.[3] Although economic growth is virtually nonexistent, it is at least not falling as precipitously as it did in the early 1930s.

The question raised by these trends is whether capital—at least in highly industrialized countries—has found the institutional mechanism whereby it can get the downturn it "needs" without simultaneously suffering a collapse in effective demand. If so, this development was the result of a number of structural reforms improvised out of material already at hand, but intensified as specific responses to the crises of the 1930s. As successful as they might have been in the early post-World War II period, each of these reforms had built into it, however, its own limitations. These limitations have now been reached in the current period of economic difficulties. In short, the distinction between the crisis of the 1930s and the downturns of the 1970s and 1980s signals not the final remedy to capitalist economic difficulties but a wholly new stage.

In what follows I will concentrate on three responses to the crisis of the 1930s and how each of these, in turn, established the conditions for the economic difficulties of the 1980s. First, there was what I will call an intensification of Fordism—the mass production of consumer goods using labor which agreed to relative docility and ever-increasing productivity levels in exchange for higher and higher wages, a trend which occurred in conjunction with expanding consumer credit which permitted the absorption of the new product. The second response—that is clearly connected to the first—was the rapid incorporation of non-traditional sectors of the population into the ranks of waged workers. Though this second trend affected many types of workers, both here and abroad, I will concentrate on that one stratum that had been, relatively speaking, outside the ranks of labor for a considerable amount of time—that is, wives and the mothers of young children. A third development, which I will mention only in passing since it goes beyond the immediate interest of this paper, is the fact that the state became a major absorber of goods and services both directly—through its own purchases—and indirectly, through a variety of welfare reforms.

These innovations—vastly expanded consumer markets facilitated by new arrangements with labor and expanded consumer credit, the increased labor activities of wives and mothers, and vastly increased welfare payments—are uniquely resistant to economic downturns. They are responsible for the contrast between the crisis of the 1930s and that of the 1970s and 1980s since they are the secret of continued consumer demand even in the face of depression levels of unemployment. Let me offer one very compelling piece of evidence. In 1930, if wives' earnings, additional credit, and welfare payments had been entirely eliminated from disposable household income, that income would have been reduced by not quite 6 percent. If the same sources of funds had been eliminated in 1982, disposable household income would have been reduced by close to 49 percent.[4]

In short, almost half of household income during the current crisis is drawn from sources that are "a harbor in the storm" of economic difficulties. First, women are much more likely to be employed in sectors that are recession-proof (Niemi 1974). Although female unemployment is classically higher than that of males, during recessionary periods the rate at which men are unemployed climbs to, meets, and then exceeds that of women.[5] At the peak of the most recent recessionary period, male unemployment exceeded female joblessness by close to a full percentage point. In 1930, male unemployment was close to three percentage points higher than that of women.[6] Even more importantly, it was precisely during the recurring recessions of the 1970s that wives and mothers flocked into the wage labor force through the doors of the service sector, which remained largely open in spite of the contemporaneous economic downturn of the period (Smith 1984).

Second, although there has been a constant recurrence of pressure from the Federal Reserve Bank to curtail consumer credit, and political pressures on states and the federal government to reduce welfare payments, neither effort has been particularly successful even in the face of the current slump. Credit restrictions were introduced during the peak of each of the recessionary periods throughout the 1970s and early 1980s, only to be rescinded each time within a matter of months.[7] An in spite of the verbal backlash against welfare mounted by the Reagan administration and the New Right, during 1983 only three states lowered welfare payments while twenty-two states increased benefits, and in 1984 only one state decreased payments while thirty-two states increased them. Although the peak of the recessionary period saw a benefit decline in constant dollars, it was a very modest one—just 2.5 percent. Between 1970 and 1984 the average monthly benefit increased by 80 percent for families and by more than 130 percent for individual recipients. From 1971 to 1981 the number of AFDC families rose more than 50 percent.[8]

## Crisis and the Restructured Household

Our current economic troubles appear mild compared to those of the past, principally because we are using a yardstick that was more appropriate for measuring past difficulties than current ones. That effective consumer demand has not been eroded is a function of a vast rearrangement in the economic and social practices of working class households. These rearrangements were the necessary condition for implementing new structures of accumulation on the part of capital—structures that were designed to bring the economy out of the depression of the 1930s and to fend off another in the immediate post-World War II period. But, these rearrangements—through their absorption of ever greater quantities of unwaged work—have depleted working class households' capacity to respond to the current crisis without eventually demanding considerably higher wages and even a realignment of the labor process itself.

As Hobsbawm has pointed out, each of the solutions to past crises creates the conditions for the next one (1976). What he did not say, but what follows from his observation, is that the nature of the next crisis may be hidden behind the illusions created by the former. In our own period, the maintenance of effective demand—a solution to the crisis of the 1930s—has provided the illusion that the country is, at worst, in a momentary slump. However, the creation of what appears to be recession-proof demand had fundamentally altered the nature of working class households. More importantly, these changes have altered the capacity of households to respond to economic difficulties in any other way than that which will require higher and higher overall wage bills for capital. Notwithstanding the current cutbacks and give-backs (and I believe that these are inaugurated precisely because of the latent upward pressure on wages), this suggests that the years to come will see an increase in labor militancy—not the kind usually associated with organized labor, but a wholly new sort of militancy that we might have trouble recognizing for what it is.

In short, working class households in the United States have entered the cash economy with a vengeance and in ways that they have never done before. They have been propelled there by the structural changes that brought the country out of the 1930s slump, changes that worked through and on the household. It is this process that I now want to investigate.

### Fordism and the New Labor Force

Recent increases in the number of wives and mothers of young children who are now permanent members of the U.S. labor force have been vast. The astronomical growth of married women in the labor force during the 1970s outstrips the new labor that had been provided by immigrant workers in any ten-year period during the so-called great migrations of the early part of the century (Smith 1984). It represents a sea change in the ordinary activities of working class households that has largely gone unnoticed—mostly because of the ideologies that surround women's waged and un-waged work.

When this growth in women's labor is addressed by economists, it is from one of two points of view. There is an increased *supply* of this labor, according to these commentators, because of reduced fertility levels and the introduction of labor-saving household appliances. Secondly, there is an increased *demand* for women's labor because of the vast increases in the number of so-called women's jobs in the expanding service sector. Both of these explanations contain small threads of reality, but both fail to place what is nothing short of a revolution in household structures and relations in its proper perspective—that is, in the context of the structural changes in households that have attended revisions in investment policies necessary to meet the increasing pressures faced by capitalist firms.

There is no question that in order to realize post-war production strategies—the expansion of the market for relatively low-priced consumer durables—wages available to households had to be substantially increased. Such goals led to the intensifications of Fordism. But this strategy had built into it two upper limits. First, while wages to individual workers could be increased, the total wage bill for individual firms had to be kept within acceptable limits. In order to maintain *relatively* low wages, the pressure on productivity and so-called efficiency, a pressure intrinsic to capitalist production, became the economy's driving force.

While there are limits at any given moment on "efficiency" and productivity—limits that are partially political and social, and partly technical—there are no such limits on what capital must produce. In short, the possibilities for increased productivity are quickly outpaced by the constant pressures to continue to produce. The current recomposition of the U.S. labor force is precisely a product of this dilemma. The number of low-wage jobs in the service sector and in manufacturing (both domestically and overseas) has now outstripped that of highly paid manufacturing jobs (Smith 1984). In addition, recent wage concessions have reduced even the wages of the unionized workers in blue collar industrial jobs.

In this context it should come as no surprise that few, if any, working class households now have the privilege of offering up the labor of only one of its members. There are two reasons for this. New "cheap" jobs were created for women in new sectors as the possibilities for accumulation in older sectors were progressively exhausted. The need for wives and mothers to take these new jobs had precisely the same source. Total cash income of working class households had to be increased in order to absorb the overall downward pressure on wages and to pay for the increased product that was the result of the increased emphasis on the production of consumer durables.

Both of these developments were in the wings by the mid-1960s, only waiting to be called upon the stage. All that was required was a slight dip in the economy to call forth this restructuring of the labor force—a restructuring that forced working class households to find additional labor to pay for the goods that were spewing forth from more traditional sectors.

## The Need for Cash and the Restructuring of Household Debt

In order to assure the absorption of the new industrial product, not only did new workers have to be found, but new credit mechanisms had to be devised. To be sure, consumer credit was on the scene long before the advent of the 1930s crisis. Singer Sewing Machine Company led the way, to be followed very rapidly by Ford and other automobile manufacturers.[9] However, consumer credit of the first half of the century bears little relationship to that of the latter.

First, the number of items that could be bought on credit has been vastly increased to include almost everything that is on the market. In its initial competition with Montgomery Wards in the 1920s, Sears extended credit to include some household items, and this was thought by some to be unsound, if not revolutionary.[10] Secondly, credit terms have been substantially liberalized. In the earlier period, large down payments were required; there were hefty monthly payments and a relatively brief time allotted for retiring the debt.[11] Third, credit eligibility in the earlier period was restricted to higher income households and based almost exclusively on net worth. Currently, eligibility requirements have been almost totally relaxed.

Each of the restrictions on consumer credit were substantially eroded during the late 1930s and in the immediate post-World War II period. Leading the way were two pieces of federal legislation which established the mechanism for increasing the extension of credit for goods that, up until that time, had been largely available only for cash; and for making credit available to households which, given earlier credit terms, simply could not have afforded it.

The Electric Home and Farm Authority—organized by the federal government in 1934—functioned as a government finance company for the purchase of home appliance papers from local retail dealers.[12] Home repair and modernization installment loans came into general use in 1934 when the FHA Title I program was initiated. It was not until this point that stockers and automatic furnaces became retail items.[13]

Between 1934 and 1955, total debt for households increased by 408 percent, outstripping the growth in total household assets by close to 60 percent.[14] While in the early part of the century consumer liabilities were less than 10 percent as large as total business liabilities, they have grown in the post-World War II period to roughly the same level as that of businesses (Jester 1966). The growth of consumer borrowing relative to that of firms had been steady but not particularly spectacular up until 1929—from 8 to 14 to 23 percent over periods that corresponded roughly to the first three decades of the century. But since 1935, the growth of external liabilities in the household sector has been nothing short of explosive. Further, to an increasing degree, household capital formation has been financed with debt rather than equity capital. The ratio of changes in household external debt to changes in tangible assets has declined steadily. In 1925, for every dollar of assets held in owner occupied housing and in consumer durables, households had incurred 18 cents of outstanding debt. By 1960 this figure had reached 30 cents, and by 1970 for every dollar's worth of assets, households had incurred 50 cents in debt.[15] (Jester, 1966)

More important, perhaps, is the ratio between disposable personal income and consumer debt. In 1925, for every dollar earned, households had incurred 20 cents in liabilities. By 1983, for every dollar earned there were

68 cents in liabilities. In short, consumer debts are increasing almost twice as fast as disposable income, with no sign of slowing down.[16]

Between 1910 and 1950, extensions of installment credit (the annual difference between new credit and debts retired) provided consumers with roughly $30 billion more than they received in income. Between 1973 and 1983—a period of just ten years—the difference between liquidations and extensions of installment credit amounted to more than $248 billion.[17] In other words, this extension of credit has added to household purchasing power $248 billion beyond the amount received from all other sources of income. It also added immeasurably to households' pressing need for cash.

During the worst of the economic downturns of the earlier period— 1929 to 1933—interest payments as a percent of disposable personal income decreased by nearly 50 percent, even though personal income decreased as well. Whatever else was going on, households severely curtailed installment buying as a key to economic survival. The pattern for interest payments between 1974 and 1981 stands in sharp contrast. During those seven years the proportion of disposable income dedicated to interest payments increased by over 17 percent.[18] Debt repayments for poor households took up 25 percent of their total disposable income in 1977 (Curie, Dunn, and Fogarty).

The production strategies of the post-depression period—strategies which were explicitly designed as a reaction against the depression of the 1930s—had built into them two opposing tendencies. On the one hand, they were designed to produce an increasing volume of consumer goods. On the other, because of the downward pressure on profits, they entailed a rapid shift of the labor force away from high wage manufacturing jobs. In order to maintain sufficient household income and to absorb the increasing abundance of consumer goods, households went increasingly into debt. In order to pay that debt, women were drawn massively into the labor market. These responses did not occur initially as a reaction on the part of households to economic crisis, but were inaugurated during periods of economic expansion.

## Surviving in "Normal" Times

By the onset of the recessionary period of the mid-1970s, two resources that working class households might have drawn upon to meet the new financial exigencies were *already* being utilized simply to accommodate the recovery strategies of capital initiated some twenty years before. Consumer credit was already reaching unacceptable limits; and the labor of wives and mothers was already being tapped just to meet the normal needs of households during periods of relative economic calm. To be sure, these strategies for survival were intensified by working class families throughout the rest of the decade and into the 1980s, but it appears that they may now have reached their outer limits.

There was yet a third resource that working class households had traditionally used to meet the demands of economic crisis, and this was the substitution of unwaged household labor for waged income. During the crisis of the 1930s, for example, housewives gave up a substantial amount of commercially available goods and services in favor of their own increased labor at home. Two years before the 1929 financial panic, 37 percent of households had at least a portion of their laundry done in commerical establishments. By 1933, that proportion had been reduced by over 28 percent, even though the sale of household laundry appliances remained virtually static. In 1927, 65 percent of households reported buying some portion of their baked goods from commerical establishments. Six years later that proportion was reduced by close to two-thirds. In 1927, households reported purchasing almost a quarter of their canned goods commercially. By 1933 they had reduced that proportion by close to 40 percent (Morgan 1939, 33).

This strategy of substituting unpaid household labor for goods and services formerly purchased on the market was not available to working class individuals by the 1970 recessionary period. This was not because they were unwilling to perform extra non-waged labor at home, but because the available pool of unwaged labor had already been drawn on by capital as a necessary companion to the new so-called labor-saving devices that were the backbone of capitalist production strategies of the earlier period. It was not that there were fewer hours to do "housework," but that what housework was had changed completely, and in that change has ceased to be a viable substitute for waged work.

A good example of this phenomenon is personal laundry. By the 1830s, commercial laundries had appeared in a number of urban areas. By the first decade of the twentieth century, social workers noted that even some of the poorest families in urban areas sent out at least a portion of their wash. In 1909, 60 percent of working men's families, according to one report, spent at least some money each week on commercial laundry services (Strasser 1982). Though a considerable portion of laundry was done at home, as families increased their earnings, more and more was sent out. This trend in commercialization of what had heretofore been unwaged housework was brought to a halt with the development of the automatic washer and dryer. The automatic washer and dryer not only brought laundry back into the home, but increased sales of detergents and other "washing aids," electric parts, plumbing supplies, and a variety of gadgets for ironing—everything from a mangle for flat wear to a special steam iron for collars and cuffs. Finally, the increase in home laundry led the way for the development of a whole new branch of the textile industry—synthetic fabrics that could, according to their manufacturers, simply be washed and worn.

There are two crucial points to be grasped here that may go unnoticed—either as a matter of theoretical interest or of practical concern. First, it was not "sales" effort that resulted in the great proliferation of washers and dryers and other household durable goods.[19] Rather, their appearance is nothing more than the objective traces of a vast rearrangement in production strategies—a rearrangement that responded, as previously argued, to the economic crisis of the thirties, and that was a measure for staving off a new crisis at the end of the Second World War. Washing machines and dryers, home tools, portable sewing machines, video-recorders, small power lawn mowers—I am listing just those I can either see or hear as I sit here at my typewriter—are all evidence of the intrinsic connection between production strategies on one hand and on patterns of consumption on the other.

The second crucial point is that the consumption of these household appliances was hardly voluntary. Within a few years of their initial appearance, the automatic washer and dryer offered the only affordable and convenient alternative for accomplishing a necessary task. Every other alternative had all but disappeared. It is important to note that these appliances did not imply a net savings of labor. Despite their adoption, between 1920 and 1968 there was an *increase* of one half hour per week spent doing laundry via the unwaged labor of household members (Walker 1969). The point to be understood is this: *The intensification of household labor—in this case doing one's own laundry—is no longer a means of extending the value of the wage.*[20]

To work harder at doing the laundry does absolutely nothing to stretch the household wage. It would, in all likelihood, cost money since appliances would depreciate more quickly, more fuel would be required, and a greater expenditure on laundry products would be involved. To forego the use of the washing machine and dryer and return to the scrub board would save money, but only a fraction of the initial costs of the appliances themselves which would then sit idle.

Laundry, of course, was not the only household activity that was initially commercialized as a mass service only to later be redivided and individualized as isolated unwaged housework. The preparation and preservation of food offers a similar example.[21] The annual per capita consumption of fruits and vegetables in 1970 was virtually identical to that consumed in 1930.[22] But between those two dates there was a 130 percent increase in the proportion that arrived in the home via pre-prepared cans, jars and boxes. The purchase of these products in new forms, like the purchase of home laundry equipment, implied greater consumer expenditures. It did not imply, however, a reduction in the unwaged labor invested in the preparation of food.

Long before the Civil War, the industrialization of food production was well on its way. By the turn of the century, technical developments such as rotary pressure cookers, automatic soldering of cans, and the further development of transportation insured that the way had been prepared for the total commercialization of eating (Braverman 1974, 261ff.). Principally because the technologies adopted for commercial canning were developed side by side with the technology for home canning, as late as the 1930s the provision of food via home methods was still a viable alternative to cash outlays for the commercial product.

Every country store and neighborhood urban hardware store not only had its supplies of glass bottles and earthenware jars but, by the 1850s, the self-sealing can and a rudimentary form of pressure cooker were also available for home use. In one survey of urban working class families conducted in 1917, only a small proportion reported they did no preserving at all (Leeds 1917, 41). The vast majority used home canned food to meet a substantial proportion of their needs. During the 1930s depression, the U.S. Home Extension Service found it still feasible to advise housewives on the use of home canning as a money saving measure. One survey indicates that that advice was taken seriously. Eleven million glass and tin containers were sold for home canning in one state in 1930, 30 million in 1931, and 50 million in 1932 (Cummings 1940, 181–82).

By the recessionary periods of the 1970s and early 1980s, home canning had ceased to be an activity available to most urban dwellers. Bulk supplies of fresh fruits and vegetables, which previously had been available at relatively low prices even in urban markets, had all but disappeared. They were replaced by commercially prepared goods that paradoxically still required *extensive household labor* for their final preparation, at the same time that they *cost considerably more*. The household labor time now expended on cooking is not a money saving practice, but is absolutely required given both the form in which the new commercial products are made available and the new standards of food preparation established in the postwar decades.

The home-baking craze of the 1950s and 1960s was the intimate companion of the expanded production of kitchen gadgetry. Nevertheless, these new appliances were not a substitute for products already available on the market, but were instead a stimulant to more commercial production. In a slightly later period, cuisinarts, microwaves, self-cleaning ovens, and dish-washers, masqueraded as viable alternatives to commercial products. Yet all had as their basic premise both a considerable amount of time spent cooking, as well as the use of food products that are available only commercially. Thus, the neighborhood bakery went the way of the local laundry, making room for household durable goods in combination with the commercially prepared "raw" ingredients that sold on a cash basis to private households.

As in earlier periods of economic difficulty, during the downturn of the 1930s, unwaged household labor and the relationships that guaranteed that labor were a means of stretching a dollar—a way of making do. By the 1960s, unwaged household labor and the relationships within which these activities are embedded had been appropriated by capital as the necessary condition in the production of a vastly expanded array of consumer goods. Services that had been increasingly purchased in the marketplace in the early part of the century were forced back into the home long before the onset of the contemporary recessions, not as a strategy of survival for indi-vidual households but as a condition for the consumption of mass produced durables.[23] Between 1929 and 1981 the proportion of annual household ex-penditures absorbed by the purchase of appliances increased by 22 percent.[24] As working wives and mothers know, these new products did not replace labor in the home but merely reorganized it in a fashion that al-lowed "free" time for wage labor if necessary. And the sale of that labor eventually became necessary in large measure to pay for the costs incurred in the purchase and use of these items.

## Housing and the Need for Cash

There is no need to go into the extensive suburbanization that characterized U.S. housing patterns in the boom years of the 1950s and 1960s, except to point out that it was one more reason why households were increasingly depen-dent upon cash to sustain themselves during periods of economic downturns.

First, in spite of the ethic of the self-reliant nuclear family composed of two parents and their biological children, over the course of the century families continued to display a remarkable dependence on a variety of kin and non-kin relations to guarantee their survival during periods of eco-nomic stress (Sussman 1959). In one study conducted during the 1930s de-pression, 7 percent of families reported that dependent relatives other than husbands, wives, and children had lived with them in 1927. In 1933 that proportion had increased by over 40 percent. A still larger difference was found in the proportion of families aiding relatives outside the home. In

1927, 8.8 percent of families studied reported aiding relatives who lived outside the immediate residential unit. By 1933 that number had increased to 21 percent (Morgan 1939, 23).

Most of the aid offered beyond the confines of the strictly nuclear family came in the form of tangible services that required some modest degree of residential propinquity (Sussman and Burchinal 1962; Adams 1968). Sewing, baby-sitting, small repairs to cars and housing, laundry, cooking and cleaning, and an extra room all were part of the menu of benefits that members of extended families offered each other during hard times. With the trek to the suburbs, both lack of housing space and geographic dispersion worked against the exchange of these sorts of services. There is no question that families still extend their net of protection far beyond their own immediate doors, but because of the limitations noted above, that aid must come in the most easily transportable form possible—money.[25]

Second, the boom in private housing signalled by the growth of the suburbs locked families into housing costs that quite frequently exceeded their ability to pay using "normal" income sources. Between 1972 and 1978, the price of an average one-family new home increased by 72 percent, while median family income in current dollars increased only 40 percent in the same period (Currie, Dunn, and Fogarty 1983). U.S. families are now paying 35 percent of their disposable income for housing and housing-related costs—double the average ten years ago. The 5.8 million families in the lowest income bracket pay over half of their income for shelter. Since most investment has gone into private single-family housing, the availability of rental space has been seriously curtailed. Thus, a seriously inflated housing market and an acute shortage of rental space have combined to lock families into housing they can ill afford without an additional infusion of cash.[26]

This is in marked contrast to earlier economic crises. In these earlier periods, families reported two major methods for cutting back on expenditures: substituting public transportation for private automobiles, and finding less expensive housing. Both distance from work—a prominent feature of suburbanization—and the demise of public transportation make automobile travel mandatory during the current crisis. Secondly, rigid housing patterns have locked most working class households into housing costs that are absolutely insensitive to the falling value of their disposable income.

## Conclusion

There are many difficulties facing the United States as it attempts to regain its position of economic strength abroad and to discipline its working class at home. In this paper I have confined myself to the latter problem and have suggested that the effort to reduce the overall wage bill reached its outer limits in the 1980s for two reasons.

First, the reserve army of workers composed of wives and mothers of young children was all but exhausted by this time. To be sure, there are other surplus workers—young people, the old, and ethnic minorities—and the policymakers of the Reagan era did all they could to press them into the labor force at wages compatible with desired levels of profit. Nevertheless, these efforts have been, on the whole, relatively unsuccessful. Efforts to reduce the minimum wage for children have failed, as have those that would have reduced the value of social security payments. And in spite of an all-out effort to reduce civil rights advances to a mere shadow of themselves, there have been modest wage gains on the part of minorities.[27]

Thus, when working class households find themselves in the position of having to come up with additional supplies of labor during the current crisis and the slumps that are sure to follow, they will in all likelihood come up empty-handed. When capital seeks new surplus workers in order to reduce their overall wage bill, it will be progressively unsuccessful.[28]

The second option for the working class during periods of economic downturns—intensifying unwaged household labor—has also been significantly eroded. It has become all but impossible to substitute unwaged labor for declining or lost wages. The fungibility of the two in earlier periods has been destroyed by the strategies of accumulation employed by capital in its attempts to overcome the crisis of the 1930s and to avoid another at the end of World War II. Unwaged household labor has ceased to be an alternative to waged work and instead has become its necessary companion.

Two final points must be stressed here. First, although *precapitalist* forms of unwaged household labor have been absolutely destroyed by the movement of capital, this in no way implies that unwaged labor in the household has been eradicated as well. To the contrary, while unwaged household labor takes a variety of forms in the world economy, in core countries the mass production of consumer durables and the commodification of almost everything else have absolutely required it, and in fact have called entirely new forms of unwaged labor into being. Similarly, to argue that the commodification process is but a partial one even in highly industrialized countries is to misread events.[29] It is not that capital eradicated only a portion of unwaged labor; it eradicated *all* unwaged labor and replaced it with an entirely new variety, one that was determined by the processes of commodification itself.[30] Unwaged household labor is one of the *results* of capitalist production, and as such is guaranteed by capitalist relationships and not by some precapitalist social form.

It was the malleability of household relationships and patterns which gave rise to the mechanisms of the recovery of the post-World War II period, but built into that process was a basic and absolutely fundamental contradiction. The economic dependency that had been drawn upon to promote new capitalist strategies has been increasingly challenged during the previous two decades. The women's movement and the civil rights movement more than testify to that. In attempting to resolve its current difficulties, old norms of racism and sexism and the inter- and intrahousehold relationships which those norms anchored are no longer available to capital. In addition, the entire working class is now equally exposed, willy-nilly, to the attempts to reduce the overall wage bill. In the confrontations to come—and indeed there must be confrontations—these developments will be decisive.

# Chapter 8

## Servants to Capital:
## Unpaid Domestic Labor and Paid Work

### *Nona Glazer*

This paper* argues for an interpretation of women's unpaid domestic labor that links the work *directly* to the everyday routines of the social relations of capitalism, far removed from the household. Unpaid domestic labor is seen usually (by those who do the work as well as those who theorize about it) as linked only in *indirect* ways to the reproduction of capitalism (e.g., Vogel 1973; Fee 1976; Molyneux 1979). It is argued here, however, that domestic labor is integral to capitalism and the capitalist state in ways that are not recognized completely in theories about its indirect contribution to capitalism through social reproduction.

This paper was provoked initially by Zaretsky's (1973) discussion of the ideological construction of the boundary between family and household, and work and the workplace, an outgrowth of nineteenth century bourgeois concerns. Social scientists have tended to adopt the view of a fundamental split between the family and other social relations rather uncritically, making it difficult to understand specific issues of domestic labor such as the division of labor in the family.[1] Recently, the boundary as conceptualized in mainstream social science has been scrutinized more critically and the questionable nature of seeing the family as more or less on the margins of "public" social life has come to be seen by many as a severe limit on understanding how capitalism shapes "private" life.[2]

Questioning the adequacy of the present conceptualization of a relatively impermeable boundary between family and the social relations outside it leads to another way of approaching domestic labor. It is to shift perspective and to view domestic labor from outside the family, asking how social relationships outside the household (in capitalist firms or state agencies) require very particular unpaid domestic labor from women. From the standpoint of capitalism and the state, women as consumers enter into definite social relationships—their labor enters into the work process,[3] but in the instances to be discussed here, they are exploited and their labor appropriated without their entering the wage relationship. Women's labor is appropriated (and women are exploited as domestic workers) by corporations

142

which are able to structure consumption in the commercial and service sectors (e.g., by the way in which goods and services are obtained in retail enterprises). Domestic labor, thus, includes some work which is both part of *social reproduction* and *production*.

Domestic labor's public face, it will be argued, is, as involuntary unpaid labor, part of how work is organized in the workplace and in state agencies. This unpaid domestic labor results from what is here called a *work transfer*. Work that may once have been done in the home and subsequently taken over by capitalism (or the state), as well as work that came into existence only because of capitalism, is reorganized. The reorganization takes the form of shifting once-paid work to consumers, making it part of consumption, and either eliminating or otherwise changing the work of paid workers. (Consumptionism is used here to include the myriad relations that people have in the marketplace and to state agencies as "clients," "users of municipal services," "patients," "defendants and plaintiffs," "tax payers," "bill payers," "kin of dependents," as well as "buyers" of goods and services.)[4]

This paper presents an analysis of the *work transfer* as it occurred since 1916 in retailing, and discusses the crisis of capitalism and other characteristics of capitalism that make the changes possible and maintain them. Class differences, the impact on female-typed occupations in retailing, the mythology of the price benefits of the work transfer, and implications of the changes for the theory of women as a reserve army of labor, and for continued female subordination will be discussed.

The focus of this paper is on women rather than both sexes because of the persistence of the traditional gender division of labor in the family and sex segregation in the labor force; women rather than both sexes bear most of the burden of the *work transfer*. Only in rare instances, such as self-service in gasoline stations, is the work done more often by men than women. Also, while the basic analysis of this paper applies to state activities as well as to those in the private sector, the discussion here will be limited to one case in the latter: retailing. Analyses of health care, *in propria persona*[5] law and clerical work will be topics of future publications.

## Theories About Work

### Views of Unpaid Labor: In and Outside the Household

Mainstream and radical theories of unpaid domestic labor converge in several ways that are challenged by this paper.

First, both approaches see women's unpaid domestic labor as private, performed by wives and mothers. Women's unpaid labor is seen as related to the world outside the family (i.e., to capitalism or to society) through the labor they do for their families. Under the press of feminist critiques, the importance of women's domestic labor for the social reproduction of capitalism has been made central to much of Marxian feminist analysis. Women are seen as reproducing the working class materially and ideologically, and on a daily and generational basis by caring for adult paid workers and rearing children (Dalla Costa 1972; Vogel 1973; Morton 1978). The social reproduction of the working class includes the daily work of preparing meals, cleaning house, doing laundry, negotiating relationships with kin and friends (as well as among household members), being emotionally nurturing, and perhaps trying to create a haven.

In mainstream social theory, the work that women do is seen only somewhat differently, with an emphasis on women's domestic work as being for "society" rather than for capitalism. Women are seen as maintaining the society and the culture by socializing the next generation into appropriate behaviors and beliefs, into readiness for school, and into other precursors of adult statuses (Parsons 1955; Lopata 1974; Oakley 1974). Of course, both radical and mainstream theorists recognize that increasing proportions of married women are paid workers and, increasingly, the sole heads of households. The point is, however, that for both radical and mainstream theorists, domestic labor is privatized and seen as having only *indirect* implications for the world outside the family.

Second, though consumption is seen by both mainstream and radical analysts as an important part of unpaid domestic labor, usually women's domestic labor is seen as centered basically in the household and done for the family. Radical theorists see consumption as essential to capital accumulation and also as having consequences for families, e.g., increasing commoditization makes households more and more dependent on the marketplace. Consumption is, however, not seen as meaning direct "labor for capitalism" but is seen as the final step in the process of capital accumulation.[6] Mainstream theorists also recognize women's consumption work as central to capitalism. For example, Galbraith (1973) labels women "crypto-servants" whose work makes it possible for their families to consume pleasantly at high levels—just as servants did and still do for the rich. In either case, women's domestic work is *directly* for the family, whether in or outside the household.

Among the social critics, only Ben Seligman (1968, 229) sees that consumers (mostly women) may actually work directly for capitalists and that their work may be included literally in measures of productivity computed by managers for stores, banks and other organizations. The sole theoretical challenge to conventional analyses of domestic labor has been the pioneer work of Batya Weinbaum and Amy Bridges (1976). They argue that part of women's domestic labor in capitalist society is consumption, that "capital organized consumption for women" and pulls women into the *work process* (Weinbaum and Bridges 1976, 88) in such disparate places as the supermarket, the doctor's office, and the laundromat (Weinbaum and Bridges 1976, 94–95). Unfortunately, these insights have not been taken up by social scientists, except in the recognition that women's domestic work in capitalist society includes aspects of "consumption."

In their analyses, Weinbaum and Bridges emphasize the chaos that results for women as consumers; the conflict that women experience in trying to reconcile family need with what the market has to offer. Also they suggest that women are forced to do unpaid work that threatens the jobs women do for pay.

This essay is complementary and yet emphasizes the logical and straightforward attempts to some capitalists to insert the consumer into the work process. It emphasizes how capitalism eliminates services in the struggle for markets, in an increasingly monopoly-like sector which, in turn, provides the condition for forcing most consumers into participating in the work process. This essay also emphasizes the impact of the work transfer on paid workers. The underlying theoretical concerns remain the issues of the dualist view of work, the inaccuracy of seeing only paid work as subject to appropriation, and the need to rethink the nature of the boundary between the private and public spheres.

## The Problem of Conceptual Opposites

Most of the views summarized above see *work* as either *for* the household or *in* the workplace. Women are, of course, recognized as doing both kinds of work. That is not the point. Rather, it is that work itself is conceptualized as being one of two kinds.

Dualistic thinking about work seems to follow from observations of a particular historical process—the change from work for subsistence, concentrated in the household, to the emergence of a market economy where waged labor became critical to the survival of the working class. The analysis of the separation of much paid work from the household and the development of the marketplace as central to capitalism beings with it a whole set of categories reflecting an either/or view of work: exchange value vs. use value;[7] productive vs. nonproductive labor; market vs. nonmarket work; the public realm of work outside the family vs. the private realm of the family. Each pair reinforces the view that there is a sharp boundary between the economy and the workplace on the one side, and the household economy and the family on the other. This conception may be accurate for describing critical changes in production that emerged from the late seventeenth century through the early twentieth century. Today, the use of these contrasts and the assumption of tight boundaries between domains of work prevent us from observing how work has been reorganized, pulling the consumer into the work process.[8] Within commercial capitalism, women as consumers substitute for once-waged workers; their work becomes a source of capital accumulation as their labor within the service sector is appropriated.

In theory and practice, there has been an emphasis by Marxists on organizing at the point of production, that is, organizing wage workers around the conditions of employment in contrast to organizing around issues connected directly to gender, race, or sexual orientation. Though there has been a good deal of organizing around other than workplace issues over the last twenty years, the question of the relative importance of different organizing issues and the forms of the groups themselves continue to be open to discussion (Rowbotham 1981; Adlam et al. 1981). Given the concern with the point of production, it is hardly surprising that the domestic labor debates were preoccupied with whether or not domestic labor generated surplus value (Glazer-Malbin 1976). This issue seems to have been skirted, not resolved, by theorists observing, albeit correctly, that attention needed to be given also to the relation between paid and unpaid work (Fee 1976; Molyneaux 1979). While one cannot pretend that recognizing some of women's unpaid domestic labor as direct labor *for* capital (that of both working class and middle class women) solves all problems of understanding domestic labor, ideology and organizing, etc., at least it may provoke new thinking about the issues. Finally, continuing a dualistic view of work prevents our considering if the appropriation and exploitation of women's labor occurs not only for waged work but for some unwaged domestic labor, too. If it can be shown, empirically, that the boundary between work women do *for* the family and *for* capitalism disappears for certain activities, there is a concrete basis for connecting some of women's domestic labor directly to the social relations of capitalism. A theoretical analysis of women's everyday struggles as shoppers, patients, clients, and users of state-provided services can show the importance of organizing women doing unwaged labor.[9]

## The Exploitation of Unwaged Domestic Labor

Commercial capital (e.g., the retail food industry) hires wage labor that does not itself add to surplus value, but is a way by which capitalists appropriate "a fraction of the sum total of surplus value accruing to the entire capitalist class" (Mandel 1981, 59). The *work transfer* to consumers means that commercial capitalists hire fewer workers: consumers work in their place and the organization is altered to eliminate some steps in the work process (e.g., consumers locate and collect merchandise, while the pre-packing of goods eliminates measuring and bagging). Thus, in place of the wage labor hired to appropriate a portion of surplus value belonging to the capitalist class, women as consumers do the necessary work. Women's un-paid domestic labor may still have only an indirect relation to increases in surplus value, but they now have a direct relation to attempts by commer-cial capitalists to appropriate a portion of surplus value.

This analysis means not seeing the wage as the only connection to the appropriation of value and to exploitation. In a sense, women may be said to be even more exploited than paid workers since their labor is appropri-ated without a wage. There are other situations of the appropriation of labor without a wage. For example, during the Great Depression, waitresses in some New York restaurants not only were not paid a wage for their work, but they had to share their tips with their employers. Furthermore, if an employer fires, say, farm workers without paying them, we would not say that the workers had not been exploited and that no surplus value had been extracted just because of the absence of the wage. Thus, *wages* are not the absolute critical issue: *work* is. The appropriation of women's work in the consumption of goods and services is essential to the particular form that distribution has taken over the last forty or so years.

What may make it difficult to see the activity as work is that each individual woman does a trivial amount compared to paid workers in the organization and does so on an irregular basis, i.e., once or twice a week perhaps, for twenty-five minutes rather than five days a week for six hours each day. The work of the individual women, however, added together, sub-stitutes for the work of many paid workers. It is this substitution that orig-inally made the use of consumer work so attractive to capitalists, though other unexpected benefits continue to make it attractive. As will be dis-cussed later, for the consumer there is no necessary *quid pro quo*, no price reduction that reflects the savings of the retailers on labor. In fact, in some cases of the transfer, the beneficiaries include those who do not even par-ticipate in it.[10]

*Disentangling Concepts*

The terms "service sector," "service worker" and "unpaid work" need discussion. Taking the first two, it may appear that the growth of these since World War II means more services to the consumer, and contradicts the theme of this paper. Indeed, theorists of "post-industrial" society ar-gued that more services would become available to people with the switch from a production-centered to a service-centered economy, and pointed to health care and education as examples (Galbraith 1973; Bell 1973; Schumacher 1979). The slowdown in growth and the cutbacks in these areas cast doubt on the thesis (Gershuny 1978). However, there is also a confusion in terms: "service sector" contrasts with extractive and manufacturing sectors which themselves actually also include "service workers." Finally, many service workers and much of the service sector are part of the infrastructure of business and industry, not "service" to consumers, e.g., most service workers maintain factories, offices and stores, not private homes (Bureau of the Census 1973, 749).

The concept of "work" (paid and unpaid) also needs to be used with an awareness of the theoretical implications of various usages. Some social scientists have suggested that the work applies to just about any human activity that is not "leisure." This obliterates two crucial points: that consumers are forced by capitalists into participating in the work process to further capital accumulation and that there are consequences of the work transfer for paid workers (Strauss et al. 1981, 404–412).[11] It also means accepting the logic of capitalist expansion—and its attempts to extend the marketplace to all domains of human life (Wadel 1979, 397).[12]

Work cannot usefully be defined in universal terms, without a recognition of how one gender—women—is exploited by the social relations of capitalism outside the wage relation. The definition below recognizes activities socially assigned to women and also exploited by capitalism (Meiksens 1981, 32–42).[13] Therefore, *work* is defined as those activities which produce goods and/or provide services and/or provide for the circulation of goods and services which are directly or indirectly for capitalism. Hence, this includes both paid work which is an indirect source of accumulation and unpaid work, inside and outside the home, which is organized by and for capitalism. This definition means that work for capital includes: (1) the commercial sector with its unproductive labor; and (2) unpaid domestic labor *in* the home and unpaid domestic labor outside the home, insofar as the labor is inserted into the work process in private firms.

## The Emergence of Involuntary Unwaged Work: The Case of Retail Sales

The assumption of a tight boundary between work in the home, *for* the family, and paid work outside the home, *for* capitalism makes the emergence of involuntary unpaid work invisible. It restricts understanding of how changes in capitalism may lead to changes in the social consequences of unwaged domestic labor, and restricts understanding of how changes in unwaged domestic work have consequences for paid work. This paper examines retailing in the United States to explore the issue of the boundary between paid and unpaid work, and the changing nature of domestic labor, drawing on historical documents as well as secondary material and some interviews with retail workers.

The widespread adoption of self-service by retailers in the United States is one source of the expansion of women's unwaged domestic labor. Here, domestic labor takes the form of privatized labor which is, at the same time, labor inserted into the public sphere. This privatized yet public labor grew side by side with expanding commercialization of domestic labor. For example, self-service emerged side by side with the convenience foods. Perhaps it is these twin developments that make it relatively easy to overlook the appropriation of women's unwaged labor by commercial firms.

It is my hope that by examining the emergence of self-service in retailing, we shall be able to locate some of the crucial causes and the consequences of the *work transfer,* that is, the elimination of certain elements of work from the jobs of paid workers, not by new technologies, but by how firms restructure the work process so that the buyer must do work once done by paid workers. The findings may alert us to other changes now underway and to areas in which such changes may occur in the near future. The following comments on self-service in retailing will explore (a) the changing structure of capitalist enterprises that allowed the work shift to function for the benefit of capitalism, and the intentions of the owners and managers in using self-service. I will also examine (b) the consequences of the work shift for paid workers as shown in work patterns, earnings, the market value of work experience, and interclass tensions between workers and buyers; and (c) the content of the new unwaged work, such as increased product knowledge, and actual steps in the work process in shops, for which women became responsible.

*Overview*

Self-service in capitalist society derives from the pursuit of profit and the social legitimacy of profit-making at all costs, even the elimination of waged workers by pulling the consumer into the work process.[14] The reliance of consumers on the market for commodities, in turn, narrows options making it difficult for them to find an alternative to self-service. Also, the development of monopoly-like conditions (through the growth of chains, mergers of stores, and the vertical integration of much retailing) allows corporate control over the organization of work in retail stores with relatively little fear that consumers will shop elsewhere, seeking clerk-service.

The mythology of consumer "convenience" and rewards to the customer in the form of reduced prices serves to legitimate the system for many consumers. Women, who are 60 percent of retail workers today, have had their jobs changed by self-service.

## Retail Sales: The Emergence of Self-Service

Prior to World War I, most food and other kinds of merchandise were sold in small, family-owned specialized shops. For example, meats were sold in butcher shops, and fabric in dry goods stores. Large food markets can be traced back to colonial days, to the public markets such as Faneuil Hall Market (Boston) and to the Pike Street Market (Seattle) (Markin 1963; Bluestone et al. 1981). By the 1870s and 1880s, there were also larger, diversified dry good stores such as Filene's (Boston) and Marshall Field (Chicago). Smaller, diversified stores often served neighborhoods and small communities while the "general store" was traditional in rural market towns.

Typically, stores were organized on a clerk-service basis, meaning that the consumer had a variety of services available to her. Stores employed a staff (Mom and Pop stores used the unpaid labor of family members) whose jobs required knowledge of goods (and often of customer needs), and who also located and collected merchandise, totaled the cost, charged the account and delivered the order to the customer's home. Lists could be left at the store by a child or the housewife, to avoid waiting for the order to be filled. Credit was used for convenience, to survive from one week's wages to the next, and in times of great economic hardship.

In contrast, self-service involves work for the customer. Some work begins before the shopping trip: reading customer education materials and advertising to familiarize oneself with the functions and quality of various products. The clerk-service store provided such information though, no doubt, the clerk was encouraged to put the interest of the store before that of the buyer. The interests of the buyer had to be considered, however, if the customer was to be retained. Clerk-service did not ensure, therefore, some kind of paradise-like shopping. The poor, the vulnerable and the despised suffered at the hands of the clerk just as today other practices in the self-service store may be difficult for the infirm, those with small children accompanying them or those not literate in English.

Today, shoppers themselves do work in the self-service store. In a food store, for example, the shopper locates the merchandise by following signs or by memorizing the location of goods, and makes selections without consulting clerks, loads the cart and pushes it to the checkout stand. Even at the checkout stand, the consumer often works by loading goods onto the counter, placing purchases in bags and portering them home.

Self-service was first introduced into food retailing in 1912 in southern California because of the relatively higher costs of wages and because of the widespread use of the automobile. The auto gave customers access to these innovating markets which were often outside the inner city, away from public transportation (Schwartzmann 1971, 22; 144). Self-service was also introduced to chains in 1916 in Memphis by Clarence Saunder's Piggly Wiggly stores. Saunders introduced and patented the technology of the floor layout, the turnstile and checkout stand and his advertising copy, and franchised his system nationwide. The Piggly Wiggly stores went bankrupt by 1924 because of manipulations on the New York Stock Exchange and the firms (Kroger and Safeway) that took over Piggly Wiggly operations discontinued self-service (Zimmerman 1955, 22). During World War I, retailers, facing labor shortage and rising labor costs because of competition from war industries, extended self-service. Some stores tried a combination of self-service and clerk-service to attract new customers by cutting prices and yet keep the old customers who wanted an array of services (Zimmerman 1955, 24).

The rapid expansion of self-service occurred because of a combination of changes in capitalism that accelerated in the late 1930s: the increasing competitive advantage of chain stores in rivalry with independent and associated food stores, the development of supermarkets which threatened specialty stores[15] and the intense competition for customers during the Great Depression.[16]

Chain store organizations first became serious competitive threats to independent retailers in the 1920s. In 1890, there were only ten chains in the United States; by 1920 there were 808 chains which grew to over double that in eight years, to 1,718 by 1928 (Haas 1939).

Some indications of why the independent retailers believed themselves so threatened by the chains is evident in the growth of the market share of chains during the first years of the Depression (see Table 1). In 1929, independents had about 89 percent of the retail stores and 78 percent of the sales. By 1933, independents decreased their share of stores by one percent but reduced their share of sales to 71 percent. Though the chains also lost stores, they increased their share of sales from 20 percent in 1929 to 25 percent in 1933 (see Table 1). Total retail sales decreased drastically and dramatically by nearly 50 percent between 1929 and 1933, from 49 million to 25 million, a reflection of massive unemployment and the loss of family income.

The chains are of particular importance in understanding the pressures under which the independent grocers found themselves and why they introduced self-service eventually and changed the gender of the work force, from men clerks to women cashiers. The chains began to develop about 1914 with a distinct advantage that came from quantity buying. They forced food wholesalers to give them sizeable discounts that independents were refused. In the late 1920s, some grocers joined associations such as I.G.A. (Independent Grocers of America) and Red and White, and buying groups that tried to get sizable discounts and carried on joint advertising compaigns. However, the chains maintained their competitive advantage legally until the passage of the Patman-Robinson Act of 1936[17] which set "fair pricing practices" and outlawed different treatment of retailers by wholesalers. However, the Patman-Robinson Act was evaded and hurt small buyers (Bluestone et al. 1981). Independents attempted unsuccessfully to control competition from the chains with other legislation, e.g., special local taxes. Independent grocers then adopted self-service which decreased the labor costs that some retailers considered to be "too high" even in the 1920s (Harrington 1962, 2).

The supermarkets that boomed in the 1930s made self-service an integral part of their organization.[18] The supermarkets were attacked both by chains and independents who attempted to outlaw their lower prices. They urged wholesalers not to sell to the supermarkets, and tried to make selling at or below costs illegal (the "loss leaders" were the object of attack). They convinced some newspapers to refuse the advertising of major self-service markets on the grounds that the stores were engaging in "unfair trading practices" and were eliminating jobs for working men (Peak and

**Table 1**
**Chains Made Disproportional Gains in the**
**Early Years of the Great Depression**

|  | 1929 | 1933 |
|---|---|---|
| **Stores** | (1.5 million) | (1.5 million) |
| Independents | 89.1% | 88.4% |
| Chains | 9.6 | 9.3 |
| Other | 1.2 | 2.3 |
| **Sales** | ($49,114) | ($25,037) |
| Independents | 77.3% | 71.2% |
| Chains | 20.0 | 25.2 |
| Other | 2.3 | 3.6 |

Source: Based on Harold Haas (1939:19)

Peak 1977). Nevertheless, some associated grocers began to use self-service, though clerk-service remained typical (*Progressive Grocer* 1941, 65–66).

The initial reason for introducing self-service was to lower labor costs by eliminating workers and making the customer do the clerks' work (Murphy 1917, 20; Dipman and O'Brien 1940, 32). However, retailers saw that higher profits were an immediate result of the new system because customers were "impulse buying," selling themselves on mass displayed goods (Zimmerman 1955).

Eventually, supermarkets eliminated the clerk not only from the sale of goods that came to the store already packaged, but also from the sale of goods that grocers once thought demanded clerk-service such as meats. The success of cash and carry self-service supermarkets encouraged chains and the associated grocers to convert from clerk-service to self-service as well as to eliminate other services such as credit and home delivery (Peak and Peak 1977).

By 1940, self-service was both sufficiently widespread in the United States and of interest to would-be adoptors that the national association of retail grocers did a nationwide study. The self-service store was described in the report as more profitable than comparable service stores though some expenses were higher, such as advertising (used to "attain and hold a large volume") and the rent of a "more favorable location." But the explicit recognition of self-service as decreasing wages and of the consumer as doing work reveal the intentions of the retailers: "Wage expense, the biggest single item of operating costs, is as a rule lower in the grocery departments of self-service stores. Insofar as consumers wait on themselves in a store with a fairly good volume, clerk expense is smaller. Insofar as other services may be curtailed by self-service arrangement and operation, operating expense may be reduced" (Dipman and O'Brien 1940, 266–267). In a follow up report issued in 1946, the self-service operation was called "labor and expense saving." The increasing post-war activities of labor unions were noted as meaning higher wages for employees (Dipman et al. 1946, 5; 8). Shorter working hours and higher wages made self-service desirable because, as the Progressive Grocer Association stated," . . . by getting consumers to do some of the work now done by employees, . . . a merchant [can] make the greatest use of the fewer hours available to the store and employees" (Dipman et al. 1946, 9).

During and after World War II, the shortage of labor and goods speeded the adoption of self-service (Wingate 1942; Thompson 1942); stores had no problem in attracting goods-hungry customers. Unionization drives meant the possibility of a shorter work week and higher wages for clerks, making self-service attractive to department and variety stores, too (Dipman et al. 1946; Canfield 1948, 104).[19]

While the original reason for self-service was to lower labor costs, other changes in merchandizing and transportation help to explain its success. The wide use of the automobile, beginning in the 1920s, and increasing with suburban and highway development in the post-war years, made shopping center construction with the self-service store a major form of investment for land developers. The centers were the only readily available stores for suburban shoppers. Clerk-service was available only to those willing and able to travel to the city.

Many services other than the clerk's help and knowledge of where the products are have been eliminated from stores. Retailers today rely on national manufacturers to provide services such as product information, guarantees, return and repair services, and quality control (Fuchs 1968). In addition, self-service is supported by national advertising and by national brands; in turn, the reliance of retailers on national brands is possible, indeed virtually forced, by other changes. These changes include vertical integration, mergers of stores and takeovers of family-owned, locally-based stores by national chains and holding companies. This made it possible for national advertising to be an effective seller of national brands. By 1982, the concentration of capital in manufacturing and retailing, and the cooperation of supposed competitors culminated in 28 major American department stores with a total of 353 branches and 17 affiliated overseas stores actually owning jointly the international Associated Merchandising Corporation (AMC). AMC advises its owners on all aspects of retailing, providing monopoly-like conditions and homogeneity in the marketplace (Salmans 1982, 1). Regional preferences for products can be reduced sharply by national advertising; the national tastes established in some products means that the retailers and independent manufacturers can assume ready-made customers, nearly anywhere in the country. Furthermore, national chains can easily abolish local purchasing so that manufacturers have relatively homogeneous markets though customers do, of course, buy differently in various regions and their preferences are not ignored completely.

Self-service began as a relatively small-scale attempt by food retailers to lower operating costs by shifting work to the consumer. It succeeded as retailing in the United States changed increasingly from local production, sales, and control to national control. The giant supermarket chains and holding companies took over the major variety markets. Today, the giants in retailing sell almost everything a family might want in the self-service store.

## Class Differences

Retailers have not been able to cut services identically across class lines. The reorganization of stores which require middle and low income consumers to substitute their own time and labor for once-waged workers have had less success among the rich and more affluent—except perhaps in grocery retailing. Retailers have responded to the wealthy by providing the services of sales clerks, locally-available guarantees, free delivery and special orders. The increased concentration in the retail industry may mean that there is the loss of clerk-service and other services except for the very rich, or for those who buy in small, privately-owned specialty shops. Retailers selling to the more affluent often provide their customers with a wide array of personal services. They may also try to use less costly tactics to attract customers, trying to create special images (such as the "preppie" nickname "Bloomies" for Bloomingdales, or the most ostentatious form of conspicuous consumption promoted by the Neiman-Marcus Christmas catalogue) in the hope of cultivating customer buying loyalty (Bluestone et al. 1981).

Working class consumers do not have the ready cash nor credit necessary to pay the higher prices in the stores that give services to the more affluent. Though employed women, including working class women, are advised by the mass media to turn to services in the marketplace to substitute for their own now-absent work in the household, low wages prevent this. Working class women, especially those who are sole heads of families, are unlikely to have sufficient income to buy services or shop where services are available. Stores in working class neighborhoods are unlikely to provide services to the consumer. The domestic mystique, that can be traced back to Catherine Beecher's wise consumer and frugal housewife, promoted an image of the ideal mother and wife as the women whose sacrifices for her family's well-being were more important than her own (Cowan 1976). This certainly supports women—working class and middle-class—believing that they ought to spend their own time and energy to serve the family rather than spending family income. Employed women, thus, continue to do the "double day" (Glazer 1980).

Self-service cannot automatically be interpreted as bad for consumers just because it is good for capital accumulation; nor is it automatically good because retailers and some customers say so. Certain aspects of self-service may be a convenience to the consumer; others may be an annoyance or set unsuspected limits.[20] Whatever benefits or losses there are for the consumer, the theoretical point about the insertion of the consumer into the work process remains: the consumer does work, unwaged, that was once done by a paid clerk.

## The Reinforcement of Gender Subordination

*Women as Self-Service Customers*

The following section will consider the gendered nature of the unpaid self-service workers, and how advertisers and grocers viewed women as self-service customers. In addition, the claim that self-service is an activity in which women customers are paid back for their work with lower prices and with benefits loosely called "convenience" will be examined.

Although not every self-service customer is a woman, the majority are. The customer is usually portrayed in the marketing literature as a woman. An economist in 1939 described why women used self-service: "There is one type of shopper whose importance is magnified by the feeling that she makes her own selections, serves herself, and gets the most for her money" (Haas 1939, 98–99). The implication was that the sense of importance is on rather banal grounds, though it can be used to the retailer's advantage to reduce labor costs. Advertising aimed at encouraging women to shop in self-service stores played heavily on themes of choice, control and freedom (*Ladies Home Journal* Oct. 1929, 185; Dec. 1929, 137). Another historian of supermarkets posits " . . . a 'shopping instinct' in the average home-maker's make-up which can be satisfied only by introducing her to the great variety of foods and goods which the present Super Market displays" as if behavior were determined genetically rather than socially (Zimmerman 1955, 145). Mass advertising and consumerism are not seen by marketing historians as implicated in what others have noted to be advertisings' construction of women's preoccupations with shopping (Ewen 1976).

Elaborate rationalizations were presented by marketing specialists from the 1920s onward to legitimate self-service. Distinctions between work and leisure were blurred in advertising self-service shopping—called an "adventure" (*Ladies Home Journal* 1929, 137) and described as a form of socializing for the housewife (which for some it was and may continue to be despite the few social contacts in self-service stores). Shopping was also turned into a kind of preventative maintenance for the family car with an implied slur on women's ability to make reasonable choices about how to use their time. Thus, one analyst wrote that:

> The consumer-buyer with available time for various activities might prefer shopping to attending a tea, say, and even if food buying were recognized as a task instead of a form of socializing, she may not be able to use the time any more profitably in another activity. Moreover, if not used in connection with shopping, the expensive automobile purchased for pleasure might sit in the garage with only the saving of the marginal cost of this

operation (the cost of one gallon of motor fuel, say), and in time might indeed deteriorate even more than if utilized for shopping. (Cassady 1962, 262)

The same writer states that the reason for merchants using self-service is to shift "much of the time-consuming unorderly marketing burden" from employees to customers and reduce "wasted [sic] time of employees waiting on each customer" (Cassady 1962, 101).

Though retailers eliminated the services of clerks, they saw themselves as providing customers with a whole range of new "services." In supermarkets, these services include such features as wide aisles, "kiddie corrals" and clearly marked prices.[21] In evaluating retailers' claims to increased service, the main convenience appears to be a chance to do one-stop shopping and to select from a large number of items (the supermarket averaged 9,000 items in 1973) (Quelch and Takeuchi 1981). But most of the "services" supplied by retailers are necessary or desirable exactly because other services, including clerk-service, have been eliminated. For example, "kiddie corrals" are "service" because self-service means that the customer with young children cannot telephone an order or drop off a list at the store and expect the clerk to do the work of assembling the goods. Retailers portrayed both the customers' opportunity to examine goods and standardized sizes and measures as "services." Yet, prepackaging, recognized as a necessity by grocers and manufacturers if clerk-service were to be eliminated and goods successfully presold through advertising (*Printers' Ink* 1921a, 1921b), actually prevents most customer examination of goods. In turn, prepackaging was possible in the 1920s because of an earlier accomplishment of manufacturers, the standardization of much packaging, and the sizes of various dry goods (Frederick 1917). Hence, except for fresh produce which has become increasingly prepackaged over the last three decades, and some soft goods, the consumer's examination usually is limited to packaging.[22] Also, it is not particularly accurate to see "convenient" size and quantities as a service. Customers do not gain much of a service if this is supposed to mean that the buyer gets the amount needed now and for the forseeable future. Foods are packaged in sizes standardized by the manufacturers and fit customer needs only accidentally.[23] Indeed, low income customers may be at a particular disadvantage insofar as cost per unit declines with increase in the amount bought.

Finally, the view that self-service means low prices to consumers is not supported by current retail pricing policies. When self-service was introduced widely in the 1930s, some of the reduction in labor costs was passed on to the customers as low prices (Haas 1939). According to business consultants, since World War II, self-service retailers have been able to replace price competition (which cuts down on profit margins) with activities that do not. Loss leaders, for example, are used to attract customers, but as market consultants who advise about strategies for sales explain, these can be "used to create the general impression of over-all low prices" with the knowledge that customers cannot be aware of more of than a few prices among the thousands of items stocked in markets (Markin 1963, 82).[24]

### Women as Retail Workers

Over the last fifty years, as self-service has become widespread in retailing, women have become the majority of paid workers.[25] In 1930, before the spurt in the adoption of self-service in food retailing, women were a minority (about 20 percent) of retail workers (see Table 2). Within a decade (by 1940), the proportion of women workers had jumped to 40 percent. By 1981, 60 percent of retail clerks and 85 percent of cashiers were women (Rytina 1982).

There are no census data on cashiers before 1950, reflecting the relative lack of division of labor in retailing: sales clerks handled the cashier work. However, in the 1940 census, "clerical workers" are included for the first time with sales clerks, showing the emergence of the "cashier" as a distinct occupation. Starting in 1950, the dominance of women in cashier jobs (80 percent) is evident.

**Table 2**
**Increase in Women Workers in Retailing**
**1930–1978[26]**

| | 1978 | 1970 | 1960 | 1950 | 1940 | 1930 |
|---|---|---|---|---|---|---|
| | | | Percent Females | | | |
| | | | (Numbers in thousands) | | | |
| **All Retail** | 58 | 53 | 50 | 44 | 40 | 20 |
| workers* | (8,677) | (4,492) | (3,694) | (3,218) | (2,468) | (4,211) |
| **Managers,** | 29 | 20 | 22 | 19 | 13 | 7** |
| salaried | | | | | | |
| **Cashiers** | 86** | 90 | 79 | 89 | 45 | N.A. |
| **Sales Clerks** | 64 | 58 | 54 | 49 | | 29 |

*Excludes stockers, delivery persons, cleaners, and other miscellaneous occupations
**Data for 1930 includes proprietors. Data for 1978: "clerical" includes also office workers, i.e., typists, accountants, bookkeepers. The data in Table 2 are *estimates* of women in retailing given these Census changes in occupational categories from 1930 to the present.

Compared to general retailing, the work force in food retailing was open to women workers less rapidly (see Table 3). In 1940, women were 40 percent of all retail workers compared to 26 percent of *food* retail workers; probably this was because of the stronger male craft unions in the food industry compared to other retailing, which made jobs here attractive to men until the expansion of jobs in war industries. The relatively more powerful butchers and teamsters unions maintained male dominance in the food industry longer than in department and variety stores where women moved rapidly into jobs, but where clerk unions were weaker. Also, women entered the retail industry as the overall proportion of cashiers was increasing relative to sales clerks. There were 50,000 cashiers in 1950 compared to 622,000 clerks. By 1970, a sharp shift had occurred, a majority of workers were cashiers—342,000, compared to 269,000 clerks.

Within food retailing, most jobs were done initially by men. As women entered, they tended to be hired for only certain jobs so that sex segregation replaced sex exclusion. Thus, since 1940, the proportion of male sales clerks has declined; men have moved into management while only a relative minority of them have become cashiers. Within twenty years, from 1950 to 1970, women workers (after their initial growth in sales work) were shifted to cashier work, not management. In 1950, 83 percent of women were sales clerks; by 1960, only 58 percent were. By 1970, only 35 percent of women sold and 60 percent were cashiers.

Weinbaum and Bridges (1976) suggest that capitalism pits women against each other, consumer against worker, shopper against cashier; the consumer is the potential strikebreaker ready to take over from the cashier as new technologies can shift more and more work away from paid work-

**Table 3**
**Changes in Women Workers in Food Retailing**
**1940–1970**[27]

|  | 1970 | 1960 | 1950 | 1940 |
|---|---|---|---|---|
|  |  | Percent Women | | |
|  |  | (Numbers in thousands) | | |
| **All Food Workers** | 56 | 46 | 42 | 26 |
|  | (805) | (862) | (786) | (94) |
| **Managers, salaried** | 12 | 7 | 11 | 6 |
|  | (194) | (137) | (113) | (80) |
| **Cashiers** | 80 | 72 | 82 |  |
|  | (342) | (221) | (50) |  |
| **Sales Clerks** | 59 | 46 | 44 | 30* |
|  | (269) | (504) | (622) | (460) |

*Clerical and sales categorized together

ers. In the 1970s, the cashier and the consumer do appear to be pitted against each other. However, earlier changes in retailing resulted in women workers being pitted against men workers, and workers of both genders against consumers. Actually, women workers were brought into food retailing as sales clerks, doing jobs once open to men, usually, and not as cashiers. Until 1970, more often women continued to be clerks than cashiers in food retailing. As sales jobs were eliminated, men were not hired, but women were, and for the cashier job. Capital then brought women into *paid* employment at the same time that women consumers were increasingly asked to do self-service. The result is a new division of labor: women shoppers do *some* of the work that men once did as sales clerks; women paid workers do *some* of that work as cashiers. Unpaid women were pitted against paid women only after paid women and men were pitted against each other. Hence, the *work shift* involves a further division of labor in which women were hired for jobs once held by men, but now the women did parts of what had been a single job. The retail food industry is one among many in which available cheaper female labor was substituted for more expensive male labor in the process of a detail division of work and a cheapening of labor. Wages in retailing did not drop absolutely, however, but the rate of wage increases dropped relative to the rate of wage increase in other industries.

The same two-step change occurred in retailing as a whole. As women increased from 20 percent to all retail workers in 1930 to 44 percent of all workers by 1950, they did so first as increasing proportions of sales clerks.

**Table 4**
**Women Move from Sales to Cashier**
**and**
**Men to Management in Retail Sales[28]**

|              | 1970  | 1960  | 1950  | 1940  |
|--------------|-------|-------|-------|-------|
|              |       | (Numbers in thousands) |       |       |
| **Women**    |       |       |       |       |
| Managers     | 5%    | 3%    | 4%    | 3%    |
| Cashiers     | 60    | 39    | 13    | 97    |
| Sales Clerks | 35    | 58    | 83    |       |
|              | (454) | (401) | (327) | (142) |
| **Men**      |       |       |       |       |
| Managers     | 49%   | 28%   | 22%   | 19%   |
| Cashiers     | 19    | 14    | 2     | 81    |
| Sales Clerks | 32    | 59    | 76    |       |
|              | (350) | (462) | (458) | (398) |

Until 1978, women retail workers were more likely to be sales clerks than cashiers (Haas 1939).

The increase in women workers in retailing parallels the general economic expansion following World War II. Employers continued to divide the work of selling, reorganizing the job, so that temporary workers could learn the tasks rapidly. Sales work changed to an intermittent source of income from a long-time, primary source of employment through management eliminating commission sales, full-time and year-around work, and by a relative lowering of wages (Bluestone et al. 1981). In turn, women workers were increasingly hired (along with youths), brought in by employers instead of adult men who were entering other areas with higher earnings. The preselling of goods and services through advertising reduced the dependency of the retailer on the selling skill of the sales clerk; because of this most clerks are no longer hired for their knowledge of products and of the psychology of selling. Therefore, commissions on sales are not used to encourage clerks to increase sales. A vastly expanded pool of workers whose skills do not have to include the product knowledge and sales skills once required allows wages to be lowered.

In contrast, in grocery stores and in supermarkets, women's entrance as paid workers was relatively more difficult. Women's wages in food retailing historically have been closer to men's than elsewhere for, as has been noted (Bluestone et al. 1981), strong unions fought for high wages even if they interfered rarely with management attempts to rationalize the work-process.

Today, women retail sales workers earn considerably less than men, sixty-seven cents for every dollar men earn, partly because of sex segregation within retailing (Rytina 1982). Women are segregated in the sales of less lucrative items of "white goods" such as clothing, general merchan-

### Table 5
### Women in Retail Industry Shift from
### Sales Clerk to Cashier
### 1950–1978[29]

|  | 1978 | 1970 | 1960 | 1950 |
|---|---|---|---|---|
|  |  | (Numbers in thousands) |  |  |
| Managers, salaried | 16% | 10% | 8% | 9% |
| Cashiers | 44 | 22 | 14 | 8 |
| Sales | 39 | 68 | 77 | 83 |
|  | (5,070) | (2,469) | (1,858) | (1,431) |
| % of all workers | 58 | 53 | 50 | 44 |

dise, and in the smaller retail food stores, where hourly wages are typical. Men clerks dominate in the sales of "brown goods" such as motor vehicles, furniture, and home appliances where commission sales increase earnings. Most important, self-service, and hence, lower wages characterize variety, department, and apparel stores where women were over two-thirds of workers in 1970 (U.S. Department of Commerce 1970, 798–800).

Some writers suggest that the gender division of labor in retail sales is tied to the sex of the buyer (Brandt 1978). Yet the sex of the buyer and the sex of the seller are not consistently identical. For example, women usually sell apparel to women, and men to men. However, furniture and household appliances (high commission items) are sold by men, but bought and used by women. Motor vehicles (another high commisssion item) are sold by men, but by the later 1970s, nearly one-half were bought by women.

Historically, women's lower wages resulted also from their lower rates of unionization (Canfield 1948, 102). Many organizers believe that women workers were difficult (if not impossible) to organize compared to men. While some obstacles do exist, men's traditional view of women has meant that even the women's militancy displayed in the retail clerk strikes in Oakland (California) during the 1940s was not seen as convincing evidence to the contrary. Hence, the clerk unions organized in food stores, where in the 1920s and 1930s men dominated, but, relatively, ignored department store clerks (Harrington 1962, 5).[30] Other characteristics contribute to women's lower wages compared to men's. Women are more likely than men to be hired as part-time workers in food (Schwartzmann 1971) and department stores (Bluestone et al. 1981, 105). However, taking into account the difference between full- and part-time work, the earnings of all retail clerks have dropped substantially over the last forty years, in comparison with other occupations, and in comparison with the gains that clerks made in earlier decades (Schwartzmann 1971; Bluestone et al. 1981). Full-time workers, in contrast with part-time and seasonal workers, once could have expected to increase their earnings through commissions on sales (Bluestone et al. 1981, 109). In turn, commission earnings depend on skill, on workers' knowledge about merchandise, and their interpersonal skills and knowledge to build a following of customers. Commission sales created conflicts and rivalries among workers (Lombard 1955), put pressure on clerks to provide as many services as possible to customers and, no doubt, encouraged some manipulation of the customer by the clerk. While the elimination of commission sales and the substitution of straight wages reduced competition over customers (and thus one source of interpersonal stress between clerks), the loss of commission sales supported the efforts of employers to deskill jobs. They did this not by dividing them into more detailed work, but by combining jobs that were once wage-stratified. Hence, sales clerks who once concentrated on learning about products and on selling began to have to wrap, tag, and restock goods, to clean dressing rooms, and also to do cashier work. Most employers have little or no interest in training workers beyond the bare minimum required in how to manage the sales transaction itself and, perhaps, some minimal instruction about customer treatment. Though there are some exceptions among national chains, today few stores do more than perfunctory training.[31] For workers, the result is that job experience is not likely to be valued or rewarded by higher wages from succeeding employers.

The tensions that once characterized the relation between the often working class clerk and the wealthy customer were around interclass disdain and working class resentment of the attempts of their employers and their customers to force them to conform in manners and deference to upper class expectations (Benson 1982). Today, the tensions are more directly tied to the structure of selling: clerks are comparatively untrained in what might be called old-fashioned selling and often without much knowledge about product use, let alone availability. Without systematic sales training and rewards in the form of commissions on sales and increase in wages, clerks have neither the knowledge nor the incentive to respond to customers questions and demands for help in finding goods. Furthermore, the clerk-customer ratio is kept high by management as a way of keeping down the wage bill; cost-benefit analyses attempt to hit the highest ratio possible without driving away impatient customers. Today, it is true, management has begun to recognize that "reduced store staffs, inadequate employee training . . . [and] erosion in selling quality may hurt" (Barmarsh 1983). The Fair Labor Standards Act in the mid 1950s gets the blame for retailers dropping commissions, though significantly, these were kept for the goods that men are more likely than women to sell, i.e., for appliances, television and related goods, men's clothing and women's shoes.

These characteristics of women in retailing suggest the continued applicability of the concept of the reserve army of labor, in spite of the percentage of women who now seem a permanent part of the labor force (Simeral 1978, 164–179). There is an extremely high turnover rate, including both high quit rates by workers and high rates of layoffs by employers, comparable to the rates for agricultural labor. Employers hire in times of their need and lay off in times when workers are not needed. The work has become sufficiently "deskilled," i.e., relatively few selling skills or clerical skills are required so that workers are easily interchangeable. Wages have dropped relative to other occupations and are low for women who cannot usually earn a living wage. The result is that for women, but *not* for

men, employment is seasonal and part-time, subject to the business cycle
and to employer attempts to lower labor costs.

The other side of the conditions of employment of women sales workers is the reinforcement of women's traditional economic dependency on
their husbands and traditional responsibility for domestic work in the home.
For women workers, the organization of retailing means that there is no job
ladder, no increase in earnings with age, or a peak in earnings after years of
work; in earlier decades, middle-aged women did earn more than younger
or older workers (Bluestone et al. 1981, 103–104), but this is no longer
typical.

In turn, women's economic dependency is supported by their being
more likely than men to depend solely on their sales jobs for earned income
(36 percent of women compared to 42 percent of men), and women are
more likely than men to report that their sales job is their primary one.
Men are likely to be "moonlighting." The low earnings of women means
that their traditional economic dependency on spouses (or increasingly, on
the state) is reinforced.

The intermittent and irregular employment of women in retailing also
reinforces traditional responsibility for domestic labor. The part-time and
seasonal character of the work means that women can more easily than men
do housework and child care than with other work. The lack of a job ladder
makes it relatively easy for women to quit retail jobs to meet temporary
family demands (e.g., a geographical move for a spouse's new job, or to
care for a sick relative).[32]

## Conclusions

The conventional view that women's domestic work is directly for the family and only indirectly for capitalism must be rejected as an artifact of sexism; a blindness to how women's domestic labor has been forced into the
work process outside the home. Women as consumers must work in order
to buy goods (and services, too, though this has not been considered in the
preceding analysis). The concept of "social reproduction" captures only
the indirect contribution that women (as wives and mothers) make in their
daily routines to the maintenance of capitalism. Most important, the view
that the family and, hence, women's domestic work is *in* and *for* the private sphere, while only paid work is *in* the public sphere can be rejected.
Daily life is actually organized so that women's unpaid work *outside* the
household is a critical aspect of the very basis of consuming in capitalist
societies. There is no need to argue that only "in the last analysis" is women's work connected to capitalism through social reproduction. There is

no need to argue that women's domestic labor is only embodied as dead labor within the living labor of the workers today and in the future labor of the generation women now raise. Instead, we can look directly at the present material conditions of women as consumers and see that our work is essential to retailing and to other aspects of distribution.

The ideology of convenience and the myth of cost-savings to consumers, used to make self-service palatable to women, has been questioned. The ideology and myth fit, in turn, with the ideology that applauds the housewife for frugality and good household financial management. These ideologies and supporting myths are important to examine, because capitalism and the state in capitalist societies, under cover of the continued "economic crisis," attempt to promote other *work transfers* (Glazer 1983). These are put forth as beneficial to family members, to the community, and to the unpaid workers themselves. Shifts in the responsibility for health, the funding problems of public schools, the threatened demise of the public law corporation, and the pretense that corporations can (and will) take over social programs eliminated from the federal budget, make the social situation ripe for capitalists and the state arguing that women must do more unpaid work. What this means for women must be recognized: the *work transfers* are mainly to wives, mothers and the other women with family responsibilities. (Of course, everyone in the United States—men as well as women, women living alone and responsible only for themselves—experience the work shift to some extent.) The increased occurrence of the work shift means that analysis and organizing ought to take into account this newer exploitation of women's labor.

*Work* must be reconceptualized to recognize that the boundary between the family and other social relations is permeable, especially for working class women. As defined by current social relations in capitalism, work includes the following:

(1) *Domestic labor in the household:* unpaid, *directly* supportive of family life and indirectly supportive of the social reproduction of capitalism (of the present generation of workers and future workers). The extreme privatization of this labor appears to have been shaped by the emergence of industrial capitalism, supported by earlier forms of gender stratification and the later characteristics of capitalism.

(2) *Paid labor:* work for wages or salary, done usually outside the home; a direct source of capital accumulation.

(3) *Voluntary unpaid labor:* the labor voluntarily contributed to projects and activities that are attempts to solve problems thrown up by the social relations of capitalism. This work may also be linked to an ideology that "explains" away the personal and social crises as unconnected to cap-

italism and as a result of personal failures. American *women* are the backbone of the myriad organizations whose goals run the gamut from providing social welfare services and cultural activities to fund raising for an array of organizations.

(4) *Involuntary unpaid labor:* this labor has the appearances of being work *for* the family, done for the benefit of family members. The labor has the appearance of being privatized; the isolated work that is women's domestic labor. However, if one shifts perspective, a different interpretation is possible: our work can be seen as central to the distribution of goods in retailing and to the performance of services. Women's unwaged work can be understood to be appropriated by capital.

The feminization of retailing has accompanied a complete change in paid work. Women workers in retailing still have the qualities of a reserve army of labor, where a majority work part time and seasonally, do not earn a reasonable living, and rotate in an out of the work force based largely on employer's needs.

Capitalism's emergence was a watershed for the oppression of women because of the resulting division of social life into, apparently, two spheres—the public sphere of social production and the private sphere of social reproduction. Value was attached to wage labor in the former, domestic labor was relatively devalued in comparison to wage labor, and the dominant ideology that emerged rejected more than a tenuous connection between the alleged "two spheres." (This is not to discount the work of feminist historians who have examined the lives of middle class women and men in the nineteenth century through the framework of separate spheres. But it is to warn against how the reification of those separate spheres today can mean ignoring where the boundaries have been dissolved.)

The trends in capitalism appear to intensify the pressures on women while weakening whatever relatively impermeable boundary may have existed between the public and private spheres of work. Our world is, now, firmly in both realms, and the belief in separate spheres of work is outdated imagery. The changes in the content of domestic work and in paid employment during most of our adult lives mean that we will experience fully the contradictions of life in capitalist society. The haven is fully mythic. We must now (1) maintain our traditional responsibilities for the household (for there is little evidence of any significant shift in the gender division of labor in the home from women to men, whether in emotional or instrumental activities). But, the double day is normalized because (2) we are increasingly expected to do paid labor outside the household, regardless of family responsibility. Also, we are, (3) the backbone of the volunteer force in the United States, the source of the labor that does work of running cultural institutions such as museums and symphonies, substituting for paid aides in the schools, and providing personal contact and nurturing in hospitals. To these widely recognized categories of our work in capitalist societies must be added, (4) the exploitation of our labor in consumption.

For paid women workers, the transfer often reinforces the traditional gender division of labor in both the paid work force and in the home, while when we consume we face more work. Given women's work in "four spheres," it is no wonder that feminism is seen as a basic force for social change in the United States and other capitalist countries: for in our lives all spheres of work in capitalism come together.

# Chapter 9

# Making Ends Meet:
# Unwaged Work and Domestic Inequality in Broome County, New York, 1930–1980

## Randall H. McGuire and Cynthia Woodsong

> Family is a close group, sharing and caring. Love—naturally that would be at the top of the list. . . . The family will always be there thru thick or thin. Family is family, no matter how you slice it.
>
> Broome County resident

Working people in Broome County, New York, see the family or the household as the fundamental social unit in their lives. It is sustained even as it is wreaked and buffeted by the forces of a constantly changing world. In the midst of uncertainty and confusion beyond their control, it is an anchor, a constant that gives meaning to their lives. Many social scientists have taken a similar view of the family or household, seeing it as a universal building block of social organization which takes on differing functions depending on the circumstances into which it is cast. For them, too, it is an anchor, a universal unit which provides the basis for making observations and comparisons through time and across cultures.

We have taken a different perspective, derived from our participation in the Research Working Group (RWG) on the household and labor force formation in the world economy at the Fernand Braudel Center (Smith et al. 1984; McGuire, Smith, and Martin 1986). This group defines the household as a set of relations rather than as a primordial unit. It is not a purely emotional arena of reproduction separate from the real productive work of the marketplace, but rather the relations of the household are both created by and create the relations of the marketplace. One cannot be understood without reference to the other because each could not exist without the other. Household members constantly negotiate and renegotiate these relations among themselves within the context of the larger social formation; the relations do not result from the inevitable joining of complementary functions. The ideology of the household as a unit masks the relations of power that shape these negotiations, obscuring their existence in the house-

168

hold and, more importantly, the processes by which relations of power and exploitation are reproduced and sustained in the larger social formation.

The relations which produce households are the products of specific historical realities and circumstances; to understand them requires an understanding of the larger set of relations in which they are embedded, as well as their historical development. Our research within the RWG has sought to understand these processes using data from Broome County, New York, covering the fifty years from 1930 to 1980. In this article we wish to focus on inequality in Broome County households, the centrality of unwaged work to this inequality, and how the burden of such work initially fell to both women and children but later shifted primarily to women. We find that the so-called "family wage," that is, a single "male" wage adequate to meeting the needs of the household, never existed for a majority of working class households in Broome County and that the adequacy of wages varied greatly over our fifty year period. Consequentially, the form and degree of importance of unwaged work also varied, and its performance was linked to other kinds of demands on household members. Our discussion will proceed from an explanation of our theory and method to an historical overview of changing household relations in Broome County.

## Conceptualizing the Household

We will not in this short paper attempt to summarize the immense literature on the "family" and "household." Suffice it to say that most of this literature links these concepts with units that are often transhistorical in character. They are frequently regarded as primordial institutions that have changed as a result of phenomena such as modernization, industrialization, or capitalism (Anshen 1959; Laslett 1971; Gough 1975; Minge-Klevana 1980; Bender 1967; Netting, Wilk, and Arnould 1984).

This conceptualization of family and household as hard bounded "things" encourages several false conclusions regarding their variation in the world economy through time. It leads many researchers to differentiate household and the marketplace as discreet spheres of activity or to characterize activities within these places as reproductive or productive (Lamphere 1986; Hareven 1984). Often when researchers encounter productive activities in households, they conceptualize them in terms of a separate informal sector (Beechey 1977; Fox 1980). With production and reproduction separated, the marketplace becomes the locus of power and exploitation, and the household or family becomes the locus of reciprocal relations which have survived from a simpler, more egalitarian past (Laslett 1971; Seccombe 1980; Molyneux 1979; Edholm, Harris, and Young 1977). These distinctions reproduce an ideology which places a higher value on productive (male) work, as opposed to reproductive (female) activities, and which views age and gender relations in the household as complementary and constant through time.

Rejecting such approaches, our empirical work leads us to the conclusion that we must reconceptualize the household for the purpose of understanding power relations and exploitation within households. Our reconceptualization proceeds from three major points.

First, we conceive of households as that set of relationships that impose on their members the obligation to share the income from their labor and its product, thus enabling the group to renew its capacity to labor on a daily basis and replenish that labor generationally. Our definition concurs with other research that equates households neither with family/kin membership nor with co-residentiality (Yanagisako 1979; Swerdlow et al. 1981). Many cases exist where families or kin do not share a common residence or consumption fund, and many more cases where households are not composed of kin (Guyer 1979; Schildkrout 1983; Reyna 1976). Family refers to kinship ties which may or may not compose an economic household. Just as family may or may not imply sharing, members of households may or may not live in propinquity to each other. In Broome County the relationships between kinship, co-residence and income-pooling change markedly through time.

Second, we focus on those social networks and processes that bring together resources from a variety of labor activities. It is only through these linkages that the resources originating in the different labor relationships have the capacity to sustain that labor and replenish it across generations. For lack of any other term, we refer to these practices as "householding." Householding brings together a variety of resources derived from multiple labor forms. Only the *combination* of these resources through the practice of householding provides the bases for sustaining and reproducing the household members.

The literature on household income tends to narrowly define income or treat income sources as discrete entities. Household income is often restricted to money from wage income, or some "production" activity. The labor of "reproduction" is thus devalued because it does not generally result in monetary return. Many challenges have been raised to this view, especially in the women's studies and the Marxist-feminist literature (Fox 1980; Molyneux 1979; Holstrom 1972). However, even when income from non-wage sources is included in household income calculations, its value is treated as having a definite quantity independent of the other forms of income with which it is combined through householding. For example, childcare may be given one value, cooking another, wage labor another, and so on, the total of these constituting or equaling the household income. Yet this is a major departure from reality, for the value of each source is a product of its being in relationship to the others. The systematic relationships of householding determine the household consumption fund, and the value of each type of income derives from its position in this system of relationships.

Our considerations go beyond the issue of monetary returns or equivalencies. The separation of housework and other reproductive activities from production devalues the market price of labor invested in this work because women routinely perform these duties for no pay. We therefore have also examined labor time as a way of establishing equivalent values between different types of work. Housework and other reproductive activities are conceptualized as "subsistence" activities which generate subsistence income, usually non-remunerated. Comparison of labor time to the monetary value of reproductive activities provides a measure of the extent to which these duties are undervalued.

Our emphasis on the relationships that impose the obligation to share incomes in no way assumes that such income is shared equitably within the household, as other have pointed out (e.g., Folbre 1985). Indeed, a major interest of our research is to identify the sources of inequality in these relationships. We do not feel that the inequalities within households can be fully understood without reference to the larger system of relations of which they are a subset.

## Methods

Our research in Broome County questioned the notion of the so-called family wage, a wage sufficient to provide for the social reproduction of the family. We expected that households in many time periods would achieve such reproduction only by pooling incomes to create a household consumption fund. To these ends we collected data on income sources (waged and non-waged), household composition, internal division of labor, and labor force participation for working class households for three points in time: the late 1930s, the late 1950s, and the late 1970s.

We chose these three time periods because they represent the nadirs and zeniths of long term fluctuations in the U.S. and the world economy. These fluctuations, or Kondratieff-cycles, may be characterized as expansion and contraction phases in the growth and development of the world economic system (Barr 1979). The first time period chosen is a period of contraction, the depression 1930s; it is followed by an expansionary phase, the prosperous 1950s, and then the recessionary 1970s, another contraction phase. The RWG argues that householding practices in existence at the peak of an expansionary phase are subject to pressures to change during the contraction, which results in newly constituted pooling practices in the subsequent expansionary phase (McGuire, Smith, and Martin 1986).

In order to collect the information we needed for the three time periods we utilized a combination of primary sources, oral history, and secondary source research. Our efforts included the examination of government statistics, the collection of oral histories in the community, and the examination of national time budget studies of housework.

## Broome County

Broome County is located in southern New York along the border with Pennsylvania and is one of the smaller urban counties in the state. The major city in the county, Binghamton, grew as a manufacturing center in the late nineteenth century. In the early twentieth century, the Endicott-Johnson (E-J) shoe company came to dominate manufacturing in the area, employing 60 percent of the work force by 1935. E-J established two new towns, Johnson City and Endicott, around its factories near Binghamton. These tree communities formed a single urban area which in 1940 had a population of 145,159 and in 1980 of approximately a quarter of a million people (Table 1).

The thriving shoe plants brought large numbers of immigrants to Broome County. Many of these people came from the impoverished rural areas of western Pennsylvania, while an equal or greater number came from eastern and southern Europe. Slovaks made up the largest European immigrant group, followed by Italians. Whether originating in Pennsylvania or Europe, these families established chain migrations which continued into the late 1920s.

Throughout its history the Endicott-Johnson company sought to forestall worker unrest and unionism through a system of welfare capitalism. The welfare system included free medical care, a cafeteria that served three meals a day at nominal cost, and public markets. E-J bought large tracts of land in Endicott and Johnson City and hired contractors to build homes which they sold back to their employees. These policies allowed E-J to pay some of the lowest wages in New York state prior to World War II (McGuire and Osterud 1980, 71).

E-J's policies rested on an analogy to the family, for each worker became a member of the "E-J family". The Johnsons, who owned the company from World War I to the 1940s, lived among and regularly socialized with the workers. The company encouraged (and the wage rates required that) more than one member of the household be employed in the factories.

Table 1:
Composite Census Data

| | 1935<br>(1940 Census)[a] | 1955<br>(1960 Census)[b] | 1977<br>(1980 Census)[c] |
|---|---|---|---|
| Population<br>Broome Co. Pop. | 145,159(BMD)<br>165,749 | 212,661<br>212,661 | 301,336<br>213,648 |
| No. in Labor Force | 71,704 | 87,141 | 139,651 |
| No. ♀ in Labor Force | 21,943 | 30,348 | 59,354 |
| % ♀ of in Labor Force | 45%(BMD) | 38% | 50% |
| % of Labor Force ♀ | 31% | 36% | 43% |
| % of Youth in Labor Force | N/A | 20% of youth<br>14–17 | 40% of youth<br>16–19 |
| % of ♀ in Labor Force with child under age 6 | N/A | 39% | 46% |
| % of Married ♀ in the Labor Force | N/A | 33% | 50% |
| No. ♀ Married in Labor Force | N/A | 17,143 | 34,158 |
| Median Schooling | 8.5 | 10.9 | 12.5 |
| Manufacturing Wage Adjusted to 1967 CP | $1,100(1939)<br>2,644.23 | $4,000(1958)<br>4,578.94 | $10,596(1977)<br>5,838.02 |
| Median Family Income | N/A | $6,251 | $19,707 |
| % below poverty level | N/A | 12% | 6.7% |
| %Dwelling units owner-occupied | 46.5(BMD) | 65% | 68% |
| Household Composition[d]<br>non-nuclear relative<br>"other" non-relative | N/A<br>N/A | 12%<br>2% | 3%<br>3% |
| Persons per household | 3.81 | 3.26 | 2.74 |

N/A = not available

a. 1935 figures are for Broome County unless marked BMD (Binghamton Metropolitan District).
b. In the 1960 Census, Broome County was the Binghamton SMSA (Standard Metropolitan Statistical Area).
c. Figures are for the Binghamton SMSA, New York portion.
d. Percentage of the total number of persons living in households.

E-J encouraged married women to work, and many did (Inglis 1935). Women made up from 25 percent to 33 percent of their work force and received wages of 50 percent to 75 percent of those paid men (McGuire and Osterud 1980).

E-J began to decline following World War II and was replaced by a more diversified industrial base which is often described as "high tech." IBM was established in Broome County early in the century and became the most prominent firm in the area, followed by General Electric, and Singer-Link. These firms employed 11 percent of the work force by 1980 and paid relatively high wages. Despite the high wages in the "high tech" areas, Broome County remained, throughout our period of study, a low-wage area when compared with the rest of the state. Beginning in the 1950s and accelerating in the 1970s, there has been a trend towards increased employment in the service sector, but as late as 1980 manufacturing remained the primary sector of employment.

Throughout the period from the 1930s till 1980, Broome County was a small-to medium-sized manufacturing center. At all times average wage rates in Broome County lagged behind those in other upstate New York industrial areas, as did the cost of living. Female employment has consistently remained high, with 45 percent of adult women working in 1935, 38 percent in 1960, and 50 percent in 1980.

## The Late 1930s

During the late 1930s the Endicott-Johnson shoe company dominated the Broome County economy and employed over 65 percent of the work force. Over 50 percent of the individuals in this work force were immigrants or the children of immigrants. Our research initially distinguished between Slovak, Italian, and rural migrant households. Slovak and Italian informants stressed to us that the essence of their ethnicity lay in their families, that it was their family lives that defined their identity and uniqueness. It soon became clear that, although ethnicity played a major role in structuring interactions and the social lives of the Broome County working class, it had little impact on the composition of households, the division of labor in the households, and the nature of household consumption funds.

The households of "native" Americans who had migrated from rural Pennsylvania also showed few structural differences from the immigrant households, except for their retention of family farms in Pennsylvania. Informants indicate that these households depended in part on subsistence income from members left on the family farm. These farms were clearly not commercially viable entities in their own right, and the shoe plants at

E-J had come to provide an alternative to the coal mines of Pennsylvania as a source of off-farm income. Some members stayed on the farm to provide for their own subsistence and to provision the Broome County household. On weekends the Broome County household members often returned to help with farm tasks. So many people in Broome County were involved in this type of household that they established regular car pools to facilitate the movement between city and farm. The farms provided the Broome County household with dairy and meat products, as well as fruit and vegetables. Our informants indicated that the only foodstuffs purchased by such households were flour and imported goods like coffee, tea, and sugar. These households showed a far higher portion of subsistence income than the immigrants, and a higher level of petty market production.

E-J workers earned an average wage of $936.00 a year in 1938, only 85 percent of the average Broome County manufacturing wage of $1099.26. E-J company benefits, however, probably made up for much if not all of the 15 percent difference in pay so that the living standards of most non-E-J employees did not differ significantly from that of E-J workers, with the notable exception of workers in skilled trades (such as machinists), who earned considerably more than the county average.

The adequacy of this wage can be assessed against several standards. Applying Stecker's 1935 study of the cost of living to a four-person household in Binghamton indicates that this wage would exceed the "emergency level" of $878.10 a year but not the "maintenance level" of $1,243.00 a year (1971). E-J claimed that company benefits increased their wage by 25 percent (Inglis 1935) and, if that was true, the average E-J worker was paid at the "maintenance" level. Both of these standards fall considerably below what at the time was considered a "satisfactory American standard of living"—an income of $1,600 to $2,000 a year (Andrews 1935, 119). We are certain that the households in our study were seeking to obtain this higher level. From informants and other sources it is clear that automobiles, radios, savings, home ownership, insurance, and the other material indicators of an "American standard" were considered necessary and that most households had these things. It is worth noting that households routinely sacrificed one of the characteristics of an "American standard"—high school education for children—in order to obtain the other characteristic factors. The consequences of this strategy in part defines the structure of households in our next time period—the late 1950s.

Wage labor in Broome County during the late 1930s did not provide the majority of the working class with a family wage, making it necessary for several individuals from the same household to enter the factories and engage in a host of other non-waged activities. Households routinely incorporated non-nuclear family relatives to increase the size of the income-sharing pool. We have referred to these individuals in our discussions as "others."

In all cases adult males entered the work force, if possible, because their potential wages exceeded that of teens and women. A normal work week at E-J was forty-eight hours, and a man could earn $24 a week. Employees received two weeks unpaid vacation a year, and informants indicate that this was routinely taken (Inglis 1935, 144; Zahavi 1983), so that a typical adult male's yearly salary would be $1,200. Adult women also worked a forty-eight hour week, but women's jobs paid one-half to two-thirds the rate of men's jobs (McGuire and Osterud 1980, 69). Teen-agers could enter the factory at age fourteen, and informants indicate that it was common to lie about one's age in order to start work earlier. Teens usually did women's jobs and were paid at the same lower rate. Oral histories suggest that older teen-agers, ages sixteen to twenty, kept from one-half to two-thirds of their wages while younger teen-agers remitted the total wage to their parents (BCOHP n.d.).

Most E-J workers were paid based on piece-rates, and the above wage calculations assume full production in the plants. During most of the 1930s this was not the case, and work slowdowns were the rule. Rather than dismissing workers, the company routinely cut back the number of shoes in production, reducing the possible piece-rate wage. The annual salary estimates we have used in our tables clearly over-represent the contribution of waged work to householding at this time.

Children between the ages of eight and fourteen engaged in a variety of waged activities, including mother's helpers, sales, and baby-sitting. For example, one of our informants indicated that at age ten she baby-sat after school for three hours a day, five days a week, and received $3 weekly. Children would remit all of their wages to their parents, or the wages might be paid directly to the parents.

It is difficult to put a monetary value on the host of activities that women routinely performed for free for their families and which we commonly refer to as housework. We base the price for housework on the wages for full-time houseworkers in 1935 (Andrews 1935, 74). It is important to bear in mind that such domestic work is normally undervalued (New York State Department of Labor 1973a). Housework hours were derived from time budget studies and other sources (Cowan 1983, 159; Waite, 171;). Although a housewife performs more tasks than would a housekeeper (Andrews 1935, 75; Oakley 1974), we have considered the cost of her replacement with a waged housekeeper, taking a conservative estimate of $863 annually (Andrews 1935, 75;).

In those families where the mother did not work in the factory, the majority of housework was her responsibility with assistance from female children or a female "other," if present. If the mother did work in the factory, she delegated much more of this work to female children or a female other. Both our informants and contemporary studies of housework indicate that children took on household duties as soon as they were mature enough to do them and that they spent much of the time that they were outside of school doing household chores. Men and teen-age boys would rarely perform any of these duties.

Virtually all of the E-J families had gardens, either on their house lots or in fields provided by the company, where they raised almost all of their yearly requirements for fruits and vegetables (Inglis 1935, 194; BCOHP n.d.).[1] In addition to their gardens, almost all of the working class families kept small stock in their yards, principally chickens, rabbits, and turkeys. All of the oral histories indicate that a significant amount of the families' meat and most or all their eggs came from these enterprises.[2] The division of labor by gender and age was least pronounced in gardening and small-stock-raising, although women and girls would do housework before tending gardens or small stock, and men and boys would tend gardens and small stock before doing housework. The exact distribution of these activities in a household depended on the size and composition of the household and changed as these characteristics of the household changed over time.

E-J built houses and sold them back to their workers on favorable terms. Consequently, home ownership among E-J workers in 1935 was approximately 75 percent, as compared to 45 percent among Broome County households in general. Oral history data indicate that the males of the household performed the maintenance work on these dwellings. E-J houses varied in price from $3,000 to $4,000 in 1934, and the company deducted a typical mortgage payment of $7 from each week's pay check (Inglis 1935, 91; BCOHP n.d.).[3]

For the most part, working class families engaged in petty market production on a seasonal and/or sporadic basis. Most women sewed for their families, producing women's and children's clothing and mending (Andrews 1935, 391; NICB 1926, 83).[4] They may have also brought cash income into the household by sewing for others. We cannot at this time quantify the income contribution of most of these activities. Women would sew, bake, or take in laundry on a regular basis. Informant data suggest that these activities were roughly equivalent in return, and that personal preference played the biggest part in choice of activity.

We know that the adult males in some families produced wine and hard cider for consumption and sale, a particularly important activity during prohibition. We have not been able to determine the contribution of this activity to household income, either as a contribution to the consumption

Table 2:
Household Labor Time in Hours and Percentage of Total

| 1935 | 4-person[a] | 6-person[b] | 8-person[c] |
|---|---|---|---|
| waged work non-waged work[d] | 48.0 / 36% 85.0 / 64% | 111.0 / 52% 103.3 / 48% | 159.0 / 61% 102.3 / 39% |
| total hours | 133.0 | 214.3 | 261.3 |

| 1955 | Household I[e] | | Household II[f] | | Household III[g] | |
|---|---|---|---|---|---|---|
| | 4-person | 6-person[h] | 4-person | 6-person | 4-person | 6-person |
| waged work non-waged work[1] | 40 / 39% 62 / 61% | 40 / 35% 73 / 65% | 55 / 48% 59 / 52% | 55 / 44% 70 / 56% | 75 / 57% 56 / 43% | 75 / 53% 67 / 47% |
| total hrs. | 102 | 113 | 114 | 125 | 131 | 142 |

| 1977 | Household I | | Household II | | Household III | |
|---|---|---|---|---|---|---|
| | 4-person | 6-person | 4-person | 6-person | 4-person | 6-person |
| waged work non-waged work[j] | 40.0/35% 73.5/65% | 40.0/32% 84.0/68% | 55.0/43% 73.5/57% | 55.0/40% 84.0/60% | 75.0/55% 60.0/45% | 75.0/51% 71.0/49% |
| total hrs. | 113.5 | 124 | 128.5 | 139 | 135 | 146 |

a. Four-person household consists of mother, father, two children ages 5 and 8.
b. Six-person household consists of mother, father, relative ("other"), three children ages 3, 8, and 11.
c. Eight-person household consists of mother, father, relative ("other"), five children ages 3, 8, 11, 14, and 17.
d. Hours are adapted from Bigelow's 1935 data with childcare adjusted for age-specificity from U.S. Bureau of Human Nutrition (1944) based on 1926–1931 studies (in Vanek 1973; 124). Includes rent and market production. The example for market production here is taking in laundry. The example for rent is care of two boarders.
e. Household I has father in waged labor full time, mother not in waged labor.
f. Household II has father in waged labor full time, mother part time.
g. Household III has father and mother in labor force full time.
h. Six-person household consists of mother, father, four children age 3, 5, 8, and 11 for the 1955 and 1977 households.
j. Hours taken from Gauger and Walker (1980).

fund or as petty commodity production. Households would produce a batch of cider or wine and sell to other households, and then at a later time buy these beverages from other households.

Almost all households kept boarders, often two to a room. Although the national ideology of the family at this time discouraged the taking of boarders, the influx of people into Broome County seeking jobs resulted in housing shortages from the 1920s until World War II. Boarding was an economic necessity for the households with space, as well as for single working people. Newspaper ads in the 1935 Binghamton Press indicate that boarders paid about $6 a week in the late 1930s. Care of boarders included meals and heavy cleaning. Some households would not take in boarders when the household was at its peak size and productive power, but would resume taking in boarders as the children moved out, vacating space and reducing income. The care of boarders would have fallen most heavily on the adult or teenaged female most responsible for housework.

Wage income was the crucial nexus for the mix of incomes and was the largest single income source. Reproduction required multiple wage earners in each household and necessitated the inclusion of non-nuclear family members in younger households and the earliest possible employment of children. Wage income, however, rarely accounted for more than 60 percent of total income, and in most cases accounted for no more than 50 percent (Table 2).

The relative importance of wages and the relative and absolute amount of labor required of household members differed depending on household size (Table 3). Except in the largest households, waged work accounted for less than half of the labor time required for the household. Members of smaller households worked harder, and the labor requirements of a member of a four-person household were approximately 60 percent of those of an eight-person household and exceeded seventy hours a week. Subsistence income was most important in smaller households. Increasing the number of adult or teen-age household members did not result in a proportional increase in the time invested in subsistence activities but did lead to a proportional increase in wage income. As the family grew, the absolute and relative labor contributions of the mother decreased because older children took her place in the factory and picked up many of the unwaged activities. In the largest households, the hourly labor contribution of the husband may have exceeded that of the wife.

## Broome County 1955

By 1958 Broome County economy had undergone a number of changes. E-J remained the predominate employer, but its 45 percent share of the work force represented both a relative and absolute decline in the number of workers it employed. The company dismantled almost all of its welfare programs in the 1940s, and the declining prospects of the company were clear in the community. As E-J declined, the work force in Broome County became more diversified with growing participation in the manufacture of electrical instruments and in the service sectors. Many former E-J employees faced the search for new jobs, and their children could no longer plan on moving into jobs with the company.

By this time, ethnic identity was no longer an important way of characterizing the work force. The ethnic composition of neighborhoods began to break down and children were more likely to marry across ethnic lines and to establish households away from their parents' neighborhoods. Although ethnic communities persisted as sources of cultural identity, none of

Table 3:
Household Division of Labor in Hours and as Percentage of Total*

| 1935 | 4-person[a] | 6-person[b] | 8-person[c] |
|---|---|---|---|
| total hours[d] | 133 | 214.3 | 261.3 |
| % mother<br>% father | 53<br>46 | NA<br>NA | NA<br>NA |
| # of hrs.<br>per prod.<br>member | mother 71.2<br>father   61.8 | 53.6 | 43.5 |

| 1955 | Household I[f] | | Household II[g] | | Household III[h] | |
|---|---|---|---|---|---|---|
| | 4-person | 6-person[i] | 4-person | 6-person | 4-person | 6-person |
| total hours[j] | 102 | 113 | 121 | 129.5 | 117 | 128.1 |
| % mother<br>% father | 55<br>45 | 58<br>41 | 62<br>38 | 64<br>36 | 61<br>39 | 64<br>37 |

| 1977 | Household I | | Household II | | Household III | |
|---|---|---|---|---|---|---|
| | 4-person | 6-person | 4-person | 6-person | 4-person | 6-person |
| total hours[k] | 113.5 | 124 | 135 | 135 | 128.5 | 139 |
| % mother<br>% father<br>% teen<br>% child | 50<br>44<br>—<br>6 | 45<br>41<br>6<br>8 | 56<br>39<br>—<br>5 | 51<br>36<br>5<br>8 | 55<br>39<br>—<br>5 | 51<br>36<br>5<br>8 |

Notes a–d and f–k same as previous table.
e. Productive members are mother, father, "other," teen, working child.
*totals may not equal 100 due to rounding.

the growing employment sectors in the community was clearly dominated by any one ethnic group.

With the decline of E-J, the children of the 1930s found themselves in a dilemma. Most had not completed high school and therefore found it difficult to gain employment at the expanding and more highly paid firms such as IBM. If they were lucky enough to obtain jobs, they found their advancement in the company blocked, a pattern described throughout the United States at this time. This experience led to an emphasis on education for their children. In 1950 92.2 percent of Broome County's fourteen and fifteen-year-olds were in school, and 84 percent of the 16 and 17-year-olds remained in school. Between 1950 and 1960 the median school years completed increased from 9.8 to 10.9 years (Table 1). Advanced schooling eliminated full-time wage contributions to the household by teenagers.

We see at this time a major shift in the ideology regarding children's work. Whereas in the 1930s the child was expected to serve his or her parents and substantially contribute to the well-being of the household, by the 1950s the emphasis was on the household serving the child and preparing the child for adulthood (Graebner 1986; Ogburn and Nimkoff 1955; Sears, Maccoby and Levin 1957). This meant that children began to require more than they contributed to the household. The majority of this burden fell on their mothers.

Adolescence had been "created" at the turn of the century as a way of prolonging childhood and postponing adulthood among the middle and upper classes (Graebner 1986). The creation of adolescence is related to a relative decline in the demand for labor, and an increase in productivity. This was reinforced by an emergent child-centered ideology which stressed the importance of a nurturing home environment. This child-centered ideology with its concept of adolescence only became a reality for the working class of Broome County in the 1950s.

The increasing significance placed on adolescence caused a decrease in children's contributions to the household waged and non-waged income. Their labor contributions were limited as advanced schooling required not only that more time be spent in school, but also in other activities such as sports and school clubs (Bigelow 1953, 16). Children continued to "help" with housework, primarily by taking responsibility for cleaning up after themselves and doing dishes, but our interviews confirm other studies which indicate that they rarely participated in major housework activities such as heavy cleaning and laundry (Ogburn and Nimkoff 1955).

Information on teen employment is extremely difficult to obtain for all our time periods in Broome County, as elsewhere (Oppenheimer 1982, 448). The census reported that 20 percent of teens aged fourteen to twenty were formally employed in 1960. The majority of teen jobs in this time were part-time, often paid under the counter and poorly paid at that (New York State Department of Labor 1967b). Teenagers assisted in Mom and Pop groceries, delivered papers, worked in gas stations, and in a variety of other unskilled part time or irregular jobs. With the exception of families which owned small businesses, teen-age work differed in both location and kind from that of their parents.

Our interviews indicate that most teen-agers did not work, or worked erratically, and that those who did retained control over their own income. The household benefited from such work only to the extent that teen-agers assumed responsibility for buying their own clothes and other items, such as radios and records, and for paying for their own entertainment. This is a marked shift from the pattern of the 1930s, when most working class teens worked along side their mothers, brothers and/or sisters at E-J and turned much or most of their income over to their parents for household expenses.

Broome County remained an area of high female labor force participation, with women comprising 35 percent of the work force in 1960 as compared to national averages of 32.3 percent. This, however, represents a substantial drop from 45 percent of the work force in the 1930s (Table 1). The majority of working women continued to work in factories. We also observe an increase in the number of women engaging in part-time work during this time period.

The national ideology of a family wage and the growth of consumerism placed conflicting demands on women. Women also had to respond to the perceived increase in the economic needs of the family. Yet women's employment was often cited as a factor contributing to juvenile delinquency (Keller 1968; New York State 1956). Working mothers were held accountable for their children's problems. Many attempted to meet these conflicting demands by working part-time jobs. (New York State Department of Labor 1967a).

Conflicting views concerning the appropriateness of women's work are reflected in labor force statistics for the time and contribute to problems with quantifying the extent of women's wage labor. National studies indicate that women in most low income families worked in either full-time or part-time jobs, as did many women in the middle income level. We know that part-time workers were more likely to be omitted form the census data and that these workers were predominately women (Durand 1948). The 1950 federal census noted that "housewives . . . who are in the labor force only on a part-time or intermittent basis may fail to report that they are employed or looking for work unless carefully questioned" (US Bureau of the Census 1950:xxii).

There is some evidence to suggest a decline in household size and in the number of households containing non-nuclear family members. In 1950 grandchildren or parents of the household head comprised 8 percent of the population in households; most of these were women over age sixty-five. We still today see a relatively significant number of "other relatives:" 7.5 percent. This category consists primarily of adults in their peak earning years. The inclusion of other family members to assist with the childcare of working mothers or take the place of mothers in the work force appears to continue, but at a lower rate. In addition, it was common for teen-agers living in outlying areas to board with relatives in town in order to attend high school or junior high. In return for their board, the child might perform household services, pay for a room, or both. Overall the percentage of "others" living in households was 22 percent in 1950, and by 1960 had dropped to 13 percent.

The 1960 housing census indicates that most of the household members were residing in their own homes, only half of which were mortgaged. Nineteen percent of the homes in Broome County were two-family houses, down from 29 percent in 1940. It is not possible to state how many of these two-family homes were owner occupied, but interviews with realtors active in the 1950s indicate that this was a frequent occurrence. It appears also to have been common to rent the other half to kin, making further income-pooling possible.

A number of non-wage activities had either declined or virtually disappeared by 1955. In the 1950 census, only 6 percent of the population in households in the Broome County area were "lodgers." The practice of keeping boarders appears to have declined, and with it both the income and additional housework generated by the practice. By this time the practice of keeping small stock was certainly in decline. In 1958 the city of Binghamton passed a zoning ordinance prohibiting animals from "running at large." This was probably only a first step in regulating livestock since they could still be kept if properly penned. However, by 1969 the keeping of any livestock was prohibited.

People were also no longer turning their lots into miniature farms. Gardening continued as one of the few subsistence activities to involve husbands, children, *and* wives. Gardens were primarily planted to furnish fresh vegetables for summer eating and to provide quantities for the canning of family favorites such as pickles, jellies, and tomatoes. Buying in bulk from fruit and vegetable stands in the country became common, with the produce often kept in home freezers. National data indicates that the savings from buying bulk and home preserving could have been greater than growing and processing the foods at home (Bigelow 1953, 162). This trend was accentuated in the early 1960s by the establishment of "U-Pick-It" farms in the area. The purchase and storing of food in this manner required ownership of a car and a freezer.

Home economists encouraged such home production, but an attitude of "consumerism" worked against it. Ads in the local papers reflect this consumerism, advertising store-bought cupcakes which "taste so good that mother stopped baking." Our informants indicate that the practice of home baking declined during the 1950s, with the baking of bread going first and the baking of specialty items, e.g., cookies and cakes, continuing but at a lower frequency than in the 1930s.

There are no indications that the amount of time spent on housework declined in any significant manner. The acquisition of household appliances probably did not appreciably decrease the amount of time spent in housework (see J. Smith in this volume). Much of the savings in household time created by household appliances was accompanied by an increase in personal attention given to children, as well as in the standards of housework (Bigelow 1953, 15; Ogburn and Nimkoff 1955, 150). Studies show that when the amount of time spent in housework decreases, this is generally due not to "labor-saving devices" but to a lowering of standards (Cowan 1983; Oppenheimer 1982; Berk and Berk 1979); the practice of lowering standards does not seem to occur until our later time period—the 1970s. In addition, the acquisition of appliances contributes to perceived increased cash needs of the household, which have been strongly associated with women's willingness to enter the work force (Vanek 1973).

The smaller four-person household with an unemployed wife was the ideal of the 1950s. The number of hours of labor required for the wife of such a household in the 1950s was considerably less then for the same size household in the 1930s, and compares favorably with the hours required of wives in larger households in the 1930s (Table 3).

For the majority of working class households the ideal required a part-time or sporadically working wife. We would estimate that the standard of living that our informants regarded as necessary in this period required an income of approximately $4,500 a year for a four-person household. With an average manufacturing wage of $4,000 a year, such an ideal situation was available to a sizeable portion of the working class, but not to a majority. The declining real price of goods made the returns from extensive gardening, small-stock raising, and boarders increasingly marginal, while increasing wages meant that the only way women could contribute significant cash income to the family was by obtaining waged work.

**Broome County 1977**
In 1977 manufacturing continued to be the largest employment sector, with over half of the manufacturing jobs in "high tech" electrical instruments and machinery. These industries paid wages higher than national averages. The largest employers were IBM, Singer-Link, and General Electric.

There were no dramatic changes in the distribution of labor responsibilities within households between the 1950s and the 1970s. The portion of households with working wives, however, increased significantly (Eberts 1984). In 1955 the average manufacturing wage was 89 percent of the amount we calculated as necessary for the socially determined cost of reproduction for a family of four. In 1977 we calculated this cost to be approximately $13,700 a year. The average manufacturing wage of $10,596 in that year accounted for only 77 percent of this total.

Few women were employed in the high-waged industries, but were rather to be found in service sector jobs paying below minimum wage (Coleman et al. 1984, 25). In 1977 women constituted 43 percent of Broome County's labor force, with fifty percent of the working-aged women employed and 50 percent of married women in the labor force (U.S. Bureau of Census 1980; Table 1). A recent study of Binghamton's economic development notes that "although high tech industry does create more high-wage, high skill jobs, . . . it creates a substantially greater number of low-skill, low-wage, seasonal jobs" (Coleman et al. 1984, 54).

Not surprisingly, the low-waged jobs also had the highest rates of part-time employment. Two-thirds of the low-waged industries counted more than half of their employees as part-time (less than thirty hours per week) (New York State Department of Labor 1977, 26). The low-waged, part-time businesses which relied most heavily on women were clothing stores, department stores, variety stores, and confectioneries.

It is difficult to obtain figures for part-time employment in Broome County, yet secondary sources and interviews indicate that many women who continued to assume the major responsibility for childcare and housework worked part time outside the home. Since part-time employment was defined as thirty hours or less weekly, a person could be expected to work six hours a day, five days per week, and be considered only as a part-time worker. For the majority of women who worked this type of "part-time" job, as well for as those in "full-time" employment, the additional work performed at home combined to present the women of the 1970s with the equivalent of two full-time jobs, or the "double day" (Berk and Berk 1979).

Once again, little information is available on teen-age employment. Census and Labor Department data from the area do not detail the jobs performed by youths, although they report that forty percent of those aged sixteen to nineteen were in the labor force, up from twenty percent (aged fourteen to seventeen) in 1955. Interviews with city officials, as well as with individuals who were teens or parents of teens in 1977, indicate that it was common for teens to have part-time jobs at one time or another. The most often-cited jobs confirm new York State Department of Labor (1973b) records for teen employment and include fast food work, clerking, and delivery. The jobs most likely to be available to teens were in the low-waged sector: at movie theaters, retail shops, supermarkets, eating and drinking places, and amusement and recreation businesses (New York State Department of Labor 1977). Employers in these businesses often applied for and received certificates from the state which allowed them to employ persons under age eighteen at below the minimum wage in order "to prevent curtailment of opportunities for employment" (New York State Department of Labor 1973b, 2). A survey of Broome County businesses from the 1955 and 1978 city directories indicates a dramatic increase in such business establishments, from 296 in 1955 to 554 in 1978, despite the fact that the county population only increased by 987 people in the same time period. The expansion of these types of establishments in the 1970s both allowed and required dramatic increases in teen employment since teens were both employees and the consumers of their goods. Other sources of employment for teen-agers (especially younger teen-agers and pre-teens) included babysitting, yard work, and paper routes.

By 1977 a combination of economic necessity and ideological shifts had resulted in changes in household form and function. Broome County households were smaller than in the previous periods, with 3.27 persons per family according to U.S. Census data (U.S. Bureau of Census 1980). Women faced increasing pressures to provide for the emotional, economic, and logistical needs of the family. Unlike the 1950s, when society sanctioned the role of "housewife" as good and proper, very little prestige accrued to the "homemaker" of the 1970s (Vanek 1973, 190). Forty-six percent of women in the Broome County labor force were mothers of children under age six, up from 39 percent in 1960 (Cowan 1983, 203; NYS 1956).

The women's liberation movement had, in the interim, "freed" women to participate in the work force, yet it did little to free men to participate in the work at home required to run a house and raise children. As the time required to keep a home clean and operating did not decrease, and as the sexual division of labor within the home did not markedly change, women who entered waged-labor were faced with two choices: to intensify their own labor, or to reduce their standards for housework. Many, surely, did both (Berk and Berk 1979: Gauger and Walker 1980).

Interviews with Broome County women helped shed light on the everyday practices of juggling job, housework, and children. Women reported that their part-time jobs allowed them to come home around the time that their children returned from school so that they could drive kids to music and dance lessons, sports, etc., take time off when children were ill, and change jobs more easily according to household demands. Children in the 1970s participated in more school and extracurricular activities than in previous times, and they did so at younger ages.

The number of hours spent in housework (approximately eight to ten hours a day per two-child household) did not change significantly from the previous periods, although the distribution of labor expended in certain tasks shifted. For example, less labor time may have been invested in such activities as laundry and dishwashing, but more was likely to be invested in the care of children (Gauger and Walker 1980). Informants speaking of this period note a decline in their housework standards. "When the kids were little I had more time, but then when I was working. . . . Who cares? There's more important things to do. But when I was a kid, oh, the house was ripped apart from ceiling to floor [when being cleaned]."

A woman's employment status had little effect on her husband's participation in household work. According to a study conducted in Syracuse, New York, in 1977, husbands contributed one to three hours daily whether their wives worked or not, as compared to five to ten hours daily for wives (Gauger and Walker 1980). It may be argued that husbands of the 1970s constituted a reserve pool of household labor, for they would sometimes assume childcare responsibilities in the evening while wives finished the housework.

In addition to housework, subsistence activities included gardening and hunting. Generally speaking, women continued to practice home canning and preserving family favorites, either raised at home or bought in bulk. By this time U-Pick-It operations had become popular. Gardening was an activity which still involved both wives and husbands. Men continued with and even increased their participation in their hunting traditions, mostly seeking white-tailed deer. This activity was viewed not as a contribution to the household food supply, but as leisure activity (Severinghaus and Brown 1982). Home-sewing also continued, but the savings this activity implied varied.

Home maintenance was likely to occupy some time in the majority of households, as home ownership in Broome County was high. Census data

indicate that sixty-eight percent of occupied dwelling units were owner occupied. Changes in household membership followed trends established in
the earlier periods. Household size dropped from 3.81 in 1940 to 3.26 in
1960, and was down to 2.74 by 1980. Non-nuclear family members, who
had comprised 13 percent of the persons in household in 1960, now constituted less than 1 percent. The percentage of two-family homes was now
lower (20 percent or less), for new homes were built to be single-family
dwellings. The two-family homes were less likely to have been owner occupied, and when the other half of the home was rented to family members
(perhaps in only 19 percent of the cases), the rent was often below the
going rate. For this reason the practice of renting to one's kin was in decline.

Real income in Broome County as measured by the U.S. consumer
price index only rose 26 percent from 1958 to 1977, as compared to 75
percent between 1936 and 1955. More importantly, real income remained
flat from 1974 to 1977 and fell by 7 percent between 1974 and 1980
(NYSDL 1980; NYSDL 1975; NYSDL 1977) Households also incurred
greater expenses in some areas, especially education, for by 1977 the median level of education in the area was 12.5 years. Whereas a high school
diploma had been required in the 1950s, in the 1970s employment increasingly demanded some college or other technical training. All of our interviews indicate that children's demands on household resources had
increased.

Households responded to increased cash needs by sending more married women into the work force. The wages of the wife were pooled with
the household fund and, unlike in the 1950s, were regarded as necessary for
the survival of the household rather than as a means of purchasing extras.
The increased commodification of goods and the time required for women
in waged work mitigated against a return to the unwaged activities of the
1930s.

Teen-agers did not increase their contributions to the household, but
their time in the labor force increased. The teen-ager's wages benefited the
household only obliquely, as teen-agers bought some of their own clothing
and consumer goods. Even so, teen employment was sporadic and wages
were low, while their demands were high and constant.

The increased number of teen-agers seeking waged work provided employers with a ready supply of part-time labor which, with a few constraints, could be exploited at a much lower cost than adult labor. The rising
pool of employed teen-agers also created greater sales for the same employers because many of the businesses dependent upon teen-age employees also
catered primarily to teen-aged consumers.

The ever-increasing requirements of education for children and the social institution of adolescence prevented households from relying on the
contributions of teen-age workers. Furthermore, if teen-agers entered the
full-time workforce without completing at least twelfth grade, they would
not be able as adults to reproduce the standard of living of their childhood
households. The period of teen-age dependency on the household established in the 1950s was lengthened, and adolescence became an even more
expensive drain on household income and labor, the cost of which was primarily carried by the wives.

In the declining economic conditions of the mid-to-late 1970s, the reproduction of working class households in Broome County was sustained
by an ever-increasing reliance on women's labor. Whereas in the 1950s
married women could regard employment as a temporary or supplemental
activity (U.S. Bureau of Labor Statistics 1955, 75), by 1980 it had become
a necessity for household survival. Household work continued to be classified according to cultural expectations as "women's work." These normative assumptions allowed husbands to shirk responsibility for the increased
labor required to sustain the household.

## Discussion

Working class households in Broome County responded to changing economic conditions in the fifty years from the 1930s to the 1980s by changing
the nature of their activities and by shifting the proportionate burden of
labor between women and children. These reactions were not simple responses, for they occurred on a large scale in Broome County and the nation in general, and they shaped the subsequent nature of the economic
shifts that occurred. The structure of households in each of the three periods that we discuss constrained and/or determined the form that households
would take in a subsequent period.

Over the fifty years we have considered here, the labor inputs of the
wives and mothers of the households increased while those of children decreased and those of the husbands and fathers remained virtually unchanged
or declined (Table 3). In the 1930s working class mothers, by increasing
their family size, could attain a higher degree of authority in the home, as
well as lower levels of labor for the household members, especially for
themselves. This was possible because, as children grew older, they increased their contribution to the household consumption fund, primarily by
taking on tasks previously accorded the mother. The mother in the household supervised and directed the labor of older children, teen-agers, and
other relatives of her own generation. The fathers also benefited from the

contributions of the children, as they allowed him to reduce those contributions he made over and above his waged labor. Through a large family, a comfortable standard of living was attained with a relatively equal distribution of labor within the household. This strategy, however, required the sacrifice of a high school education for the children.

As the children of the 1930s established their own households in the 1950s, they found their occupational opportunities limited by lack of education. They, therefore, placed a high priority on the education of their children. Dramatically increasing real incomes and an active ideological campaign to put women in the home both allowed and forced a greater number of women to forego participation in the work force, or to participate on a more limited basis than in the 1930s. Increased income also reduced the need for and return from informal sector subsistence practices such as petty market activities and the keeping of boarders, lowering the amount of non-waged labor this implied for the household. This meant that older children and teen-agers were released from a range of household duties to attend school and participate in the other rites of adolescence.

Mothers took virtually full responsibility for non-waged housework and the increased demands of the children. If the wife did not also have waged work, she could do this without increasing her labor contribution much beyond that of her mother in the 1930s. The disparity in contributions from the husband and unemployed wife did not exceed one to two hours a day. We do not think that the majority of married men working at anytime in the 1950s or 1960s obtained a "family wage." However, most women moved in and out of the labor force throughout their life cycle. This allowed them to regard the periods of increased labor when they had jobs as temporary, anomalous, and linked to specific large-ticket, extra consumption goals.

Declining economic conditions and increasing social requirements for the reproduction of the household, including at least a few years of college for the children, forced more and more women into the labor force in the 1970s. The creation of a virtually separate sphere of consumption and labor which involved teen-agers in waged work benefited the household only incidentally. Both women and children labored harder, but the contributions of men appear to have changed only slightly or not at all from the 1950s. The majority of households included wives with full-time employment, and in these households the disparity in contributions of labor to the household fund between men and women increased to the point that women worked twenty percent more than men, at least three to four hours a day more (Table 3).

The labor of men changed very little in Broome County households between the late 1930s and the late 1970s. Adjustments to changing situations were accomplished by shifting the labor requirements of women, older children, and teen-agers. The one major example of duties being shifted from women to men occurred in the case of rent income. In the 1930s the majority of such income came from boarders whose care, as residents in the house, was the responsibility of women. In the 1950s and the 1970s the majority of such income came from the rental of separate houses, or apartments in the owner occupied house. Household work which takes place outside the house was more closely associated with men, and the majority of the labor necessary for this income therefore fell to men. Despite this exception, patriarchy manifests itself in this case primarily in the men's ability to avoid changes in their contributions to the household (England and Farkas 1986), while those of women and children are greatly altered.

Recent national studies have confirmed Robinson's contention (1977, 68) that men, particularly college-educated men, take more responsibilities for household duties, easing the wife's burden and making the sharing of the work load more equitable (Pleck 1983; Berk 1985). We have some indication that a comparable shift maybe occurring in our working class households. Several of our informants indicated that their husbands, who had not taken responsibility for housework in the 1970s, were now beginning to do so.

Nevertheless, our research interviews indicate that women are clearly aware of the discrepancies between their labor and that of their husbands. Since the late 1970s it has been apparent that women's participation in waged labor is essential for the household and that this necessity will not change during the household's life cycle. We suspect that this awareness has led to an ongoing controversy within the households and a renegotiation of household duties which continues today.

## Conclusion

Our detailed diachronic analysis of changes in householding in Broome County, New York, from 1930 to 1980 leads us to three conclusions regarding the significance of unwaged work and domestic inequality. First, throughout this fifty-year time period, unwaged work was always important and essential for the reproduction of Broome County working class households, but its form and degree of importance varied over time. The "family wage" never existed for a majority of working class households. Second, the performance of unwaged work was linked to other kinds of demands on household members, especially to education for the children. Finally, the distribution of labor in the households was rarely equitable between all household members, and those who shifted between waged and unwaged work as necessary were primarily women and children.

There is a very close correspondence between shifts in the labor demands on household members and changes in the labor market, such as growth of the service sector and part-time work, declining or rising real wage rates, and greater educational requirements for employment. Indeed, households are shaped by these changes, even as they influence the relations of the market place. By combining a historical perspective with a broader conceptualization of the household as a set of relationships, it is possible to see how households are, have been, and continue to be reproduced. In the very heart of the developed world, unwaged and undervalued labor remains central to the well-being of individual households, and such labor is a pervasive element of daily life.

# Chapter 10

# Family Wheat Farms and Third World Diets: A Paradoxical Relationship Between Unwaged and Waged Labor

## Harriet Friedmann

Family farming took its modern form to serve people newly dependent on purchased foods—the counterpart to wages as incomes. Although its origins may be traced very far back,[1] in practical terms the specialized, commercial family farm originated in the late nineteenth century with the establishment of the world economy in foodgrains.[2] It arose first in areas of European overseas settlement and then forced peasants and capitalists alike to adapt in European countries. It grew out of the conjuncture of two fundamental changes in the nineteenth century world: first, the widespread transformation of food into commodities to be bought by new proletarians; and second, the supply of foods as commodities on a world scale through extensive settlement by European agricultural colonists of temperate regions outside Europe. The agents of settlement were states seeking the most extensive territorial claims, and private capitals seeking profits from railway construction and international trade in wheat and meat (Fowke 1957; McMichael 1984; Friedmann 1978). With the typical American colonist homesteading an area roughly equivalent to that of a Junker estate in Prussia (Weber 1958), the result was farming on a scale as unprecedented as the markets they both served. Specialization went beyond anything yet seen in Europe, but was nonetheless modest compared with what was to occur later in the twentieth century.

Purchased diets and specialized regions of monocultural production are still the hub of agro-food relations, but the scope of these relations now encompasses the globe, and they penetrate ever more deeply into daily life. The basis of post-war accumulation was mass production and mass consumption of standard products, such as automobiles and household appliances. However, mass production in industry was underpinned by transformations in both agriculture and domestic relations.[3]

First, *agriculture* converted from horses to tractors in the 1940s in the United States. Thus began the rapid shift into practices geared ever more intensively to mechanical and chemical inputs. Just as mechanized agriculture had been the motor for a distinct type of capitalism in the nineteenth century United States (Post 1982), post-war technical changes became a major source of demand for the crucial vehicle and chemical industries (Kenney, Curry, and Stockwell 1987). At the same time, growth in size of farms and decrease in the number of farms meant that many people left the land to enter labor markets in industry and services—some related to food manufacturing and restaurants.

Second, commodity relations penetrated more deeply into daily life than ever before. The new importance of mass consumption for the accumulation of capital depended on a specific reorganization of *domestic relations.* Creating "Mrs. Consumer," in the advertising language of the 1920s, and locating her in a private house in a new suburban tract after World War II (Hayden 1984) was as crucial to the mass consumption of consumer durables, replicated in isolated households, as was the "family wage" earned by unionized male workers, many of whom were employed themselves in the expanding industries producing consumer durables.

Durable foods invented by expanding agro-food industries connected them all. Manufactured foods and meals increasingly replaced fresh ingredients in private consumption. Frozen foods, for example, relied on the multiplication of freezers of all sized in factories, warehouses, retail stores, restaurants, and kitchens, plus cooking appliances from stoves to (eventually) microwave ovens. Household appliances both made possible and (given changes in house design and location, and changes in domestic work) even required the use of processed foods. The use of household appliances was, in turn, intimately connected with changes in styles of life associated with automobiles.

However, the expansion of the durable foods industry rarely increased demand for farm products, which simply shifted from final use to industrial raw materials. It did mean more competition for farmers facing monopoly corporate buyers instead of dispersed, individual consumers. For most commodities, farming became an increasingly simplified production process (as its commercial, fiscal, and financial relations became more complex) located within a web of agro-food corporations supplying inputs to farms and using farm products as inputs for manufactured foods. After thirty years, all farmers together were receiving less than one-third of the value of food expenditures. An equivalent amount went to a handful of giant food manufacturing companies, while the lion's share went to the corporations engaged in transport, wholesaling, and retailing over the vast distances separating increasingly monocultural agricultural regions.

Wheat was especially prone to stagnant demand, compared to the agricultural products specific to new manufactured foods, such as vegetable fats, sweeteners, and meat, with its intensive inputs of soybeans and corn (Friedmann forthcoming a). Consumers with increasing incomes in the post-war years paid more for manufactured breads and pastries. But the value added came from processing, and the only ingredients whose quantities increased were fats and sugar. The "law" proclaimed by M. K. Bennett on the basis of observing dietary choices of Americans in the 1930s held: they did not eat more wheat. With stagnant domestic consumption, wheat farmers were caught in a bind. After the War, Europe continued to substitute domestic wheat for imports; American wheat farmers competed amongst themselves to increase productivity by buying machines and chemicals; and federal government agricultural support programs established in the New Deal maintained surplus stocks of wheat on a seemingly permanent basis.

Without more consumption, new consumers were needed: people who would buy wheat when they never had before. These were found in several places, but notably among new proletarians, people wholly or partly severed from historically self-provisioning relations, throughout the emerging third world. What I wish to address here is the tie between *unpaid domestic labor on American farms* and *paid (and unpaid) labor in third world countries that buy the products of those farms and consume their products in specific domestic relations*. My argument is that family wheat farms survived after World War II because of an extraordinary creation of demand for wheat as a "wage food" in the underdeveloped countries.[4] They survived only by complete internal transformation, continuing the social and technical reorganization begun in the 1920s, which marginalized women's (and children's) work. The relationship between farm work in the United States and proletarianization in the third world is key to the "wheat complex," one of several commodity complexes linking farms and consumers in the international food regime established after World War II.[5]

The essay below is in three parts: (1) regulation theory, which helps to interpret the transformations of both wheat producers and consumers, and its extension to include gender at one extreme and international relations at the other; (2) how American farm policy and food aid policy made wheat the wage food of new proletarians during the international food regime of 1947–73; and (3) how export wheat production in the same period underwent internal transformations at the expense of women's paid work. I draw these threads together, linking the American farm crisis with the third world food crisis, in the conclusion.

## Regulation Theory: Adding Gender
## and International Dimensions

The wheat complex connecting American farmers with third world proletarians was one part of the international food regime of 1947–73. The
United States emerged from the Second World War as the dominant world
power, and post-war international institutions established the dollar as
world currency. This new international position put the American government in a unique position to find an international solution to domestic agricultural surpluses, a problem stemming from New Deal farm programs
and exacerbated by the loss of European export markets through import
substitution. After 1947 the Cold War isolated the trade of West and East,
forcing the solution to be confined to the West. The solution involved two
decades of export subsidies ("food aid") to third world states, comple-
menting the price subsidies to American wheat farmers. Imported wheat
then served as a cheap wage food for the growth of paid labor forces, all
part of the elusive pursuit of industrial capitalism. In effect, the U.S. government created a new link between American wheat farmers and new proletarians in countries developing capitalist labor markets for the first time.
By the time of the crisis of the regime in 1972–73 (precipitated by the
Soviet-American grain deals), both American farmers and third world consumers were hooked on the connection, and both farmers and third world
states acquired crushing debts in the futile attempt to sustain it.

The period of the international food regime, 1947–73, corresponds
roughly to the period defined by the French "regulation school" (Aglietta
1978; deVroey 1984) as a *regime of intensive accumulation*. Most fully developed within the United States, this new form of capitalism also came to
characterize other advanced capitalist economies. Both commercial farmers
in the first world and rural communities in the third world were marginal to
the central institutions of the regime—those regulating work and wages in
mass production industries in advanced capitalism. But both underwent
transformations governed by these central institutions.

After World War II capitalist accumulation came to be based on the
mass production and mass consumption of consumer durables. In this regime of intensive accumulation (or "Fordism"), the economy was reorganized around new and higher "norms" of working class consumption,
expressed through purchases of standard commodities. In contrast to an earlier *regime of extensive accumulation*, which was based on low wages and a
narrow market—and possibly in contrast to downward pressures on wages
through international competition during the past decade or more—for the
first time aggregate demand became a significant factor in the reproduction

of capital. A new set of institutions regulated waged work in such a way that general living standards increased and mass consumption became crucial to profits for the first time in the history of capitalism. This led to a shift in industrial sectors towards consumer goods, especially durable consumer goods such as the automobile and domestic appliances. Although only a fraction of the paid labor force was directly incorporated into these new stable, high-paid (though monotonous) relations of production—male workers in unionized heavy industry—mass consumption involved a reconstitution of all spheres of life for ordinary people.

Although following Gramsci (1971, 277–316), the focus of the regulation school is laws and practices governing wage relations and wage levels, its major innovation is the new emphasis in Marxist political economy on the spheres of consumption and circulation. Thus "norms of consumption" characterize specific "regimes of accumulation." These norms refer not only to how much people use (Marx's moral and historical standard of life), but also to how they acquire goods, especially the extent and character of market (and money) dependence. As for circulation, if norms of consumption requiring many purchased goods are met, then there is an increasing density of ties between consumer goods sectors and producer goods sectors supplying equipment and raw materials.

Of course, people not only act out their roles in the reproduction of capital (and society in the narrow material sense), but live their lives and relationships in the rich totality of emotions, symbols, and practices. Decisions about what to eat, who will acquire, prepare, and serve food, and the social relations around meals, all reflect struggles to assert ourselves as we face changes in work and domestic life. As "consumption" overtakes more aspects of life, struggles to consume, and to live richly without consuming, more directly affect the structure of the economy. This emphasis enhances the richness of *historical* interpretation of concrete reality, while retaining the analytical coherence of concepts such as accumulation and labor-power.

This essay focuses on two questions not adequately addressed in the regulation literature. First, the division of labor is *gendered*. The idea of norms of consumption suggests both the crucial place of food in regimes of extensive and intensive accumulation, and attention to the specific *social relations of consumption*. From another perspective, corporate domination of all phases of the agro-food complex rests on a *gender division of labor* in family farming. In part this replicates the gender shifts of wage-dependent families, which bore an intimate relationship to the mechanization of domestic labor in a particular way—isolating and replicating the process and equipment for each family and further privatizing the work of each woman. The key to the shift from extensive to intensive accumulation in the United

States (and eventually in other advanced capitalist economies) was the penetration of commodity relations deeply into daily life, transforming all aspects of self-provisioning by individuals, households, families, and communities into commodity relations involving waged labor and purchased products. The clearest recent example is the growth of fast foods: the majority of workers are part-time housewives and teen-agers, a new labor force from the point of view of capital. Of course, the work they do for wages makes a product that replaces meals prepared at home for no pay. The shift from unwaged, self-provisioning work to paid work represents *not additional goods,* as the GNP measure suggests, but different goods whose sale in the market (plus the wages of new paid workers) represents new *value for capital* (Ekins 1984, 32–38).

Second, while Aglietta (1982) insists on the national character of all the crucial variables—labor process, norms of consumption, and state legal and fiscal supports to both the wage relation and the level of consumption—the *international economy* is clearly central and rests on its own rules which underpin (similar and complementary) national regimes (Block 1977). It is my claim that *intensive accumulation in the advanced capitalist countries was intimately bound up with proletarianization in the third world,* and that both were implicated in the rise of the international food regime after 1947 and its continuing crisis since 1973. The gender division of labor often noted there, where women increasingly concentrate on agricultural production in conjunction with men's (and sometimes also their own) waged labor, is one part of the story. It must be seen in context of a world economy reorganized around mass production and consumption in advanced capitalism. The unraveling of that division of labor in the crisis of the international food regime—and of high wage, mass production national economies generally—will ultimately, I believe, be one key to understanding the present complex of crises in all parts of the world economy.

## Third World Diets and Proletarianization

Both agriculture and diets in the third world (as in the first world) became increasingly reorganized through international markets. The prototype of the relationship can be illustrated by MacDonald's. The growth of fast foods is central to the intensification of commodity relations within advanced capitalism. Self-provisioning communities were expelled from vast areas of Latin America to provide cheap beef for mass-produced hamburgers, often directly organized by the company itself. Now MacDonald's is expanding to the third world to sell standardized food—the emerging global diet—to those who can no longer supply themselves. Even if only a minority can afford to buy it, the third world is the most important source of expansion for mass-produced food (Greenhouse 1986). This is a process full of contradictions which I cannot pursue here. But it provides a framework for posing the questions of how the complex experiences of people in core and peripheral agriculture were brutally disarticulated and subordinated to commodity relations.

The core specialized in basic grain staples, both for animal feeds (corn and soybeans) and for food (wheat). This led to the drastic simplification of farming as a *social* activity embedded in family and community relations and specific natural settings. This transformation depended entirely on creating markets for grain, specifically wheat, in the periphery. This was a crucial complement to the specialization of the periphery to supply two new kinds of agricultural products to the core. As pressures grew to increase agricultural exports, and as the prices of classical colonial crops, such as sugar and coffee, stagnated, other agricultural products became important, first meat and now fruits and vegetables (George 1981; Lappe and Collins 1979; Feder 1980; and Burbach and Flynn 1980). The consequences for first world export agriculture are almost equally disastrous in the long term (Wessel 1983). Yet export agriculture does not simply "cause" food import dependence; both are products of a unifying agro-food complex, linking diets and agriculture in each part of the international economy.

Within the United States, a new kind of food was invented to link the large mechanized farm to the small mechanized suburban household. It was manufactured with increasing complexity, value added, and distance in social and physical space between farmer and consumer. Highly processed, standardized, durable foods, subject to long-distance shipment and long storage, were appropriate to the key Fordist products in use by private households and central to accumulation—initially, of course, the car, but also the stove and refrigerator in every house, then freezers, manifold small appliances, and now the microwave oven. This implied no necessary increase in demand for farm products, since value added increasingly occurred through processing, wholesaling, and retailing. Farm products shifted from final use to inputs to industry. For some products, such as corn and soybeans, this meant a shift to supplying inputs for meat and dairy products;[6] for others, such as sugar, it meant increased consumption as an ingredient in a wide range of new manufactured foods.

For wheat, demand came from proletarianization in the periphery. In contrast to the stark divide between farm and consuming household that was occurring through intensive accumulation in the first world, capital subsumed new populations in the third world through a combination of self-provisioning and waged labor. Self-provisioning communities were disrupted and transformed, but for the most part—as in Europe and America in an earlier phase of capitalism—only half of their lives was of direct relevance for accumulation. Capitalist enterprises, supported by third world state policies, wanted labor as cheaply as possible. Except for very specific vendors such as Coca Cola, they did not want these workers as buyers on any significant scale. Capital subsumed labor haphazardly and partially, evicting people from the land without offering them employment, or employing them at wages that permitted survival only in the context of complex kin-based survival strategies, including considerable self-provisioning.

The literature on poverty and hunger in the third world either focuses on *how much* people eat, or if it addresses *what* they eat it is usually to focus on the trade-off between grains and meat. Yet meat consumption is increasing among third world elites (Yotopoulos 1985), preventing any easy match between diets and countries. More important is the shift in diets that makes meat and many other foods simply unavailable to people whose self-provisioning is disrupted by changes in land and labor forced upon them. People who work for wages, especially if they migrate to work, cannot attend to animals who need milking and feeding, or to gardens with diverse, labor-intensive crops (Dewey 1981). From the other side, sideline production of cattle is becoming less and less viable to people who find themselves unable to meet new international standards imposed by centralized purchasing by large capitalist packers. They lose more than the meat they used to raise themselves, partly to sell, partly to eat; they also lose the leather for shoes and the tallow for cooking (Sanderson 1986). All these things must now be purchased or done without. The point is that integration into markets in labor-power disconnects peoples' diets from local agriculture and forces their participation in food markets where different factors are at play, notably price.

What do people buy when local food markets become integrated into global markets? People were forced into waged work in the newly independent countries of Africa and Asia, and among the peasantries of Latin America, within the framework of the international food regime of 1947 to 1973. This regime had as its central principle increased trade and specialization. Since the largest numbers of consumers with money were in advanced capitalist countries, where intensive accumulation was developing on the basis of mass consumption, the agriculture of all countries, rich and poor, was oriented to supply the new standardized, mass-produced diets of advanced capitalist countries. The diets of new proletarians in the third world, for the first time dependent on buying food, were transformed within the cultural and material context of foods available to them in markets that were increasingly global. Unlike workers in advanced capitalist countries in this period, they were not integrated as consumers into capitalist accumulation. They were forced to buy food, but capitalist firms, with few exceptions, cared little about them as consumers, and mainly hired them for the lowest possible wages. Price—and ideology—gained new significance in what people ate.

In the 1950s and 1960s, the cheapest foodgrain on world markets was wheat. While at a national level, any food might do as long as it was cheap, third world governments rarely resisted the temptation to import cheap wheat, rarely attending to the consequences for domestic agriculture. The *international food regime* that linked the first and third worlds between World War II and the food crisis of the early 1970s depended on the transfers of surplus U.S. wheat to new waged workers in the third world. The restructuring of international grain markets, away from the traditional markets in Europe and towards a U.S.-third world trade, is a complex story of international power and economics which I have told elsewhere (Friedmann 1982). Here it is sufficient to note that cheap American grain led to the displacement rather than the increased production and marketing of traditional foods. This shows up in aggregate statistics on per capita consumption between the early 1950s and the late 1970s: while total per capita grain consumption in the underdeveloped world increased 44 percent, per capita consumption of *wheat* increased 108 percent (from 31.6 to 65.6 kg./cap.). Comparable increases for the advanced capitalist world were 21 percent for all grains and 4 percent for wheat, reflecting the shift into greater meat consumption. As a rough indicator of the displacement of traditional diets in the third world, per capita consumption of all other grains and root crops in the nonsocialist third world *declined* by 15 percent and 23 percent respectively. In real quantities, this was a per capita decline of root crop consumption from 109.2 to 88.7 kg., and of grains other than wheat from 184.9 to 157.2 kg.[7]

Thus the historically privileged grain of Europe, the mark of wealth and status, became the wage food of twentieth century proletarianization. Because the American government programs supported wheat farmers and accumulated large stores of wheat, and because it used concessional sales[8] to third world governments (''aid'') to replace European markets lost through import substitution, wheat became in effect an internationally subsidized foodgrain. When the American government sought to develop new markets for its burdensome surpluses, it developed a mechanism that overcame temporary obstacles presented by people without money and countries without dollars: food aid. Third world consumers during the 1950s and 1960s switched their diets to wheat under the incentive of this double subsidy. By the early 1970s the purpose of food aid—to develop new markets for American agricultural products—was achieved. The legacy was new proletarians determined to eat wheat at low prices, and national economies dependent on wheat imports to feed their populations. The difficulties of governments in meeting these conditions is part of the complex political situation of debt and food riots in the 1980s. And the export competition faced by American farmers is another part. But during the international food regime, new third world proletarians bought (with subsidies direct and indirect) increasing quantities of American wheat.

While proletarianization in the third world was intimately bound up with the regime of intensive accumulation in the first world, wage relations were regulated differently. In contrast to the laws and practices underpinning high wages in advanced capitalism—collective bargaining, internal labor markets, wages tied to productivity, minimum wages and social wages—new proletarians were wanted in underdeveloped countries, if at all, for cheap labor. An overriding interest in low wages meant a different configuration of domestic and paid labor, and a dietary norm simplified not by standardized commodities as in Fordism, but by the forced reduction of self-provisioning activities without compensation in income to buy commodities. Frances Rothstein (1986) shows from one perspective how migrant industrial workers in a Mexican village are forced to reduce their domestic food production and other activities, along with the time spent with family members; she concludes that they must be seen not as peasant workers but as particularly insecure and impoverished proletarians. Collins (1986, 665) emphasizes that participation in the cash economy based on coffee in highland Peru—by migrant labor, both self-employed and waged—"narrows the range of social relationships in which individuals can participate," bringing to new prominence the nuclear family household, with attendant pressures to undervalue the self-provisioning work of women. From another perspective, Kathryn Dewey (1981) shows how a project of the Mexican government to improve agricultural production *within the form of the communal ejido,* had equally simplifying and impoverishing effects through the transformation of the landscape, the living spaces, and most of all the activities and diets of the people. Although many villagers, both within the project and nearby, work for wages either for the "collective" or outside, the most immediate link to the simplification—and impoverishment—of their diets and their productive activities lies in the switch from self-provisioning through slash and burn agriculture to commercial crop production. And when they do buy food, they frequently substitute white bread for corn tortillas and cola drinks for nutritious drinks now too time-consuming to prepare.[9]

Yet this layer of simplification is hidden by the creative mix of survival strategies adopted by people in all parts of the world economy, and by the superficial variety of commodities available on the market. The original simplification of capitalist development is the separation of production from consumption. When people are separated from the land and social ties that root their material practices and cultures, there occurs a forced transformation of reciprocal and redistributive relations, concrete in each locality, into waged labor and purchased articles of consumption. From this we can move directly to the sphere of capitalist production, which has dominated analysis of the process, or we can focus, as feminist studies have begun to do, on the reconstitution of the domestic unit and the consequent reconstruction of the lives and unvalorized activities of working women and children. The excellent collection of studies entitled *Of Marriage and the Market* (Young, Wolkowitz, and McCullagh 1981) reveals the complexity of this process in the third world today, exploring the continuities and specificities of women's experiences with proletarianization, in relation to both the history and present experiences of women in advanced capitalism. What is clear from these studies as a group is that advanced capitalism is present as a proximate or distant determination of the transformation of working women's lives in the third world. At one extreme is the new isolation of women's work, either in self-provisioning agriculture or in privatized domestic activities, as community is replaced by the replication of wage-dependent family households. This isolation intensifies their dependence on husbands and fathers, in situations otherwise as various as subsistence cultivators in rural Ghana and seamstresses confined to home in urban Morocco (Maher 1981; Whitehead 1981). At the other extreme is the factory employment of young women, exploiting their traditional skills in needlework and related activities, to work in export platform industries, notably in garments and electronics—"darning with copper wire" (Elson and Pearson 1981). Their wages are low even by third world standards, and their vulnerability to employers and male relatives is high, even in relation to women in the secondary sectors of advanced capitalist economies.

Both proletarianization and the reorganization of agriculture in the third world were intimately connected with the intensive accumulation simultaneously being constructed in the core. In Mexico, where proximity to U.S. markets has brought about the most profound transformations of both agriculture and industry, integrated, communal agriculture (which should not be treated uncritically) has become divided into a capitalist sector, oriented to world markets, and a self-provisioning part for marginal workers (Bartra and Otero 1987; Sanderson 1986; Burbach and Flynn 1980). The obvious link to the core was third world export agriculture. The less obvious but equally critical link was the import of food staples from advanced capitalist countries, notably the United States. So it is crucial to outline the changes in family farming in the United States, focusing on the link between an emerging regime of intensive accumulation and the marginalization of work and products of farm women.

## Unwaged Labor in Family Wheat Farms

The family grain farm in the specialized regions of the midwest and the plains was, from the beginning, linked to and dependent on world markets. But in the era of extensive accumulation prior to the Second World War, it was at the same time a *simple commodity production enterprise* and a *family labor farm*. Although capitalist agriculture existed in some regions, notably the California "factories in the fields," the specialized character of simple commodity production coexisted with a complex of productive and domestic activities collected under the name of "mixed farming." Most of the non-specialized activities, many of which combined commercial and self-provisioning production, were the work of women. They included a long list, as reconstructed by Jane Adams (1988) for pre-war agriculture in a county in Illinois. The very shape of the farm house reflected the active involvement of women in the household enterprise. The dominant space was organized for food processing, preparation, and storage. Much of this was self-provisioning, from curing bacon to preserving fruits and vegetables and storing root crops. Self-provisioning extended to mass feedings of seasonal workers and the supervision of children's work in these tasks. Self-provisioning also merged with local commercial operations with the cleaning of eggs, the slaughtering and cleaning of poultry, and the separation of cream and its churning into butter. Some women sold to merchants, but others developed their own routes of customers. Self-provisioning was also typical for clothing, and some women developed commercial activities as seamstresses, and also sold baked goods and even flowers. Farms often took in boarders, typically the rural school teacher.

Crucial to this complex of mixed farming based on complementary women's and men's labor was a certain density of settlement. Farms were small enough to form settlements appropriate for services such as schools, banks, government extension agencies, and churches. They also supported concentrations of town dwellers. In short, the mix of activities on farms meant that their simple commodity production character was buttressed by the mixed unwaged and local commercial activities of women. Mixed farming underpinned a vital rural life, in which a variety of occupations served the social needs as well as the material inputs of farms, and in turn provided local demand for the non-specialized activities of farm households.

The changes after World War II could not have been more dramatic. They must be interpreted within the context of the general reorganization of production and consumption through the new regime of intensive accumulation, and with it to the reconstruction of the family itself. Sachs (1983) points out that poultry, eggs, and most of all processed dairy products, such as butter and cheese, began to be organized as capitalist production off the farm in New England as early as the turn of the twentieth century. Women's activities consequently became unwaged. From the opposite side, this was encouraged by a propaganda campaign by agricultural extension services through the idea of home economics. The ideology of women as unwaged domestic laborers has a long history even on the American farm.

But it was the regime of intensive accumulation, which touched commercial grain farming least directly, that brought these changes to the midwest and plains. The indirect *economic* effects were vast regional specialization, in which livestock and poultry farming, and of course horticulture, relocated primarily to the south, southwest and west. Even dairying became concentrated on special farms. The capital intensity of livestock, dairy, and horticulture operations on some farms was associated with the direct organization of markets by an emerging agro-food complex. As processing became more important in the final product, and as supermarkets became more important in retailing, corporations bought an increasing proportion of the supply and encouraged concentration of suppliers geographically and in the scale of the enterprise. Sometimes this meant contract farming. Always it meant difficulty of local farm products to compete in increasingly national and international markets.

For grain farming, the loss of supplementary markets was reinforced by intensive investment in grain monoculture, encouraged by agricultural support policies geared to single commodities. Mechanical equipment forced simplification of land use and even the landscape itself, as farms grew in size and decreased in number. Chemicals replaced the organic fertilizers and natural limits to pests provided by mixed farming. Socially, fewer farms meant lower population density and loss of the population basis for towns. The result was rural depopulation and impoverishment of rural life, abetted by agro-food capitals through the concentration of storage and transport facilities, and by state agencies through consolidation of schools, hospitals, and social services.

Some numbers will indicate the trends in farm specialization. The percentage of farms with milk cows, according to data compiled by Adams (1988) from U.S. censuses, declined from 86 percent in 1945 to 20 percent in 1964, and now stands at about 5 percent. This of course corresponded to the specialization of dairy farms, which caused the average numbers of cows per farm to rise from three in 1945 to nine in 1964; the figure now stands at twenty-five. Gilbert (1987) argues that this sort of concentration within family farming appears small in the shadow of giant dairy operations near Los Angeles, which have made use of all the elements of land speculation and associated politics so subversive to direct connections between farmers and local communities and between both and the land. The story of chickens, with the rise of factory farming, is even starker and may show the future for dairy farms. The percentage of farms with chickens fell from more than 90 percent to less than 10 percent between 1945 and today, and the average number per farm rose from seventy-three to more than twelve hundred. And with the growing size and distance among farms, transportation and marketing networks have been centralized. So have public services, such as school consolidation. Rural communities have disappeared, and farms have become isolated as the countryside has been simplified by monoculture. The ecological and social costs are mounting.

Chickens, moreover, were women's work, crucial to support of the household and through it the farm, until capitalist enterprises, encouraged by state programs and propaganda, removed it from the farm. Deborah Fink (1987) gives us a moving and well-documented account of the shift to regional and corporate concentration of egg production after World War II, and its destructive legacies for farm women, farm families, and the integration of farms into vital local communities and markets in "Open Country, Iowa." Before its capitalist reorganization off the farm, men on farms and in government derided poultry production as part of their devaluation of women's contribution to farm work. The invisible work of women was hidden in the household; they kept their egg money separate, reinvesting it in the poultry production, but also bartering eggs with local merchants in return for goods needed for the household, for herself, and for the children.

War brought two crucial changes: the beginnings of outmigration of men on a massive scale, which would drastically undercut the population base for viable rural communities and mixed farms; and an increased demand and soaring prices for eggs. The government began a propaganda effort, based on statistics showing profitability, appealing to men to reconsider the virtues of poultry. As a result, egg and broiler factories were established during the War. After the War they rapidly drove out women's production, which came to seem small-scale despite the fact that they sometimes involved as many as 500 chickens! The ultimate blow came with grading regulations, which prevented local provisioning of grocers by farm women.

It is difficult not to concur with Fink's conclusion that the result has been to undercut the positive meaning, if not the formal existence, of family farms. Women have lost their independent work and incomes on farms. With all farm work now confined to what has been traditionally defined as "men's," most women now participate in farm tasks as "assistants." More important, however, is the frequency with which they work off the farm for wages and on it in the more conventional unwaged housework of their urban counterparts. Much of this unwaged work—shopping, ferrying children to activities, and the like—is much more difficult in monocultural farming regions. With the size of farms and the loss of so many small communities, large distances separate households from population centers. A Nova Scotia farm woman told me that she drives so much that she often meets herself on the road coming the other way!

While industrial production of standardized, highly processed foods was forcing grain farms to narrow their activities, consumption of commodities (rather than self-provisioning work) increasingly became the specialized domain of unwaged women in private houses. This work was, like farm work itself, increasingly mechanized, through automobile transport and an expanding array of domestic appliances. Most of these consumption activities, whether in the prototypical suburb or in the city, were dependent on wages earned by men and often by women, too. The same process, anticipated by the home economics movement decades earlier, was brought to the farm as an ideology whose appeal lay both in easing the real hardships of women's work in complex farm households, and in filling a gap left by the marginalization of their commercial activities by regional and enterprise specialization. While even modern plumbing remains to become universal on farms today, two-thirds have home freezers (Adams 1988, Table 2).

Farm women, of course, have not been made fully marginal to commodity production. Studies by Bennett (1983) and Kohl (1976) in Canada and by Rosenfeld (1985) in the United States, detail the variety of productive, accounting, financial, and marketing tasks undertaken by farm women. As production has narrowed with increased specialization, commercial and bureaucratic management has become more demanding. Often, women have taken these tasks on without pay and without the independence that comes from a separate income (Wilkening 1981). From the perspective of family dynamics, Bennett and Kohl particularly emphasize how the conventional emotional work of woman in families becomes a crucial element of labor relations. Women at once supervise children in some spheres of farm work, and mediate between fathers and children in conflicts over productive relations in the man's sphere. Yet Rosenfeld also reinforces the picture drawn by many analysts of increasing off-farm work by both women and men. While a growing proportion of part-time farming is hobby farming, a large number of working farms are trying to survive through wages earned outside to support the flagging income of the farm.

What distinguishes the specific complex of work and family in family farming is *the combination of labor and property*.[10] Unlike working class, professional, or capitalist families, who live from wages, salaries, and profits, respectively, simple commodity production families live from the sale of their own product, alone or in combination with wages earned outside. The changes in the structure of families in each class, in periods of both extensive and intensive accumulation, took place *within* the productive household.

Family enterprises contain two distinct contradictory relationships: one between value and family, and the other (within value relations) between property and labor. Value relations undercut family ties as individual men, women, and children are confronted with increasing possibilities for calculating the relative gains of remaining on the farm and entering labor markets fully (Chevalier 1982). Especially when the farm itself is under competitive pressure, the opportunity costs of clinging to the emotional ties and traditional obligations of patriarchal household production appear increasingly high. At the same time, the survival of the farm may well depend on the ability to invoke familial obligations for women and children to participate in labor in the present and for children to inherit and ensure the continuity of the farm.

Yet value relations reinforce families as well. Property, which is valued as a source of independence from the pressures to seek employment by others, is a cement to simple commodity production households. Connection to property is a powerful incentive to accept patriarchal domination. Fathers want their sons, who have learned farm skills as apprentices, to carry on the enterprise after their retirement or death; this anticipated continuity can give meaning to lives devoted to hard work (Bertaux 1979). For women and children, abandoning work dominated by husbands and fathers means losing their connection to property—no small matter in capitalist societies. Divorce rates, though rising, remain lower in rural areas. "Independence" from the family contradicts "independence" for capital. Divorce or refusal to inherit leads, to turn Marx's phrase inside out, not only to freedom from toil, but also to freedom from the property associated with it. The unifying pressures of family property are in tension with larger social pressures to equality across genders and generations. The fight for rights for women and youth are mainly defined by the very different conditions of existence of most families which depend on wages and salaries, which are paid to individuals. In contrast to an income from the sale of a joint (but rarely equally controlled) family product, individual wages provide a material basis for individuals (especially men, who are better situated in labor markets) to act on wishes to dissolve and reconstitute families.

At the same time, the increasingly precarious competitive position of simple commodity production intersects with the increasing precariousness of patriarchy, both legally and in practice. Laws governing property and labor are principally designed for corporations and waged laborers. Consequently, many family farms are adopting the legal form of corporations. Similarly, family law is evolving principally in relation to families whose property is personal rather than productive. The dilemmas posed for family farms are extraordinary. Division of the farm is disastrous for the enterprise. At the same time, land speculation, principally related to the potential non-agricultural uses of the land, creates an incentive (and sometimes pressure from creditors) to realize capital gains at the expense of continued family production (Buttel 1986). Similarly, labor laws cannot easily accommodate unemployment, compensation for injury, maternity leave, and all the contemporary guarantees against the worst hazards of labor. If the family is a relation of production, it is unregulated by any but emotional ties under seige by both capital and the rights of women and children.

Yet Susan Rogers (1987) shows that community values—what Polanyi (1957) calls self-protection against the consequences of land and labor turned into commodities—can resist pressures of capital and state commodity programs to specialize and speculate in land values. Only if we assume, with economists, that people really embrace commodity relations does the tendency to specialization, simplification, rural depopulation, and the loss of diverse rural life become inevitable. Though these trends dominate Illinois as elsewhere, Rogers shows how different cultural values prevailed in a community that succeeded in moving in the opposite direction. The farms in Freiberg, Illinois, are owned by the descendants of the original German settlers of the 1830s. They sustain mixed farming, small farms, and owner-operation, and even intensify these characteristics against the larger trends. The farmers of Freiberg have a long-term vision, extending well beyond their own lifetimes. The commitment of each (male) farmer to maintain his farm for his descendants limits the land available for expansion through purchase or rental for the others. This produces very peculiar and local land markets, usually involving transactions within the community. While Rogers does not tell us much about gender, she does show that these arrangements are sometimes fraught with family conflict over succession or sharing. Positively, the strategy for succession in a context of land scarcity involves greater intensity of labor and land in farming, mixing animals with grains as ways to use labor and generate the extra income to support dependent children and heirs. The greater density of settlement supports a richer community life, which in turn reinforces the commitment to sustain labor-intensive, mixed farming. Negatively, we must conclude, with Fink, that the *family* is a contradictory basis for sustaining diverse agriculture in rural communities. It at once shows the possibility of cooperative and community relations, and the dangers of locking them in a patriarchal mold.

## Conclusion: The Crisis of the International Food Regime

Family wheat farms were subject to all the changes wrought by the regime of intensive accumulation: integrated sectors of mass production and consumption, the spatial redistribution of populations in cities, suburbs, and the countryside, and the changing relations among genders and generations. At the same time, they were not directly incorporated into agro-food complexes to nearly the same extent as the specialized production of other agricultural commodities. They survived, isolated in vast seas of grain, under pressure of the simplification of farm practices (though not financial and policy relations), and changing commitments of individuals to enterprise and family. They did so by selling to new proletarians in the third world.

In the 1970s, banks extended credit to expand this relation on both ends. Farms increased investments, often by expanding land, and third world countries borrowed to finance imports of (among other things) food. This extravagant expansion of the system was inspired by the very thing that was undermining it permanently. The dramatic price rise of wheat, that at once produced a price boom for farmers and a foreign exchange crunch for third world importers, was precipitated by the huge Soviet-American grain deals of 1972–73. The isolation of the Cold War trading blocs had been a condition of the international food regime. Yet the difficulties of food import dependence, and the potential political crises of new proletarians in third world countries, was not balanced by expanding markets for American farmers. Other countries, not only the traditional wheat export competitors, but also Europe, began to compete, using export subsidies and all the other items in the American inventory of international commercial strategies. Prices plummeted, and with them the inflated land prices of the speculative boom, inducing a debt crises in the grain heartland.

What can come of this? Now is the time to ask the question, when the restructuring of a regime of accumulation in crisis opens alternate paths and makes visible the human choice underlying economic arrangements. I shall note only two aspects related to the paradoxical relationship between third world proletarianization and American family wheat farms.

The legacy for the third world of the post-war wheat complex was two-fold: import dependence on food (and often a preference among consumers for wheat), and underdevelopment of domestic agriculture. The main thrust of the solution, forced by balance of payments difficulties compounded by debts, is import substitution of domestic foodgrains combined with export agriculture to earn foreign exchange. For the import substitution side, there has been a renewed emphasis in the past decade and a half on increasing productivity through a combination of high prices to farmers and introduction of improved seeds, mainly associated with the Green Revolution high-yielding varieties.

Import substitution through Green Revolution technologies does not unambiguously address the dependence on imports. Inputs of machinery and chemicals add to the import bill, even if the grain produced reduces it. Even if the gains outweigh the losses to the national balance of payments, foreign exchange is still necessary to pay for imported inputs. This may have the paradoxical and perverse effect of encouraging export agriculture to pay for inputs for switching to domestic agriculture to replace imported food. Whatever the effects in national accounting or in the balance between domestic and export production, reliance on inputs manufactured abroad ties third world agriculture into global agro-food complexes.

Higher food prices, of course, limit the size of the market by requiring higher wages to buy it, just as cheap food formerly expanded it by increasing the number of people available for industrial employment at low wages. In human terms this means more hunger. In the cheap food epoch of the international food regime, states throughout the third world introduced subsidies to urban food supplies. Now these have become more expensive, just as they are more desperately needed. State expenditures, moreover, are the target of IMF austerity measures conditional to the extension of international loans. The result has been frequent "IMF riots" as hungry people react to the removal of food subsidies that they have come to consider a right.

In farming, the Green Revolution brings the same social and ecological problems of capital-intensive monoculture that have plagued post-war American agriculture. As Kloppenburg (1984, 1988) has shown, adoption of high-yielding varieties is nothing else but the adaptation of the earlier experience of hybrid corn that eventually proved so devastating socially and ecologically in the United States. At best, success will reproduce the devastation of social and ecological simplification of post-war monocultures. Green Revolution critics have already shown how the shedding of labor and the social reorganization of mixed agricultural systems are reproducing the early negative effects of agricultural specialization in advanced capitalism.

The effects on fragile ecosystems in the tropics and subtropics may well be worse, and the genetic consequences of standardizing varieties under the control of capital are frightening indeed.

At least the marginalization of women's work associated with commercial farming is now explicitly recognized in the policies of international agencies. Under new programs focused on "women in development," the marginal food production of third world communities, and especially of women, is being acknowledged. It seems unlikely, but possible, that women's work will be incorporated and rewarded in one or both of self-provisioning or commercial agriculture. Unless patriarchal domination within families is addressed, however, transformation to simple commodity production will likely bring the relations between family and value, between waged and unwaged labor in agriculture so fraught with contradictions in the United States. The results will no doubt be specific to each case, but the concepts we can glean from the American experience may be guides to interpretation and action.

In advanced capitalism, simple commodity production is losing its political support, long disproportionate to its actual numbers or economic weight. Price support policies have become less appropriate and less politically or fiscally viable. Monoculture also requires chemicals, causes loss of topsoil, and compacts soil by using large machines, all ecologically unsustainable.

There is a way out of the impasse of grain surpluses, farm crisis, expensive public subsidies, ecological and esthetic simplification of the countryside, and chemically dangerous foods. It is to reorient American plains agriculture (and all other regional agriculture) to local consumption. In production, this implies a decision not to sustain or abolish agricultural subsidies, in the arid debate now prevailing, but to shift them to encourage specific changes for each farm within a comprehensive program of land use and food planning. Commodity-specific price supports (and associated production and trade controls) should give way to income supports and direct subsidies to farmers to redirect land towards socially desirable uses, which will vary from region to region—for instance, subsidies to plant trees. These uses would reflect a socially desirable mix of healthy food, sustainable agriculture, wilderness, and a beautiful, socially diverse countryside. The complement must be consumer education about the benefits of locally produced, low chemical-input foods, for the health of both people and the environment. The Swedish Social Democratic Party has adopted such a policy, under the pressure of parliamentary inroads by the environmental party (Vail 1987).

With a focus on regional agro-food systems and more labor-intensive methods, several possibilities open up. First, scientific and technical research and experiments in diverse, biological methods specific to ecological settings could extend the range of crops and foods available to consumers within each region. Second, greater employment in agriculture, including specific inputs and the processing of outputs as local foods, would enhance the population base for a revived rural life. Together these changes would provide the basis for experiments in new forms of property and labor. As Buttel (1986) argues, a corollary policy in the United States must involve public control of some kind over land use. On this basis it is possible to imagine both patriarchy and domination by giant corporations within far-flung agro-food complexes giving way to cooperation among equal individuals supplying local markets.

"Free markets," in the sense of operating without direct policies to manage supplies and prices of agricultural products, created the instability that inspired such policies in the first place. Now instability has returned despite price supports, supply management, and protectionism. Ironically, "free markets" are advocated as the solution to third world agriculture (Bates 1981), when subsidized exports to get rid of surpluses generated by policies introduced to save first world farmers are a major cause of third world ills. Grain monoculture was created by free trade and deepened to the point of a second crisis within the specific types of subsidy and control now used. Food import dependence was created by subsidized trade now cut off. Both will need to adapt to new realities. But as the structures of international regimes should make clear, rules always govern production and trade. If we refuse to face the political choice of what those rules will be, they will be made by those pursuing profits at costs which have become quite clear—to people, nations, and environments.

# Notes and References

## Chapter 1

*Notes*

1. Some scholars argued that what was necessary was not a reformulation
of Marx, but a re-reading of his work that would make social reproduction
more visible.

2. The concept of simple commodity production in Marx and later
works is discussed by Cook (1976).

3. This discussion of the work of Friedmann and Gibbon and Neocosmos owes much to Bernstein's perceptive paper (1986).

4. Gibbon and Neocosmos rightly point out that individual enterprises
can participate in this differentiation and class mobility, while petty commodity producers as a class will not disappear.

5. Gimenez (this volume) refers to Glazer's notion of capital pulling
women into the work process as "a powerful metaphor." She argues, however, that while capital may benefit from women's unwaged labor, it does
not appropriate it.

*References*

Alderson-Smith, Gavin. 1976. Peasant Response to Cooperativization under Agrarian Reform in the Communities of the Peruvian Sierra. In *Popular Participation in Social Change.* June Nash, Jorge Dandler, and Nicholas Hopkins, eds. Pp. 11–156. The Hague: Mouton.

Banaji, Jairus. 1976. "Summary of Selected Parts of Kautsky's The Agrarian Question," *Economy and Society* 5(10):1–49.

Barrett, M. and M. McKintosh. 1980. The "Family Wage": Some Problems for Socialists and Feminists. *Capital and Class* 11:51–72.

Beechey, Veronica. 1977. Female Wage Labour in Capitalist Production. *Capital and Class* 3:45–66.

Bennholdt-Thomsen, Veronika. 1981. Subsistence Production and Extended Reproduction. In *Of Marriage and the Market: Women's Subordination in International Perspective.* Kate Young, Carol Wolkowitz, and Roslyn McCullagh, eds. Pp. 16–29. London: Conference of Socialist Economists Books.

Benston, Margaret. 1969. The Political Economy of Women's Liberation. *Monthly Review* 21:13–27.

Bernstein, Henry. 1986. Is There a Concept of Petty Commodity Production Generic to Capitalism? Paper presented to the 13th European Congress for Rural Sociology, Braga, Portugal.

Birbeck, Chris. 1978. Self-Employed Proletarians in an Informal Factory: The Case of Cali's Garbage Dump. *World Development* 6(9/10):1173–85.

Blincow, Malcolm. 1986. Scavengers and Recycling: A Neglected Domain of Production. *Labour, Capital and Society* 19(1):94–116.

Bradby, Barbara. 1982. The Remystification of Value. *Capital and Class* 17:114–33.

Briskin, Linda. 1980. Domestic Labour: A Methodological Discussion. In *Hidden in the Household: Women's Domestic Labour Under Capitalism.* Bonnie Fox, ed. Pp. 135–172. Toronto: The Women's Press.

Bromley, Ray and Chris Gerry, eds. 1979. *Casual Work and Poverty in Third World Cities.* New York: Wiley.

Burawoy, Michael. 1982. *The Politics of Production,* London: Verso.

Chayanov, A. V. 1966. *Theory of Peasant Economy,* Homewood, Illinois: Richard D. Irwin.

Chevalier, Jacques. 1982. *Civilisation and the Stolen Gift.* Toronto: University of Toronto Press.

Collins, Jane. 1986. The Household and Relations of Production in Southern Peru. *Comparative Studies in Society and History* 28(4):651–71.

Cook, Scott. 1976. Value, Price and Simple Commodity Production: The Case of the Zapotec Stoneworkers. *Journal of Peasant Studies* 3(4):395–427.

Curtis, Bruce. 1980. Capital, the State and the Origins of the Working Class Household. In *Hidden in the Household: Women's Domestic Labour Under Capitalism.* Bonnie Fox, ed. Pp. 101–34. Toronto: The Women's Press.

de Janvry, Alain. 1981. *The Agrarian Question and Reformism in Latin America.* Baltimore: Johns Hopkins University Press.

Ennew, Judith, Paul Hirst and Keith Tribe. 1977. "Peasantry" as an Economic Category. *Journal of Peasant Studies 4(4):295–322.*

Feldberg, Roslyn and Evelyn Nakano Glenn. 1982. Male and Female: Job vs. Gender Models in the Sociology of Work. In *Women and Work: Problems and Perspectives,* R. Kahn-Hut, A. K. Daniels, and R. Colvard, eds. Pp. 65–80. New York: Oxford.

Friedmann, Harriet. 1978. Simple Commodity Production and Wage Labour in the American Plains. *Journal of Peasant Studies* 6:70–100.

——— . 1980. Household Production and the National Economy: Concepts for the Analysis of Agrarian Formations. *Journal of Peasant Studies* 7(2):158–84.

——— . 1986a. Postscript: Small Commodity Production. *Labour, Capital and Society* 19(1):117–26.

——— . 1986b. Patriarchal Commodity Production. *Social Analysis* 20:47–55.

Gardiner, Jean. 1975. Women's Domestic Labour. *New Left Review* 89:47–59.

Gardiner, Jean, S. Himmelweit, and M. McKintosh. 1975. Women's Domestic Labour. *Bulletin of the Conference of Socialist Economists* 4:1–11.

Gershuny, J. I. 1985. Economic Development and Change in the Mode of Provision of Services. In *Beyond Employment: Households, Gender and Subsistence.* Nanneke Redclift and Enzo Mingione, eds. Pp. 138–164. London: Basil Blackwell.

Gimenez, Martha E. 1978. Structuralist Marxism and "the Woman Question." *Science and Society* 42(3):301–23.

Gibbon, Peter and Michael Neocosmos. 1985. Some Problems in the Political Economy of African Socialism. In *Contradictions of Accumulation in Africa: Studies in Economy and the State.* Henry Bernstein and Bonnie Campbell, eds. Beverly Hills: Sage.

Harris, Olivia. 1981. Households as Natural Units. In *Of Marriage and the Market: Women's Subordination in International Perspective.* Kate Young, Carol Wolkowitz and Roslyn McCullagh, eds. Pp. 136–156. London: Conference of Socialist Economists Books.

Harrison, John. 1973. The Political Economy of Housework. *Bulletin of the Conference of Socialist Economists,* Winter:35–52.

Humphries, Jane. 1977. The Working Class Family, Women's Liberation and Class Struggle: The Case of 19th Century British History. *Review of Radical Political Economics* 9(3):25–41.

Illich, Ivan. 1981. *Shadow Work.* Boston: Marion Boyars.

Kuhn, Annette. 1978. Structures of Patriarchy and Capital in the Family. In *Feminism and Materialism: Women and Modes of Production.* Annette Kuhn and AnnMarie Wolpe, eds. Pp. 42–67. Boston: Routledge and Kegan Paul.

Lenin, V. I. 1899. *The Development of Capitalism in Russia.* (Collected Works, vol. 3, chapter 2, pt. 13). Moscow: Progress Publishers.

Long, Norman, ed. 1984. *Family and Work in Rural Societies: Perspectives on Non-Wage Labour.* New York: Tavistock.

Long, Norman and Bryan Roberts, eds. 1978. *Peasant Cooperation and Capitalist Expansion in Central Peru.* Austin: University of Texas Press.

Marx, Karl. 1968. *The German Ideology.* (with F. Engels). Moscow: Progress Publishers.

Mattera, Philip. 1986. *Off the Books: The Rise of the Underground Economy.* London: Pluto Press.

McDonough, Roisin and Rachel Harrison. 1978. Patriarchy and Relations of Production. In *Feminism and Materialism: Women and Modes of Production.* Annette Kuhn and AnnMarie Wolpe, eds. Pp. 11–41. Boston: Routledge and Kegan-Paul.

Medick, Hans and David Sabean. 1984. *Interest and Emotion: Essays on the Study of Family and Kinship.* New York: Cambridge University Press.

Mingione, Enzo. 1985. Social Reproduction of the Surplus Labour Force: The Case of Southern Italy. In *Beyond Employment: Household, Gender and Subsistence.* Nanneke Redclift and Enzo Mingione, eds. Pp. 14–54. London: Basil Blackwell.

Molyneux, Maxine. 1979. Beyond the Domestic Labour Debate. *New Left Review* 116:3–27.

Pahl, R. E. and Claire Wallace. 1985. Household Work Strategies in Economic Recession. In *Beyond Employment: Households, Gender and Subsistence.* Nanneke Redclift and Enzo Mingione, eds. Pp. 189–227. London: Basil Blackwell.

Perlman, Janice. 1976. *The Myth of Marginality: Urban Poverty and Politics in Rio de Janeiro.* Berkeley: University of California Press.

Portes, Alejandro and Lauren Benton. 1984. Industrial Development and Labor Absorption: A Reinterpretation. *Population and Development Review* 10:589–611.

Portes, Alejandro and John Walton, eds. 1981. *Labor, Class and the International System.* New York: Academic Press.

PREALC. 1987. *Ajuste y deuda social: Un enfoque estructural.* Santiago: Programa Regional de Empleo para América Latina y el Caribe.

Redclift, Nanneke and Enzo Mingione, eds. 1985. *Beyond Employment: Household, Gender and Subsistence.* New York: Basil Blackwell.

Roberts, Bryan. 1988. The Informal Economy in Comparative Perspective. Paper presented to meetings of the Society for Economic Anthropology, Knoxville, Tennessee, April.

Roseberry, William. 1983. *Coffee and Capitalism in the Venezuelan Andes.* Austin: University of Texas Press.

——— . 1986. The Ideology of Domestic Production. *Labour, Capital and Society* 19(1):70–93.

Rubin, Gale. 1975. The Traffic in Women. In *Towards an Anthropology of Women.* Rayna Rapp, ed. Pp. 157–210 New York: Monthly Review Press.

Sargent, Lydia, ed. 1981. *Women and Revolution.* Boston: South End Press.

Sayer, Derek. 1987. *The Violence of Abstraction.* New York: Basil Blackwell.

Scott, Joan and Louise Tilly. 1975. Women's Work and the Family in Nineteenth-Century Europe. *Comparative Studies in Society and History* 17(1):36–64.

Seccombe, Wally. 1974. The Housewife and Her Labour under Capitalism. *New Left Review* 83:3–24.

——— . 1980. Domestic Labour and the Working Class Household. In *Hidden in the Household: Women's Domestic Labour Under Capitalism.* Bonnie Fox, ed. Pp. 25–100. Toronto: The Women's Press.

Segalen, Martine. 1983. *Love and Power in the Peasant Family.* Chicago: University of Chicago Press.

Smith, Carol. 1986. The Petty Bourgeoisie as a "Fundamental" Revolutionary Class in Nicaragua. *Labour, Capital and Society* 19(1):8–35.

Smith, Joan. 1984. Nonwage Labor and Subsistence. In *Households and the World Economy.* Joan Smith, Immanuel Wallerstein, and Hans-Dieter Evers, eds. Pp. 64–89. Beverly Hills: Sage.

Smith, Paul. 1978. Domestic Labour and Marx's Theory of Value. In *Feminism and Materialism: Women and Modes of Production.* Annette Kuhn and AnnMarie Wolpe, eds. New York: Routledge and Kegan-Paul.

Vergopoulos, Kostas. 1978. Capitalism and Peasant Productivity. *Journal of Peasant Studies* 5(4)446–65.

von Werlhof, Claudia. 1984. The Proletarian is Dead: Long Live the Housewife. In *Households and the World Economy.* Joan Smith, Immanuel Wallerstein, and Hans-Dieter Evers, eds. Pp. 131–50. Beverly Hills: Sage.

Wallerstein, Immanuel, William Martin, and Torry Dickinson. 1979. Household Structures and Production Processes. Paper prepared for the Colloquium "Production and Reproduction of the Labor Force," Fiori, Italy, June.

West, Jackie. 1978. Women, Sex and Class. In *Feminism and Materialism: Women and Modes of Production.* Annette Kuhn and AnnMarie Wolpe, eds. Pp. 320–53. Boston: Routledge and Kegan Paul.

Williams, Raymond. 1976. *Keywords: A Vocabulary of Culture and Society.* Oxford: Oxford University Press.

Wolf, Eric. 1966. *Peasants.* Englewood Cliffs, N.J.: Prentice-Hall.

Wood, Charles. 1981. Structural Change and Household Strategies: A Conceptual Framework for the Study of Rural Migration. *Human Organization* 40:338–44.

## Chapter 2

*Notes*

1. By process of structural and functional differentiation I mean the process whereby household structure changes to incorporate other people who, on a temporary or semi-permanent basis, carry on activities which were previously the sole responsibility of the adult members of the household.

2. Throughout this paper I make a distinction between *social classes*, based on households and individuals relationship to the means of production (a concept of social class based on Marxist theory), and *socioeconomic status*, the ranking of individuals on the basis of indexes arbitrarily constructed using type of occupation, income, and education (a concept based on sociological theory). From the standpoint of Marxist theory, those who own nothing but their labor power—no matter how skilled that labor power may be—are members of the working class. At the level of the market, the differences in socioeconomic status *within* the working class are large; people who are working class in terms of their location in the relations of production can be "middle class" or "upper-middle class" in terms of socioeconomic status. I chose, therefore, to use the concept of propertyless class to indicate that households dependent on wages or salaries for survival face common constraints, despite socioeconomic status differences in their standard of living.

3. These "roles" are the empirically observable effects of processes of structural and functional differentiation at the level of market and individual relations which, in turn, rest upon underlying capitalist processes and contradictions.

*References*

Baldwin, Wendy H. and C. Winquist Nord. 1984. "Delayed Childbearing in the U.S.: Facts and Fictions." *Population Bulletin.* Vol. 39, No. 4 (November). Washington, DC.: Population Reference Bureau.

Bluestone, B. and B. Harrison. 1982. *The Deindustrialization of America.* New York: Basic Books.

———— . 1986. "Most Jobs in U.S. Low Paying." *Boulder Camera*, December 10.

Boserup, Ester. 1970. *Woman's Role in Economic Development*. New York: St. Martin's Press.

Braverman, Harry. 1974. *Labor and Monopoly Capital*. New York: Monthly Review Press.

Burns, Scott. 1977. *The Household Economy—Its Shape, Origins and Future*. Boston: Beacon Press.

Buss, Terry and F. Stevens Redburn with Joseph Waldron. 1983. *Mass Unemployment: Plant Closings and Community Mental Health*. Beverly Hills: Sage Publications.

Congressional Quarterly. 1983. "Problems of the Unemployed," pp. 129–156 in *Employment in America*. Washington, DC.

Cowan, Ruth Schwartz. 1983. More Work for Mother. New York: Basic Books.

Dill, Bonnie Thorton. 1987. "Race, Class and Gender: Prospects for an All-Inclusive Sisterhood," Pp. 204–213 in Ronald Takaki, ed. *From Different Shores: Perspectives on Race and Ethnicity in America*. New York: Oxford University Press.

Dollars & Sense. 1987. "Even Young Men Feel the Pinch." No. 131 (November): 10–11.

Friedan, Betty. 1963. *The Feminine Mystique*. New York: Dell Publishers.

Gimenez, Martha E. 1978. "Structuralist Marxism on 'The Woman Question'," *Science & Society*, Vol. XLII, No. 3 (Fall): 301–323.

———— . 1982. "The Oppression of Women," pp. 292–324 in Ino Rossi, ed., *Structural Sociology*. New York: Columbia University Press.

———— . 1987. "Marxist and Non-Marxist Elements in Engels' Views on the Oppression of Women," pp. 37–56 in Janet Sayers et. al, eds., *Engels Revisited: New Feminist Essays*. London: Tavistock.

Glazer, Nona. 1984. "Servants to Capital: Unpaid Domestic Labor and Paid Work." *Review of Radical Political Economics*. Vol. 16, (1): 61–87.

Hartmann, Heidi. 1981. "The Unhappy Marriage of Marxism and Feminism: Towards a More Progressive Union," pp. 1–41 in L. Sargent, ed., *Women and Revolution*. Boston: South End Press.

Holstrom, Linda L. 1972. *The Two-Career Family*. Cambridge, Mass.: Schankman Publishing Co.

Mitchell, Juliet. 1971. *Woman's Estate*. New York: Pantheon Books.

O'Connell, Martin and D. E. Bloom. 1987. "Juggling Jobs and Babies: America's Childcare Challenge." Occasional Paper No. 12, February. Washington, DC: Population Reference Bureau.

O'Hare, William. 1985. "Poverty in America: Trends and New Patterns." Population Bulletin Vol. 40, No. 3 (June). Washington DC: Population Reference Bureau.

Patton, H. M. and J. W. Patton. 1984. *The Displaced Worker and Community Response: Case Study of Portsmouth, Scioto County, Ohio.* Lexington, Kentucky: State Research Associates.

Piven, Frances F. and R. A. Cloward. 1985. *The New Class War: Reagan's Attack on the Welfare State and its Consequences.* New York: Pantheon.

Reich, Michael. 1978. "The Development of the Wage Force," pp. 179–185 in R.C. Edwards et. al., eds., *The Capitalist System.* 2nd. edition. New Jersey: Englewood Cliffs, Prentice Hall.

Rollins, Judith. 1985. *Between Women: Domestics and their Employers.* Philadelphia: Temple University Press.

Rose, Stephen. 1986. *The American Profile Poster.* New York: Pantheon.

Seccombe, Wally. 1974. "The Housewife and her labor under Capitalism" *New Left Review* 83 (January-February): 3–24.

Sivard, Ruth Leger. 1985. *Women . . . A World Survey.* Washington, DC: World Priorities.

Smith, Joan, Immanuel Wallerstein & Hans-Dieter Evans. 1984. *Households and the World Economy.* Beverly Hills, California: Sage Publications.

U.S. Bureau of the Census. 1987a. Statistical Abstract of the United States: 1987 (107th edition). Washington, DC: U.S. Government Printing Office.

U.S. Bureau of the Census. 1987b. Current Population Reports, Series P–60, No. 157. Money Income and Poverty Status of Families and Persons in the United States: 1986 (Advanced Data from the March 1987 Current Population Survey). Washington, DC: U.S. Government Printing Office.

Waite, Linda J. 1981. "U.S. Women at Work." Population Bulletin Vol. 36 No. 2 (May). Washington, DC: Population Reference Bureau.

## Chapter 3

*Notes*

1. The research on which this paper was based was funded by a grant from the Ministry of Education of the Government of Québec, various

grants from the Social Sciences and Humanities Research Council, Canada and a subvention from the Banco Central de Reserva, Peru. Some research was also carried out while a Visiting Fellow at St Antony's College, Oxford. I am grateful to all these bodies for their support.

2. This is made especially clear for the parameters of the sphere of "subsistence" for the medieval peasantry, a case which provides a useful heuristic device for rethinking the, possibly less clear, case of the auto-provisioning sphere for more contemporary domestic enterprises. Brenner (1976) shows how the medieval peasantry of Europe were engaged in a struggle over the amount of labor and means of production (pre-eminently land) devoted to subsistence as opposed to rents and taxes. In this case then, the social relations of subsistence production cannot be understood outside the context of rents and taxes and the power relationships which supported them. In this struggle—on the one hand for the retention of "subsistence" and on the other for the retention (or expansion) of rents—markets and cash played their part, on *both* sides. That is to say, markets and cash were a part both of the landlords' sphere of rents and domain produce *and* of the peasants' sphere of "subsistence" production. Now, if the sphere of what is to be socially prescribed as "subsistence" is the outcome of struggle over the disposition of the products of direct labor, then in the waxing and waning of this struggle the peasantry may be prevented from the self-provisioning necessary for their reproduction ("sub-subsistence"), or alternatively may acquire the ability to retain sufficient products of their labor to expand reproduction ("super-subsistence") (see Roseberry 1976).

3. I have placed quotation marks around these terms because, rather than accepting the domestic as an analytic category, I believe we must think in terms of "the cultural production" of the category: domestic.

4. For example, Mingione's two hypothetical cases indicate that, however much a struggle may be directed toward the securing of certain conditions—state provisioning or self-help networks—its effectiveness is conditioned by the historically-given social environment.

5. The groupings here are descriptive and relate to the issues addressed in the paper. For a more extensive discussion, see Smith 1989.

6. The Huasicanchinos' "unity" in their resistance against *hacendados* and the commercial classes of the Mantaro Valley nearby, is well known in the region (See Smith 1989).

7. Owners of larger farms and family farms tended to blame equally the high cost and unreliability of water and the high price of day labor, which they ascribe to the irresponsible behavior of the socialist union.

8. Nevertheless, making comparisons between the two cases should not obscure the differences that exist within them: I have suggested that among the Huasicanchinos, too, those with limited networks sought to expand the arena of "extraordinary domestic activities" within each domestic unit in the absence of alternatives.

9. One of the attractions of this form of production to capital is that the struggle over the division of surplus-value between wages and profits is greatly in capital's favor, owing not so much to the isolation of workers in their homes, as is often suggested, but to the pyramid-like structure of appropriation through contracting, subcontracting and sub-subcontracting. Under these conditions increases in surplus value are generated absolutely (through greater sweat and longer hours) rather than relatively, through increasing the organic composition of capital (Marx 1976, Parts 3 and 4).

## References

Bernstein, Henry. 1979. "African Peasantries: a Theoretical Framework" *Journal of Peasant Studies*, Vol 6, number 4, July.

Bradby, Barbara. 1982. "Resistance to Capitalism in the Peruvian Andes" in Lehmann, David, ed. (ed) *Economy and Ecology in the Andes*. University Press, Cambridge, pp. 97–121.

Brenner, Robert. 1976. "Agrarian Class Structure and Economic Development in Pre-Industrial Europe" *Past and Present*, LXX.

Chevalier, Jacques M. 1982. *Civilization and the Stolen Gift: Capital, Kin and Cult in Eastern Peru*. University Press, Toronto.

Friedmann, Harriet. 1980. "Household Production and the National Economy: Concepts for the Analysis of Agrarian Social Formations," *Journal of Peasant Studies*, Vol 7, number 2. July.

Harding, Susan. 1984. *Remaking Ibieca: Rural Life in Aragon Under Franco*. University of North Carolina Press, Chapel Hill

Harris, Olivia. 1982. "Households and Their Boundaries," *History Workshop*, Issue 13.

Kahn, Joel. 1980. *Miñangkabau Social Formations*. University Press, Cambridge.

Lehmann, David. 1982. *Economy and Ecology in the Andes*. University Press, Cambridge.

Lem, Winnie V. 1988. "Household Production and Reproduction: Social Relations among the Petty Commodity Wine Producers of Languedoc," *Journal of Peasant Studies*, Vol. 15 number 4.

Lenin, V. I. 1964. *The Development of Capitalism in Russia*. Progress Publishers, Moscow.

Marx, K. 1976. *Capital* Volume 1. Penguin Books, Harmondsworth

Mingione, Enzo. "Informalization, Restructuring, and the Survival Strategies of the Working Class," *International Journal of Urban and Regional Research*, Vol 7. number 3

————. 1986. "Social Reproduction of the Surplus Labour Force: The Case of Southern Italy" in Redclift, Nanneke and Enzo Mingione (Eds): *Beyond Employment*. Tavistock Press, London.

Roseberry, William. 1976. "Rent, Differentiation and the Development of Capitalism among Peasants," *American Anthropologist*, Vol 78. number 1.

Scott, Alison. 1979. "Who are the Self-Employed?" in Bromley, Ray and Chris Gerry (Eds): *Casual Work and Poverty in Third World Cities*. John Wiley & Sons, Chichester.

Sider, Gerald M. 1984. "The Ties That Bind: Culture and Agriculture, Property and Propriety in the Newfoundland Village Fishery," *Social History*. Vol 5.

————. 1986. *Culture and Class in Anthropology and History*. University Press, Cambridge.

Smith, Gavin. 1979. "Socio-Economic Differentiation and Relations of Production among Petty Commodity Producers in Central Peru 1880–1980," *Journal of Peasant Studies*, Vol 6. number 3, April.

————. 1984. "Confederations of Households: Extended Domestic Enterprises in City and Country" in Long, Norman and Bryan Roberts (Eds): *Miners, Peasants and Entrepreneurs*. University Press, Cambridge.

————. 1985. "Reflections on the Social Relations of Simple Commodity Production," *Journal of Peasant Studies*, Vol 13, number 1. Oct.

————. 1989. *Livelihood and Resistance: a Study of Petty Commodity Producers and the Politics of Land in Central Peru*. University of California Press, Los Angeles.

Williams, Raymond. 1976. *Keywords*. Fontana, London.

## Chapter 4

*Notes*

1. The quotes that are used as examples are all from the same informant, because of the clarity with which she expressed various issues. The

other members of her domestic group are her father, an elderly man, her husband, two unmarried sons, and an unmarried daughter. They are owners of a moderate amount of property (approximately thirty hectares), and they also have a small ambulatory business selling clothes. The sons work as waiters during the summer, the daughter works outside the home in a clothing workshop, and the informant makes clothes at home.

2. In the case of women, these expenses are described as "hairdresser's," "gifts," and "clothes" for oneself or the children. Various informants between the ages of approximately fifty-five and eighty-five indicate that they had worked in order to obtain the cash needed to buy items for their trousseau. They worked either in day labor on land belonging to others, or they earned a salary in domestic service in larger cities such as Valls, Reus, Tarragona, or Barcelona. They saved at least part of this income for their expenses—or sometimes combined their income from these sources with the proceeds from their own production of the trousseau. This reveals how certain investments tied to the reproduction of the work force—like the marriage trousseau—were considered to be women's personal expenses, for which they were individually responsible.

3. This does not mean that women do not have access to any income from the farm. Insofar as the farm continues to be conceptualized as "household," all of its members have access to its earnings. All members of the domestic group also have access to the household account with the Rural Credit Union, where profits from the olive crop are deposited directly in the name of *all* household members. It means, however, that women think of this income as mainly belonging to the farm and to men, and thus as somewhat remote from them and their domestic and reproductive tasks.

4. Cf. the contradiction between *rapports familiaux/rapports marchands* in the peasant domestic group studied by Alice Barthez (1982).

5. This is valid for medium-sized proprietors (five hectares to thirty hectares) and for many small proprietors with diversified sources of income. Nevertheless, it is not the case for day laborers from domestic groups without land or for some small proprietors who are at the same time day laborers: these *do* have a common fund for income that originates from various sources.

6. The same woman expressed the situation in this way: " . . . this work is not compensated. I understand this. Now, for example, when the mother is sick in bed or when she's out and can't [work], they become aware. But while she is able . . . as I see it, all of us women already work in the spirit of sacrifice; it is enough to be one [a woman]. . . . When one is young, one doesn't understand so much. The same thing happened to

me. What value did I give to what my poor mother did . . . ? I thought that it was her obligation. I don't know. But now that you are in it and, you see the weight one carries [in caring for a] house and the sacrifice it is. Well, later you understand . . . what a favor it is to have a woman at home. . . . She's the soul of the family, I believe, and when this mother is lacking, then. . . . ''

*References*

Assier-Andrieu, L. 1984. ''Representacions jurídiques i conseqüències sociològiques del model domèstic als Pirineus.'' *Quaderns de l'Institut Català d'Antropologia* 5:9–27, Barcelona.

Barthez, A. 1982. *Famille, Travail et Agriculture*. Economica, Paris.

Berkner, L. 1972. ''The Stem Family and the Development Cycle of the Peasant Household: an Eighteenth Century Austrian Example'', *American Historical Review*, 77(2):398–418.

———— . 1973. ''Recent Research on the History of the Family in Western Europe.'' *Journal of Marriage and the Family* 35(3):395–405.

———— . 1976. ''Inheritance, Land Tenure and Peasant Family Structure: A GermanRegional Comparison.'' *In Family and Inheritance: Rural Society in Western Europe 1300–1800*, J. Goody, ed. Cambridge: Cambridge University Press.

Bestard, J. 1986. *Casa y familia: Parentesco y reproducción doméstica en Formentera*. Institut d'Estudis Baleárics; Palma de Mallorca.

Covarrubias, S. 1984. (1611). *Tesoro de la Lengua Castellana o Española*, Edición facsímil. Madrid: Turner.

Flandrin, J-L. 1979. *Orígenes de la familia moderna, la familia, el parentesco y la sexualidad en la sociedad tradicional*. Barcelona: Crítica.

Harding, S. F. 1984. *Remaking Ibieca: Rural Life in Aragón under Franco*. Chapel Hill: University of North Carolina Press.

Iszaevitch, A. 1981. ''Corporate Household and Ecocentric Kinship Groups in Catalonia.'' *Ethnology* 20(4):277–290.

Ministerio de Economía y Hacienda (MEH). 1986. *El trabajo a domicilio en España*. Madrid.

Mitterauer, M., and R. Sieder. 1979. ''The Developmental Process of Domestic Groups: Problems of Reconstruction and Possibilities of Interpretation.'' *Journal of Family History*, 4(3) Fall: 257–287.

Narotzky, S. 1988. *Trabajar en familia: Mujeres, hogares y talleres.* Valencia: Institució Alfons el Magnànim.

Sanchis, E. 1984. *El trabajo a domicilio en el País Valenciano.* Madrid: Instituto de la Mujer.

Segalen, M. 1980. *Mari et femme dans la société paysanne.* Paris: Flammarion.

Terradas, I. 1984. *El món històric de les masies.* Barcelona: Curial.

## Chapter 5

*Notes*

1. The field work upon which the analysis in this and subsequent sections is based was conducted through a project, in which I was principal investigator, entitled "Petty Commodity Production, Capitalist Development and Underdevelopment in the 'Central Valleys' Region of Oaxaca, Mexico," conducted from September 1978 to August 1981 with funding from the National Science Foundation. The project's primary data corpus includes a main component consisting of a survey of 1,008 households in twenty-three communities located in the districts of Ocotlán, Tlacolula, and Centro. In addition, it includes the following components: (1) transcribed texts of structured, tape-recorded interviews with 182 direct producers (96 men, 82 women) from nine communities representing backstrap loom weaving, treadle loom weaving, embroidery, wood carving, palm plaiting, broom making, rope twining, sandal-making, fireworks making, blacksmithing, carpentry, mescal distilling, basketry, and brick making; (2) a special interview schedule for merchants/intermediaries was administered to thirty-one respondents in the embroidery industry in five separate localities, and to seventy-two proprietors of craft businesses in Oaxaca City (see Cook 1986); (3) fifteen detailed household budget studies were carried out in four villages over periods from four to ten weeks each; and (4) a series of observational studies, most important in a treadle-loom-weaving village, a palm-plaiting village (see Cook 1983), and a brick-making village (see Cook 1984a).

Hilda Cook, Alice Littlefield, Rosa Maria Salgado, Amelia Pacheco, Javier Telles, Leticia Rivermar, and Luis Garcia performed valuable roles at various stages in the collection and processing of data used in this article. Leigh Binford has played a major role in the computer processing of project data and in the subsequent analysis/interpretation of the statistics.

During the project period the peso-to-dollar exchange rate was approximately 22.50 to 1. In other words, 100 pesos was equivalent to about $4.50.

2. For reasons of expository clarity I have chosen to gloss the Spanish word *tejer*, which means both "to weave" and "to braid" (and is used by the palm workers to denote their craft), as "to plait."

3. The average age of these informants was forty-six. Thirteen were married with an average of four children each; three were single; four were widowed.

4. Reciprocity is institutionalized in the rural Zapotec Oaxaca valley as *guelaguetza*. It is operative both in the ceremonial-ritual context and in non-ceremonial economic life. It involves formal and informal exchanges of cash, commodities, and labor services between households (see Cook 1982, 65–67; 109–114; 213–216; Beals 1970; Martinez-Rios 1964).

5. Backstrap loom weaving of "traditional" woolen sashes and wrap-around skirts remains a female occupation in Mitla where, however, it has largely been displaced by male treadle loom weaving (see Beals 1975, 257–260).

6. San Tomás Jalieza's weavers produce sashes (*fajas*), belts (*cinturones*), bags (*bolsas*), slipover shawls (*cotorinas*), wall hangings and throw cloths (*tapetes*), and place mats from cotton and/or wool and/or acrilan yarn. Six of our thirteen female informants belonged to the weaver's cooperative at the time they were interviewed, and three others had been members previously but had quit. The main reasons cited for quitting were high membership fees or assessments and too few concrete benefits. Those who remained active saw the principal benefit in doing so to be wholesale purchases made by special orders from Mexico City and foreign clients.

7. The "Living Conditions Index" was designed to measure the level of material well-being achieved by households. It was formulated by assigning different numerical values to contrasting house types (i.e., thatch, adobe, or masonry construction), types of house flooring (i.e., dirt, tile, or concrete), number of rooms, tenure status of the house lot and of the house itself (i.e., owned, rented, borrowed, *ejidal*), and possession or non-possession of a television set (which is a more accurate status indicator than the radio, given the almost universal distribution of the latter in Oaxaca valley households). The assigned values were then summed up to arrive at an overall index value.

One of the income estimates used was obtained by totaling the reported average weekly income of all income-earning jobs performed by the two principal household workers. In our household survey we recorded data about the principal, secondary and tertiary occupations of the household head and the second person in the household. In nuclear family households this usually meant data from the husband and wife.

The data from Santo Tomás Jalieza yielded a median weekly income of 420 pesos (about 19 dollars) with the range from 40 pesos (2 dollars) to

3,000 pesos (133 dollars). The median Living Conditions Index was 3.5 with the range from 0 to 8.

8. The role of FONART among Mexico's artisans is controversial (see Novelo 1976; Cook 1981). My own experience has been that the effectiveness of its often well-planned and well-intentioned programs for artisan assistance/development founder because of sometimes larcenous or incompetent personnel who staff its regional offices, budgetary problems and lack of program continuity within and between *sexennios* (six-year presidential terms).

In 1985 my visit to Santa Cecilia confirmed that the embroidery program which was functioning reasonably well in 1979 had disappeared, together with the sewing machines which had belong to the program. Presumably these have been privatized—the usual fate of many wellmeaning cooperative ventures in Oaxaca valley villages.

## References

Beals, R., 1970, "Gifting, Reciprocity, Savings, and Credit in Peasant Oaxaca", *Southwestern Journal of Anthropology* 26:231–241.

——— . 1975, *The Peasant Marketing System of Oaxaca, Mexico*, Berkeley and Los Angeles: University of California Press.

Benería, L. and G. Sen. 1981. "Accumulation, Reproduction, and Women's Role in Economic Development: Boserup Revisited," *Signs* 7:279–298.

Bertocci, P. 1964. "An Artisans' Cooperative", Summer Field Training Program in Anthropology (Oaxaca, Mexico), Department of Anthropology, Stanford University, Mimeograph.

Binford, L. and S. Cook. 1986. "A Marxist Approach to Third World Rural Industrialization", in R. England, ed., *Toward A New World Economic Order*, New York: Praeger.

Blanton, R. and S. A. Kowalewski, 1981, "Monte Alban and After in the Valley of Oaxaca", in J. Sabloff, ed., *Supplement to The Handbook of Middle American Indians*, Austin: University of Texas Press.

Blanton, R., S. Kowalewski, G. Feinman and J. Appel, et. al. 1981. "The Valley of Oaxaca", in *Ancient Mesoamerica, a Comparison of Three Regions*, Cambridge: Cambridge University Press.

Bossen, L. 1984. *The Redivision of Labor*, Albany, N.Y.: SUNY Press.

Cook, S., 1978, "Petty Commodity Production and Capitalist Development in the Central Valleys Region of Oaxaca, Mexico", *Nova Americana I: Mercato, mercati e mercanti*. Einaudi, Torino, pp. 285–332.

────── . 1981. "Crafts, Capitalist Development, and Cultural Property in Oaxaca, Mexico", *Inter-American Economic Affairs* XXXV, 3:53–68.

────── . 1982. *Zapotec Stoneworkers*, Lanham, MD: University Press of America.

────── . 1983. "Mestizo Palm Weavers Among the Zapotec: A Critical Reexamination of the 'Albarradas Enigma', *Notas Mesoamericanas* (Universidad de las Americas) No. 9:39–46.

────── . 1984a. *Peasant Capitalist Industry*, Lanham, MD: University Press of America.

────── . 1984b. "Rural Industry, Social Differentiation, and the Contradictions of Provincial Mexican Capitalism", *Latin American Perspectives*, Issue 43, Vol. 11, (4):60–85.

────── . 1984c. "Peasant Economy, Rural Industry and Capitalist Development in the Oaxaca Valley, Mexico," *Journal of Peasant Studies* 12, (1):3–40.

────── . 1985. "Craft Businesses, Piece Work, and Value Distribution in the Oaxaca valley, Mexico," in S. Plattner, ed., *Markets and Marketing* (Monographs in Economic Anthropology, No. 4), Lanham, MD: University Press of America.

────── . 1986. "Entrepreneurship, Capital Accumulation, and the Dynamics of Simple Commodity Production in Rural Oaxaca, Mexico," in S. Greenfield and A. Strickon, eds., *Entrepreneurship* (Monographs in Economic Anthropology, No. 2), Lanham, MD: University Press of America.

Cook, S. and L. Binford. 1986. "Petty Commodity Production, Capital Accumulation, and Social Differentiation: Contradictions in the Oaxaca Valley, Mexico", *Review of Radical Political Economics* 18 (4):1–31.

Cook, S. and M. Diskin, eds. 1976. *Markets in Oaxaca*, Austin: University of Texas Press.

Deere, C. D. and M. Leon de Leal. 1981. "Peasant Production, Proletarianization, and the Sexual Division of Labor in the Andes", *Signs* 7, (2):338–360.

Gibbon, P. and M. Neocosmos. 1985. "Some Problems in the Political Economy of 'African Socialism'," in H. Bernstein and B. Campbell, eds., *Contradictions of Accumulation in Africa*, Beverly Hills, CA. Sage Publications.

Goody, E., (ed.). 1982. *From Craft to Industry*, Cambridge: Cambridge University Press.

Kowalewski, S. and L. Finsten. 1983. "The Economic Systems of Ancient Oaxaca: A Regional Perspective," *Current Anthropology* 24, (4):413–442.

Lenin, V. I. 1964. *The Development of Capitalism in Russia*, Moscow: Progress Publishers.

Martínez Ríos, Jorge, 1964, "Análisis funcional de la 'guelaguetza agrícola'," Revista Mexicana de Sociologia 26(1):79–125.

Novelo, V. 1976. *Artesanias y Capitalismo en Mexico*, Mexico, D.F.: SEP-INAH.

Portes, A. 1983. "The Informal Sector: Definition, Controversy, and Relations to National Development", *Review* VII, (1):151–174.

Taylor, W. 1971. "The Colonial Background to Peasant Economy in the Valley of Oaxaca, Mexico", Unpublished manuscript.

Taylor, W. 1972. *Landlord and Peasant in Colonial Oaxaca*, Stanford: Stanford University Press.

Villanueva, M. 1985. "From Calpixqui to Corregidor: Appropriation of Women's Cotton Textile Production in Early Colonial Mexico", *Latin American Perspectives* 12, 1:17–40.

Young, K. 1978. "Modes of Appropriation and the Sexual Division of Labour: A Case Study from Oaxaca, Mexico", in A. Kuhn and A. Wolpe, eds., *Feminism and Materialism*, London: Routledge and Kegan Paul.

## Chapter 6

*References*

Bastide, Roger. 1978. *The African Religions of Brazil: Toward a Sociology of the Interpenetration of Civilizations*. Baltimore: Johns Hopkins University Press.

Debien, Gabriel. 1974. *Les esclaves aux Antilles françaises*. Basse-Terre: Société d'histoire de la Guadeloupe; Fort-de-France: Société d'histoire de la Martinique.

Hall, Douglas. 1978. "The Flight from the Plantations Reconsidered: The British West Indies, 1838–1842." *The Journal of Caribbean History* (10–11): 7-23.

Lepkowski, Tadeusz. 1968. *Haiti*. Havana: Casa de las Americas.

Marx, Karl. 1966. *Capital, III*. Moscow: Foreign Languages Publishing House. 1976a. *Capital, I*. Harmondsworth: Penguin Books. 1976b. *Capital, II*. Harmondsworth: Penguin Books.

Mintz, Sidney. 1974. Caribbean Transformations. Chicago: Aldine.

Mintz, Sidney. 1978, "Was the Plantation Slave a Proletarian?" *Review* II(1): 81–98.

Mintz, Sidney. 1982. "Decrying the Peasantry," *Review* VI(2): 209–225.

Rodney, Walter. 1981. "Plantation Society in Guyana." *Review* IV(4): 643–666.

Weber, Max. 1978. *Economy and Society*. Berkeley: University of California Press.

## Chapter 7

*Notes*

1. The nature of that decline is in dispute, of course. See Samir Amin, Giovanni Arrighi, Andre Gunder Frank, and Immanuel Wallerstein (1982).

2. These data are drawn from *Statistical Abstracts of the United States*, 1984, p. 494, Table 811.

3. Median household income in 1983 dollars decreased between 1981 and 1983 by close to 3 percent, and between 1973 and 1983 by close to 12 percent. *Statistical Abstracts of the United States*, 1984, p. 442.

4. This figure is calculated from data given in the following: *Historical Statistics of the United States*, p. 229, Series F47–70 p. 340, Series H1–31; p. 133, Series D42–48; p. 304, Series G372–415. *Statistical Abstracts of the United States*, 1984, p. 432, Table 715; p. 354, Table 589; p. 394, Table 659; p. 419, Table 700.

5. The data were calculated by the author from figures given in "Current Labor Statistics," *Monthly Labor Review*, selected issues, 1982 and 1983.

6. *15th Census of the United States*, 1930, Unemployment, Vol. II, pp. 13–18.

7. See, for example, the series of *New York Times* articles throughout 1978 and 1979. See also *Business Week*, July 21, 1980, pp. 158 ff. Immediately after the "Fed" instituted controls both in 1977 and again in 1980, the following was reported in U.S. News & World Report

> More banks have picked up hefty supplies of cash, and they're out beating the bushes for borrowers. (*U.S. News and World Report*, Vol. 83, Oct. 31, 1977, pp. 82–84)

And

> Large U.S. retailers are expanding the use of bank cards . . . and some are planning to promote credit more extensively in an effort to counteract a lag in installment sales since the imposition of Federal credit controls in March. (*New York Times*, July 3, 1980) p. 27

Though throughout early 1980 various moves were made to institute strict credit curbs, all such efforts were abandoned by July 4 (*New York Times*, July 4, 1980) p. 32.

8. This material can be found in *Background Material and Data on Programs Within the Jurisdiction of the Committee on Ways and Means,* Feb. 22, 1985. Washington: U.S. Government Printing Office, 1985 (WMCP: 99–2), pp. 343 ff.

9. To be sure, it could be plausibly argued that Ford's real success was his innovation of credit mechanisms, both for dealers and customers. Issac Singer's partner, Edward Clark, introduced the installment plan in 1856, and the following year he introduced the "trade–in". See Susan Strausser (1982, p. 139).

10. Throughout the early 1930s, *Fortune Magazine* ran articles extolling consumer credit with the clear implication that serious question had been raised.

11. For the most comprehensive report see the Federal Reserve Board, *Consumer Installment Credit,* Part I, Vol. 1, Growth and Import, 1957.

12. Ibid., p. 30.

13. Ibid., p. 25.

14. Ibid., p. 154.

15. Though net worth of households rose during the recessions of the 1970s and early 1980s, it was only because of a rapidly inflating housing market. Thus, a family could actually increase its net worth without at all incurring additional debts. Banks and other credit agencies were willing to make loans on these additional "assets" even though the capacity of households to meet these new debts had not increased one whit. In 1981, "about half the loans made by consumer finance companies are . . . secured by second mortgages compared to 16 percent in 1976" (*Newsweek,* May 25, 1981, p. 73).

16. Data is drawn from the following: *Historical Statistics of the United States,* Series F6–9; F144–162; F17–30; N273–N276; X551–560 and *Statistical Abstracts of the United States,* 1985, p. 443, Table 717; p. 501, Tables 839 and 840.

17. See both Jester (1966) and *Statistical Abstracts of the United States,* 1985, p. 501, Table 840.

18. These data were compiled from figures given in *National Income and Product Accounts of the United States, 1929–1974,* U.S. Department of Commerce, Bureau of Economic Analysis, pp. 334 and 66; Survey of Current Business, July, 1983, p. 34, No. 2.

19. I am arguing that the social roots of mass consumption are precisely in production strategies themselves.

20. This is the point I have argued more extensively in other papers and am only elaborating here.

21. The immediate counter-example of fast food chains and the vast increase in eating meals out comes to mind. But in fact it is precisely the "mix" of more commercial consumption along with privatized labor to which I am referring. It is the combination of the vast proliferation of "gourmet" cooking on one hand and "fast food" meals on the other that is so interesting. Further, though I have no way of proving this except my own experience, it is *not* that one stratum of the society utilizes "McDonald's" while the other cooks from Julia Child. Rather, any given household will be found doing the one on Wednesday and the other on Saturday.

In fact, there is an interesting parallel between patterns of "eating out" in the two periods of 1929–1933 and 1974–1981. In the former, the proportion of the total household spending on restaurant meals *increased* by slightly more than eight percent. In the latter period, it increased just six percent. In 1933, families on average were dedicating four percent of their expenditures to restaurant meals. In 1981 that proportion was a mere 1.3 percentage points higher. See data given in *National Income and Product Accounts of the United States, 1929–1974, op. cit.*, pp. 88 and 336. *Survey of Current Business*, July 1983, p. 36, No. 24.

22. Compiled from material taken from *Historical Statistics of the United States*, p. 329, Series G881–915.

23. Feminists not infrequently concentrate on one or another aspect of this process. A major exception is found in Heidi Hartmann, (1974). Hartmann points out repeatedly that production strategies were responsible for retaining work in the home, but in a form that demanded fixed investment rather than discretionary spending. Ironically, Braverman was publishing his book the same year in which he concentrates on the "universal market" while simply lamenting the passing of the productive household. Obviously, he misses the point by the partiality of his view.

24. Data are drawn from *National Income and Product Accounts*, op. cit., and *Survey of Current Business*, op. cit.

25. Obviously, the suburbanization of housing patterns is considerably more true for white working class families than for people of color. I suspect—not withstanding very different levels of income—that patterns of mutual aid among household members differ by virtue of these different housing patterns. See, for example, Carol Stack, (1974). In my own childhood, it was taken as a matter of fact that Polish and Italian families lived much closer together than did the Irish, and that the former groups were much more likely to be "clanish." Of course, in Chicago in the 1930s, neither the Poles nor the Italians had as much discretion in their housing patterns as did the Irish. The irony, of course, is that the Irish took the "clanishness" of the Poles and the Italians as a mark of their inferiority!

26. See footnote 15.

27. Obviously, these wage gains are hardly evidence of vast economic advances. What they are evidence for is a tendency that, if not held in check, further erodes the ability of firms to hold the line on wages.

28. This year white males for the first time found themselves to be in the minority in the labor force.

29. For an example of this view, see Immanuel Wallerstein (1982, 24).

30. I believe it is this point which is missed by my feminist colleagues.

## References

Adams, Bert N. *Kinship in an Urban Setting*. Chicago: Markham Publishing, 1986.

Amin, Samir, Giovanni Arrighi, Andre Gunder Frank and Immanuel Wallerstein, eds. *Dynamics of Global Crisis*. New York: Monthly Review Press, 1982.

Braverman, Harry. *Labor and Monopoly Capital*. New York: Monthly Review Press, 1974.

Business Week. Untitled Article, October 29, 1979, p. 168.

Cummings, Richard Osborn. *The American and His Food: A History of Food Habits in the United States*. Chicago: University of Chicago Press, 1940.

Curie, Elliott, Robert Dunn, and David Fogarty. "The New Immiseration: Stagflation, Inequality and the Working Class," *Socialist Review*, No. 40 (Oct. 1983), pp. 149–82.

Ewen, Stuart. *Captains of Consciousness*. New York: McGraw Hill Book Co., 1980.

Hartmann, Heidi. "Capitalism and Women's Work in the Home 1900–1930." Unpublished Ph.D. dissertation. Department of Economics, Yale University, 1974.

Hobsbawm, Eric. "The Crisis of Capitalism in Historical Perspective," *Socialist Review*, Oct.–Dec. 1976, pp. 77–96.

Jester, F. Thomas. *Household Capital Formation and Financing, 1897–1962*. New York: National Bureau of Economic Research, 1966.

Leeds, John B. *The Household Budget*. Philadelphia: John B. Leeds, 1917.

Morgan, Winona L. *The Family Meets the Depression*. Minneapolis: University of Minnesota Press, 1939.

Niemi, Beth. "The Female-Male Differential in Unemployment Rates," *Industrial and Labor Relations Review*, Vol. 27, No. 3 (April 1979).

Smith, Joan. "The Paradox of Women's Poverty," *Signs*, 1984, pp. 291–310.

Stack, Carol. *All Our Kin: Strategies for Survival in a Black Community*. New York, Harper & Row, 1974.

Strasser, Susan. *Never Done: A History of American Housework*. New York: Pantheon Books, 1982.

Sussman, Marvin. "The Isolated Nuclear Family: Fact or Fiction," *Social Problems* 6 (1959), pp. 333–40.

——— and Lee Burchinal. "Parental Aid to Married Children: Implications for Family Functioning," *Marriage and Family Living* 24, 1962, pp. 320–32.

U.S. Government. Background Material and Data on Programs Within the Jurisdiction of the Committee on Ways and Means. February 1985.

——— . Census of the United States, 1930, Vol. II.

——— . Consumer Installment Credit, Part I, Vol. I, 1957.

——— . Historical Statistics of the United States.

——— . Monthly Labor Review, 1982, 1983 (Selected Issues).

——— . National Income and Product Accounts of the United States, 1929–1974.

——— . Statistical Abstracts of the U.S., 1984, 1985.

——— . Survey of Current Business, July 1983.

*United States News and World Report*. October 31, Vol. 38.

Walker, Kathryn. "Homemaking Still Takes Time," *Journal of Home Economics*, LXI (Oct. 1969), pp. 621–24.

Wallerstein, Immanuel. "Crisis as Transition" in Amin, Samir, Giovanni Arrighi and Immanuel Wallerstein, eds. *Dynamics of Global Crisis*. New York: Monthly Review Press, 1982.

## Chapter 8

*Notes*

*Reprinted with permission from Review of Radical Political Economics, volume 16, number 1, 1984. Funds to support this work came from the Center for the Study, Education and Advancement of Women, University of California, Berkeley, Fellowship—1982; and from the American Association of University Women. Thanks are due to Joan Acker, Jessie Bernard and Charles Bolton for sustained support. Joan Acker, Harry Brill, Arlene Kaplan Daniels, Norman Diamond, Jan Haaken, Rachel Kahn-Hut, Dorie Klein, Judith Lorber, Maureen Reese, Ann Schofield and Judith Wittner gave me detailed comments as did my friends in the Berkeley Women's Work Research/Study Group, 1982.

1. Glazer-Malbin (1975) includes a methodological and empirical criticism of Parsons who attempted to bridge the split by positing the employed male head of household as the link.

2. An excellent reference on the dialectic between domestic labor and the corporate development of technology for profit shows how capitalism shapes women's domestic work (Strasser 1982).

3. Women's domestic lives are also organized by the terms on which services are made available (Klein 1965). Interviews with German middle-class women conducted by the writer in 1979 confirm this. The women complain most about shopping and school hours as restricting their activities and complicating their doing paid work. In the Federal Republic of Germany the extension of the hours of shops has been fought by the large department stores who do not want to increase their labor costs; they view the smaller shops as competing unfairly since the latter are run on unpaid family labor. Though some stores have changed their hours to accommodate to the needs of employed women with family responsibilities, that change has been accompanied by the loss of services (e.g., of free delivery and knowledgeable clerks) that would make shopping relatively easier.

4. Consumerism, unfortunately, has two meanings. The older meaning refers to the social construction of buying and displaying goods and services as a measure of social position, and pursued as the basis of personal and social happiness and fulfillment. Veblen described its initial character among the late nineteenth century and early twentieth century bourgeois in his vitriolic analysis of "conspicuous consumption." Contemporary analyses includes such work as Stuart Ewen (1976) who details how capitalism used advertising to place consumption in the center of human existence. Since the early 1960s, a new meaning of consumerism has emerged, referring to the organized efforts of buyers to regulate the goods and services sold to capitalists, and services provided through state agencies (e.g., schooling, medical care, prisons, public housing). I shall be using consumer to refer to the person doing the buying and using consumptionism in the place of the older use of consumerism to avoid the newer, Nader-like character.

5. *In propria persona* law refers to individuals representing themselves in legal proceedings. Bankruptcy hearings have been the prototype of *in pro per law*. Recently, do-it-yourself divorce, temporary restraining orders against battering husbands, and eviction defense cases have been added to *in pro per law*.

6. Some theorists argue that women's domestic labor makes a direct rather than indirect contribution to capital accumulation, but still assume that women's labor is *in* the household, done in the immediate sense *for*

productive labor with "productive labor" in the technical economic sense whereby an owner makes a profit by paying workers at a level that is lower than the value added by labor power of the worker.

7. Marx's use of exchange and use value does not, of course, divide the world into two realms, but critiques how capitalism mystifies and appropriates exchange values. Ultimately, the dualism is rejected as part of the mystification of commodity production. In feminist analysis, the pair of terms does seem to be used in a way that lends itself to seeing women as devalued *because* their work does not enter into relations based on exchange value; see Margaret Benston (1977).

8. Many theorists have explored how capitalism and the state in capitalist society penetrates the family. For example, wage labor is seen to shape family dependence (Zaretsky 1973); the state regulates private life (Donzelot 1979); professionals dictate the terms of child care, marital relations, and other intimate parts of life and change how mothers educate children with the change from a peasant to a worker economy (Minge-Kalman 1977).

9. Nearly all women are houseworkers, whether or not they also do paid work. Hence, organizing women as consumers means joining disparate women together, "housewives" (women who do only unpaid work) and employed women who do paid work. Though the union of women is not likely to cross class lines, the recognition of consumption work provides a specific way for women who may appear to be divided among themselves because of their relationship to production in the marketplace to come together over issues of their unpaid work in the marketplace.

10. For example, a major medical center estimates that their "cooperative care unit" costs them forty percent less than their traditional units. The cost reduction results both from reduced building costs (e.g., the absence of expensive medical equipment in each room) and from the labor of a cooperating, live-in family member who does the work usually done by nurses. However, the patients in the cooperative care unit are billed at exactly the same rate as the patients in the traditional nurse-supervised hospital units, and the forty percent reduction in costs is shared out among all the units and all the patients. The special unit patients get some savings, but nothing commensurate with the savings from the labor of the family member. For the hospital, the use of unwaged family labor lowers costs without infringing on other lucrative sources of profit. (Source: Interview, January 1983, New York City.)

11. There is no doubt that patient cooperation is important for diagnosis and treatment. The question is whether or not "work" is the appropriate concept to use. Illich (1981, 100) even broadens unpaid work, putting ac-

tivities and emotional states together, e.g., " . . . housework, activities connected with shopping, . . . the stress of forced consumption, the tedious and regimented surrender to therapists, compliance with bureaucrats. . . . "

12. Wadel (1979) uses a mechanical, dictionary-like approach to unpaid work. His lack of a theoretical frame leads to *no* mention of women's housework. His view illustrates the uncritical incorporation of a capitalist world view. An even more extreme acceptance of the capitalist logic of the marketplace is the argument that "nonmarket time" is a "major source of untaxed income," though it is admitted that this nonmarket time generates no income that could be taxed (Leuthold 1981). One may conjure up an Orwellian-like world with IRS agents monitoring women at washing diapers (in preference to using disposable ones, or using commercial laundries) and of tax evasion through "laundered" brownies. Another economist would tax home production (if economists could figure a way of computing its value) as a way of discouraging people from producing in their homes, and encouraging buying in the market—the ultimate in attempting to force all activities into the market for the profit of corporate capitalism. (J. F. Due, cited in Leuthold ([1981, 278].)

13. As Meiksins (1981) notes in discussing productive and unproductive labor, the crucial issue for an analysis is exploitation. The same should be said for analyses of *work* and *domestic labor.*

14. The rental of expensive equipment by the consumer is a somewhat borderline case in relating unpaid work outside the household to capital accumulation. People rent the use of washing machines and dryers in laundromats, grommet-applying machines in hardware stores, and photocopying machines in libraries and often do the work of once paid workers. However, consumers who rent equipment such as carpet shampoo machines, steam cleaners for house exteriors, kits for installing door locks from locksmith shops, and chain saws to lower their own costs are not working for capitalism any more than when they add their labor to such goods as unassembled toys, unfinished furniture, fabrics and yarns and, of course, raw foods.

15. Though it has been fifty years since retail food sales began to be dominated by the supermarkets, more than 30 percent of retail food stores are still run entirely by their owners and have no paid workers (Carey and Otto 1977).

16. The following definitions should help in following the social history of food retailing. In 1920, retailers were of several ownership types and sold varying products. The small independent (often Mom and Pop) store operated with a minimum of investment and the unpaid labor of family members, selling usually an array of groceries, but no meat, or special-

izing in a single product such as food or clothing. *Independent* stores also were locally owned, had much larger inventories and investments compared to Mom and Pop stores, and some paid workers, though, usually few. Among independent food retailers some sold only groceries while others also sold meat. The *chains* included speciality shops each retailing such goods as electric appliances, food, clothing or shoes. Chains had many more stores than independents, often concentrated in a particular community or region, and were centrally owned and managed, though some local autonomy might be allowed to accommodate local tastes. The *supermarkets* were originally independents who sold a much wider variety of merchandise than either grocery or department stores, and were organized on a self-service basis from their origin even though some used clerk-service as an adjunct of self-service. There are different kinds of chains (local, regional, national) and various kinds of associations of independents (cooperatives, associated independents) but for this paper the broad categories are sufficient (Markin 1963; Haas 1939).

17. The Patman-Robinson Act of 1936 prohibited wholesalers from pricing the same merchandise differently for different retailers, from foregoing brokerage fees or giving other rebates (such as advertising) that would discriminate between different classes of buyers. Other legislation was eventually passed to set minimum or "fair trade prices" which effectively prevented discount houses from selling national brand merchandise until the 1960s (Bluestone et al. 1981).

18. The technology for self-service existed before the Depression: shopping baskets and basket carts, the turnstile, check-out stands, aisles for customers' circulation and open display counters were developed by the 1920s or before World War I.

19. Self-service was also adopted for the sales of goods in about the only area where men rather than women do the bulk of the buying, for gasoline sales. The marketing of gasoline is also the history of competition between independents and monopolies, here between the smaller independent refineries and their retailers, and the big oil corporations and the brand dealers. Price subsidies for brand dealers (of gasoline sold by the giant companies) were used in a successful attempt (in the 1940s) to curtail competition from the independent refineries and dealers. The smaller self-service operators were closed down. Self-service was not adopted again until the late 1960s. Independent dealers were driven out of business by the major oil companies withholding oil from the independent refineries during the so-called oil shortage of the early 1970s. The brand dealers then adopted self-service so that by 1982 all but two states have self-service gas stations (Bluestone et al 1981).

20. These points are made somewhat laboriously because American social scientists and humanists (mainly women) to whom this work has been presented sometimes react protectively and defensively about self-service. They point to the small European shop and the long hours of shopping by European women as the alternative, without connecting these to limited home refrigeration or to preferences for fresh foods. Open-air peasant markets also seem to leap to mind as another alternative. Why no alternative seems feasible that would combine quick service, home delivery, credit, and telephone orders for American women, especially the employed, says something about the success with which self-service has been promoted as "convenient" and about how this area of unpaid work is invisible to most social scientists.

21. The services retailers see themselves as giving to customers were introduced after price competition was virtually eliminated. Retailers sought a substitute for low prices to attract customers. Other services retailers see themselves as giving customers include adequate parking, nice colors, music, shopping carts, a wide choice of shopping hours, clearly marked department and produce signs, convenient sizes and quantities of goods, check-cashing, and efficient, rapid check-out system, and portering to cars (Cassady 1962). Air-conditioning, parcel pick-up services and premium plans (Zimmerman 1955) as well as self-opening doors and hot-air curtains have been also seen as services (Nell 1958).

22. Prepackaging also means that the customer cannot sample a product, but must buy in order to try it. Manufacturers sometimes give samples in markets when promoting new products.

23. Because prepackaging is used widely by self-service markets, self-service consumers not only substitute for clerk-service when they take over "the unorderly marketing burden," but they also absorb the expensive *storage burden*. Insofar as customers buy in large quantities, the retailers have that much less merchandise as inventory or waste losses. While the customer's ability to provide home-storage may be a convenience, it also means costly equipment such as a refrigerator, many cupboards and a freezer, and an outlay for food and other goods well in advance of use.

24. During and for many years after World War II, goods shortages eliminated the need for much price competition. Later, monopoly-like conditions especially in food retailing, but also in other manufacturing made price competition much less important for marketing. Producers and distributors actually may raise prices when profits sag because consumers are not buying.

25. Retail workers also include stock persons, delivery persons, cleaners, and other miscellaneous occupations, but the majority of workers are managers, cashiers, and sales clerks to whom this analysis is limited.

26. Sources: For 1978: Job (1980, 40–43); for 1970: U.S. Bureau of the Census: 1970 (1973, 25–28); for 1960: U.S. Census of Population: 1960 (1961, 97–111); for 1950: U.S. Census of Population: 1950 (1954, 52–59); for 1940: Sixteenth Census of the United States: 1940 (1943, 98; 100); for 1930: Sixteenth Census of the United States: 1940 (1943, 69).

27. Sources: See note 26 for sources for 1970, 1960, 1950, 1940. 1940 which is Sixteenth Census of the United States, 1943.

28. See note 25 for sources for 1970, 1960, 1950, 1940.

29. See note 26 for sources for 1978, 1970, 1960 and 1950.

30. In his history of the Retail Clerks International Association, Harrington (1962) notes that the clerks were so difficult to organize because so many were women. However, the 1946 Oakland General Strike, which he also discusses briefly, was provoked by the militant continued strike action of women store clerks. This is not to fault Harrington, particularly, but to show how uncritically analysts have accepted the view that the difficulty of organizing women workers accounts for weak unions or their absence in female-typed jobs.

31. Informants employed in a large west coast chain store described their training as a course in encouraging customers to buy the most expensive items and to push these as the highest in quality (Interview: 1982, Portland, Oregon).

32. Other domains of the *work transfer* with its implications for unpaid and paid women's work include health care, *in propria persona* law, billing systems for consumers, and other clerical work. These will be discussed in an eventual monograph, Serving Capital: Women's Paid and Unpaid Work.

## References

Adlam, Diana et al. 1981. *Politics and Power 3: Sexual Politics, Feminism and Socialism*. London: Routledge and Kegan Paul.

Barmash, Isadore. 1983. Selling-Retailing's Lost Art. *The New York Times* (March 15).

Bell, Daniel. 1973. *The Coming of Post Industrial Society*. New York: Basic Books.

Benson, Susan Porter. 1982. *A Great Theater: Saleswomen, Customers, and Managers in American Department Stores, 1890–1940*. Ph.D. Dissertation. Brown University.

Benston, Margaret. 1977. The Political Economy of Women's Liberation. In, *Women in a Man-Made World*, N. Glazer and H. Waehrer (eds). Chicago: Rand McNally.

Bluestone, B., P., Hanna, S. Kuhn, and L. Moore. 1981. *The Retail Revolution*. Boston: Auburn House.

Brandt, Ellen. [n.d. Probably 1978] *Women in Shops: A Sociological Exploration of the Saleswoman Occupation*. Norges Almenvitenskapelige Forkingsrad.

Bureau of the Census. 1973. *Occupation by Industry* PC (2)–7C.

Canfield, Bertrand. 1948. Unionization of Salesmen: An Outline of the Present Situation. *Printers' Ink* 239(9)(May).

Carey, J. L. and P F. Otto, 1977. Output Per Unit of Labor in the Retail Food Store Industry. *Monthly Labor Review* 100(1).

Cassady, Ralph Jr. 1962. *Competition and Price Making in Food Retailing*. New York: Ronald Press.

Census of Population: 1950, 1954. *Occupation by Industry* P–E, No. IC, Reprint of Vol. IV., Part I, Chapt. C.

Census of Population: 1960, 1961. *Occupation by Industry*. PC9(2)–7C.

Census of the United States: 1940. Population. 1943. *Industrial Characteristics*.

Cowan, Ruth S. 1976. Two Washes in the Morning and a Bridge Party at Night: The American Housewife Between the Wars. *Women's Studies* 3.

Dalla Costa, Mariarosa. 1972. Women and the Subversion of Community. *Radical America* 6.

Dipman, Carl W., Robert W. Meuller, and Ralph E. Head, 1946. *Self-Service Food Stores*. New York: The Butterick Company, Inc.

Dipman, Carl W. and John E. O'Brien. 1940. *Self-Service and Semi-Self-Service Food Stores*. New York: The Butterick Company, Inc.

Donzelot, Jacques. 1979. *The Policing of Families*. New York: Pantheon Books.

Ewen, Stuart, 1976. *Captains of Consciousness*. New York: McGraw-Hill.

Fee, Terry. 1976. Domestic Labor: An Analysis of Housework and Its Relation to the Production Process. *Review of Radical Political Ecomonics* 8.

Frederick, Christine F. 1917. Brands Needed by Consumer as Economy of Time and Money, Says Mrs. Frederick. *Wear* (Monday, October 29). Greensboro, Long Island. Schlesinger Library, MO 7, Reel 78–1.

Fuchs, Victor R. 1968. *The Service Economy*. New York: Columbia University Press.

Galbraith, John Kenneth. 1973. *Economics and the Public Purpose*. Boston: Houghton Mifflin.

Gershuny, Jonathan. 1978. *After Industrial Society? The Emerging Self-Service Economy*. Atlantic Highland: Humanities Press.

Glazer, Nona. 1980. Overworking the Working Woman: Portrayals of the Double Day in a Mass Magazine. *Women's Studies International Quarterly* 3.

———— . 1983. Ideologies: Understanding the Legitimacy of Women's New Unpaid Work. Radcliffe Research Scholars Colloquium Series, Radcliffe College, May 19.

Glazer-Malbin, Nona. 1975. The Husband-Wife Relationship in the Division of Labor. Paper presented at the Ford Foundation/Merrill-Palmer Institute, World Congress on Gender and Family Sociology.

———— . 1976. Housework: A Review Essay. *Signs* (Summer).

Haas, Harold M. 1939. *Social and Economic Aspects of the Chain Store Movement*. Ph.D. Dissertation. University of Minnesota. (Reprinted 1979).

Harrington, Michael. 1962. *The Retail Clerk*. New York: John Wiley.

Illich, Ivan. 1981. *Shadow Work*. Boston: Marion Boyers.

Job, Barbara C. 1980. Employment and Pay Trends in the Retail Trade Industry. *Monthly Labor Review* 103(3).

Klein, Viola. 1965. *Women Workers, Working Hours and Services*. Geneva: Organization for Economic Cooperation and Development.

*Ladies Home Journal*. 1929. June, 129:144; October 1929: 185; and December 1929: 137. (Piggily Wiggly Stores advertisements.)

Leuthold, Jane H. 1981. Taxation and the Value of Nonmarket Time. *Social Science Research* 10.

Lombard, George F. F. 1955. *Behavior in a Selling Group*. Boston: Harvard University Press.

Lopata, Helena Z. 1974. *Occupation: Housewife*. New York: Oxford University Press.

Mandel, Ernest. 1981. Introduction. *Capital*, Karl Marx. Vol. 2. New York: Vintage Books.

Markin, Rom J. 1963. *The Supermarket: An Analysis of Growth, Development and Change*. Pullman: Washington State University Press.

Marx, Karl. 1981. *Capital*. Vol. 2. New York: Vintage Books.

Meiksins, Peter. 1981. Productive and Unproductive Labor and Marx's Theory of Class. *Review of Radical Political Economics* 13(3).

Minge-Kalman, Wanda. 1977. *Family Production and Reproduction in Industrial Society: A Field Study of Changes During the Peasant to Worker Transition in Europe*. Unpublished Ph.D. Disseration. Columbia University.

Molyneux, Maxine. 1979. Beyond the Domestic Labour Debates. *New Left Review No. 116. 24 (11) (Nov)*.

Morton, Peggy. 1978. Reproduction of Labor Power: The Family. In, *The Capitalist System*, Richard Edwards, Michael Reich and Thomas Weisskopf (eds.). Englewood Cliffs: Prentice Hall.

Murphy, John Allen. 1917. In Piggly Wiggly Stores the Product Has to Sell Itself. *Printers' Ink* 101(12)(Dec).

Nell, W. A. 1958. Automation in Food Marketing—The Extension of Mechanized Shopping. *Agenda* 6.

Oakley, Ann. 1974. *The Sociology of Housework*. New York: Pantheon.

Parsons, Talcott. 1955. *Family, Socialization and Interaction*. Glencoe: The Free Press.

Peak, Hugh S. and Peak, Glen. 1977. *Supermarket Merchandising and Management*. Englewood Cliff: Prentice Hall.

*Printers Ink*. 1921a. 117(1)(Oct). Piggly Wiggly in New Line of Merchandise.

———. 1921b. 117(11)(Dec). Piggly Wiggly Develops a Chain Store Copy Angle.

*Progressive Grocer*. 1941. 10. Self-Service Layout Boosts Unit Sales From 72¢ to 1.60.

Quelch, John A. and Takeuchi, Hirotaka. 1981. Nonstore Marketing: Fast Track or Slow? *Harvard Business Review* 59(4).

Rowbotham, Sheila. 1981. *Beyond the Fragments: Feminism and the Making of Socialism*. Boston: Alyson Publishers.

Rytina, Nancy F. 1982. Earnings of Men and Women: A Look at Specific Occupations. *Monthly Labor Review* 105(4).

Salmans, Sandra. 1982. Seventh Avenue's Sharpest Eye. *New York Times* (Sunday, May 23).

Schumacher, E. F. 1979. *Small is Beautiful*. New York: Harper and Row.

Schwartzmann, David. 1971. *The Decline of Service in Retail Trades.* Washington: Washington State University.

Seligman, Ben. 1968. The High Cost of Eating. *Economics of Dissent*. Chicago: Quadrangle Press.

Simeral, Margaret. 1978. Women and the Reserve Army of Labor. *The Insurgent Sociologist*. Vol. VII. (2)(3). Vol. VIII. (2)(3).

Sixteenth Census of the United States: 1940. 1943. Population. *Industrial Characteristics.*

Sixteenth Census of the United States: 1940. 1943. Comparative Occupational Statistics for the United States. 1870–1940.

Smith, Dorothy. 1975–76. Women, the Family, and Corporate Capitalism. *Berkeley Journal of Sociology* 20.

Strasser, Susan. 1982. *Never Done: A History of American Housework*. New York: Pantheon.

Strauss, Anselm L., Shizuko Fagerhaugh, Barbara Suczek, and Carolyn Weiner. 1981. Patients' Work in the Technologized Hospital. *Nursing Outlook* 29.

Thompson, Morris. 1942. What About Self-Service? Is It an Answer to the Problem of Personnel Shortage? *National Retail Dry Goods Association,* 10.

Vogel, Lise. 1973. The Earthly Family. *Radical America* 7.

Wadel, Cato. 1979. The Hidden Work of Everyday Life. In, *Social Anthropology of Work*, Sandra Wallman (ed.). London: Academic Press.

Weinbaum, Batya, and Amy Bridges. 1976. The Other Side of the Paycheck. *Monthly Review* 28.

Wingate, John W. 1942. Wartime Personnel Problems in Department Stores. *Journal of Retailing* 19(1)(Feb).

Zaretsky, Eli. 1973. Capitalism, the Family and Personal Life. *Socialist Revolution*. Part I (Jan–April); Part II (May–June).

Zimmermann, M.N. 1955. *The Supermarket: A Revolution in Distribution*. New York: McGraw-Hill.

## Chapter 9

*Notes*

*A number of individuals assisted us in the preparation of this paper. We would like to thank the other participants in the Households Research Working Group, especially Joan Smith, Immanuel Wallerstein, Bill Martin, Mark Beittel, and Lanny Thompson, for their shared insights and support. Several people reviewed earlier drafts of the paper, including Jane Collins, Sarah Elbert, Vivian Dreves, and Lynn Clark. The Roberson Center for the Arts and Sciences allowed us to use their archives and the records of the Broome County Oral History Project. Michelle Morrison and Marge Hinman were especially helpful in arranging our use of materials at the Roberson Center. We would also like to thank our families, who verify our research by performing household duties exactly as findings would suggest they should. Our research with the Households Working Research Group was supported by grant #R02064784 from the National Endowment for the Humanities.

1. Budget studies estimate that fruits and vegetables comprise 13 percent of the food budget, including the contribution of canning and preserving (NICB 1931, 93). We have used 13 percent of the maintenance level food costs for Binghamton to calculate this figure for a four-person household and adjusted it upwards proportional to the increased number of people in the other household types.

2. The National Industrial Conference Board (1931, 93) estimated meat as comprising 25 percent of the food budget and eggs 6 percent. We considered the contribution for a four-person family to be 18 percent of the maintenance level food budget for these activities. We increased the contribution of small-stock-raising proportional to the increase in the number of individuals in the household.

3. We valued home maintenance at half of 1 percent of the home's value (Waite 1928, 166) and figured a four-person household would be in a $3,000 home and an eight-person household in a $4,000 home.

4. We have conservatively estimated the value of home-sewing to equal 25 percent of the clothing budget given for the maintenance level. The women's sewing contribution equals half of the clothing required by the family, but the cash outlay for cloth and notions reduce the contribution to 25 percent. This would have been strictly a female activity.

*References*

Andrews, Benjamin. 1935. *Economics of the Household*. MacMillan, New York.

Anshen, R. N. (editor). 1959. *The Family: Its Function and Destiny*. Harper, New York.

Barr, Kenneth. 1979. Long Waves: A Selected Annotated Bibliography. *Review* 2(4):675–718.

BCOHP (Broome County Oral History Project) n.d. Oral History Interviews. Transcripts of interviews conducted for the Broome County Oral History Project. Broome County Historical Society, Binghamton, New York.

Beechey, Veronica. 1978. Women and Production: A Critical Analysis of Some Sociological Theories of Women's Work. *In Feminism and Materialism*. A. Kuhn and A. M. Wolpe, eds. pp.155–197. Routledge and Kegan Paul, London.

Bender, Donald. 1967. A Requirement of the Concept of Household. *American Anthropologist* 59:493–504.

Berk, Richard and Sara Fenstermaker Berk. 1979. *Labor and Leisure at Home*. Sage Publications, Beverly Hills.

Berk, Sara Fenstermaker. 1985. *The Gender Factory: The Apportionment of Work in American Families*. Plenum Press, New York.

Bigelow, Howard F. 1953. Family Finance. Chicago: Lippencott.

Coleman, Cindy, Karl Debus, Fred Freundlich, Amy Halpern, Lynn Marshal, Doug Meurs, Arn Pearson, Sharon Porter, Kate Welch, Randy Wilson, and Thomas Wong. 1984. Binghamton: Case Studies in Urban and Economic Development. Report prepared by the Workshop in Local Economic Analysis. Department of City and Regional Planning Community Design Assistance Program. Cornell University.

Cowan, Ruth. 1983. *More Work for Mother*. Basic Books, New York.

Durand, John. 1948. *The Labor Force in the U.S. 1890–1960*. Social Science Research Council, New York.

Eberts, Paul. 1984. *Socio-Economic Trends in Rural New York State: Towards the Twenty-first Century*. New York State Legislative Commission on Rural Resources.

Edholm, Felicity, Olivia Harris, and Kate Young. 1977. Conceptualizing Women. *Critique of Anthropology* 3:9–10; 101–130.

England, Paula and George Farkas. 1986. *Household Employment and Gender: A Social Economic and Demographic View*. Aldine, New York.

Folbre, Nancy. 1985. Cleaning House: New Perspectives on Households and Economic Development. Paper presented at the U.N. University's Conference on New Directions in Development Theory, Boston.

Fox, Bonnie (editor). 1980. *Hidden in the Household: Women's Domestic Labour Under Capitalism.* Women's Educational Press, Toronto.

Gauger, William and Kathleen Walker. 1980. *The Dollar Value of Housework.* New York State Department of Agriculture, Bureau of Home Economics.

Gough, Kathleen. 1975. The Origin of the Family. in *Toward an Anthropology of Women.* ed. by Rayna Reiter, pp. 52–73, Monthly Review Press, New York.

Graebner, William. 1986. Coming of Age in Buffalo: The Ideology of Maturity in Postwar America. *Radical History Review* 34:53–74.

Guyer, Jane. 1979. Household Budgets and Women's Incomes. *Working Paper No. 28,* African Studies Center, Boston University, Boston.

Hareven, Tamara. 1984. Themes in the Historical Development of the Family. *Review of Child Development Research* 7:137–178.

Holstrom, L. L. 1972. *The Two Career Family.* Schenkman, Cambridge.

Inglis, William. 1935. *George F. Johnson and His Industrial Democracy.* Endicott-Johnson Co., Endicott, New York.

Keller, Suzane. 1968. *The American Lower Class Family.* State of New York, Division for Youth, Albany.

Lamphere, Louise. 1986. From Working Daughters to Working Mothers: Production and Reproduction in an Industrial Community. *American Ethnologist* 13:118–130.

Laslett, Peter. 1971. *The World We Have Lost.* Scribner, New York.

McGuire, Randy, Joan Smith, and William G. Martin. 1986. Household Structures and the World-Economy. *Review* Summer.

McGuire, Ross, and Nancy Grey Osterud. 1981. *Working Lives: Broome County New York, 1800–1930.* Roberson Center for the Arts and Sciences, Binghamton, New York.

Minge-Klevana, Wanda. 1980. Does Labor Time Decrease with Industrialization? *Current Anthropology.* 21:279–98.

Molyneux. Maxine. 1979. Beyond the Domestic Labor Debate. *New Left Review* 116:3–27.

Netting, Robert McC., Richard Wilk, and Eric Arnould. 1984. *Households: Comparative and Historical Studies of the Domestic Group.* University of California Press, Berkeley.

New York State Commission of Youth and Delinquency. 1956. Final Report. State of New York Division for Youth, Albany.

New York State Department of Labor (NYSDL). 1967a. *Structure of Earnings and Hours in New York State Industries. Vol. 4, Women Workers.* New York State Department of Labor Division of Research and Statistics.

New York State Department of Labor (NYSDL). 1967b. *Employment Statistics.* Vol. 3, New York State Department of Labor, Division of Research and Statistics.

New York State Department of Labor (NYSDL). 1970. *Employment Statistics.* New York State Department of Labor, Division of Research and Statistics.

New York State Department of Labor (NYSDL). 1973a. *Earnings and Hours. Wage Bulletins.* New York State Department of Labor, Division of Research and Statistics.

New York State Department of Labor (NYSDL). 1973b. *Labor Research Report No. 17. Minimum Wage Certificates for Under-18 Workers.* New York State Department of Labor, Division of Research and Statistics.

New York State Department of Labor (NYSDL). 1975. *Labor Statistics Relating to the Economy of New York State.* Labor Research Report. New York State Department of Labor, Division of Research and Statistics.

New York State Department of Labor (NYSDL). 1977. *Earnings and Hours in New York State Industry.* New York State Department of Labor, Albany.

New York State Department of Labor (NYSDL). 1980. *Statistical Yearbook.* New York State Department of Labor, Division of Research and Statistics.

NICB (National Industrial Conference Board). 1928. The Economic Status of the Wage Earner in New York and Other States. NICB, New York.

NICB (National Industrial Conference Board). 1931. The Cost of Living in the United States 1914–1930. NICB, New York.

Oakley, A. 1974. *The Sociology of Housework.* Pantheon Books, New York.

Ogburn, W. F. and M. F. Nimkoff. 1955. *Technology and the Changing Family.* Houghton Mifflin Company, Boston.

Oppenheimer, V. 1982. *Work and the Family: A Study in Social Demography.* Academic Press, New York.

Oppenheimer, V. K. 1970. The Female Labor Force in the United States. *Population and Monograph Series No. 5.* Institute of International Studies, Berkeley.

Pleck, John. 1983. Husband's Paid Work and Family Roles: Current Research Issues. In *Research in the Interweave of Social Roles: Vol. 3 Families and Jobs.* H. Lopata and J. H. Pleck, eds. JAI Press, Greenwich, Connecticut.

Reyna, S. P. 1976. The Extending Strategy: Regulation of Household Dependency Ratios. *Journal of Anthropological Research*. 32:182–199.

Robinson, John. 1977. *How Americans Use Time: A Social-Psychological Analysis of Everyday Behavior.* Praeger Publishers, New York.

Schildkrout, Enid. 1981. Dependence and Autonomy: The Economic Activities of Secluded Hausa Women in Kano, Nigeria. In *Female and Male in West Africa.* Christine Oppong, ed. pp. 107–126. George Allen and Unwin Publishers, Ltd., London.

Sears, Robert Eleanor Maccoby, and Harry Levin. 1957. *Patterns of Child Rearing.* Row, Peterson and Company, Evanston, Illinois.

Seccombe, Wally. 1980. Domestic Labour and the Working Class Household. In *Hidden in the Household: Women and Domestic Labour Under Capitalism.* Bonnie Fox, ed. pp. 25–100. Women's Educational Press, Toronto.

Severinghaus, C. W., and C. P. Brown. 1982. History of the White-Tailed Deer in New York, Addendum. New York State Department of Environmental Conservation.

Smith, Joan, Immanuel Wallerstein and Hans-Dieter Evers. 1984. *Households and the World Economy.* Sage, Beverly Hills.

Stecker, Margaret Loomis. 1971. *Intercity Differences in Costs of Living in March, 1935–59 Cities.* Da Capo Press, New York.

Swerdlow, Amy, Renate Brindenthan, Joan Kelly, and Phyllis Vine. 1981. *Household and Kin.* The Feminist Press, Old Westbury, New York.

U.S. Bureau of the Census. 1940. Census of Population: Vol. 2, Characteristics of the Population.

U.S. Bureau of the Census. 1950. Census of Population. Characteristics of the Population.

U.S. Bureau of the Census. 1960. Census of Population: Vol. 1, Characteristics of the Population.

U.S. Bureau of the Census. 1980. Census of Population: Vol. 1, Characteristics of the Population.

U.S. Bureau of Labor Statistics. 1935. *Statistical Abstracts of the U.S.* U.S. Department of Commerce, Bureau of the Census, Washington.

U.S. Bureau of Labor Statistics. 1955. Economic Forces in the U.S.A. *Facts and Figures.* U.S. Department of Labor, Washington.

Vanek, Joan. 1973. *Keeping Busy: Time Spent in Housework, United States 1920–1970*. University Microfilms, Ann Arbor.

Waite, Warren. 1928. *Economics of Consumption*. McGraw-Hill, New York.

Yanagisako, Sylvia. 1979. Family and Household: The Analysis of Domestic Groups. *Annual Review of Anthropology*. 8:161–205.

Zahavi, Gerald. 1983. Negotiated Loyalty: Welfare Capitalism and the Shoeworkers of Endicott-Johnson, 1920–1940. *Journal of American History*.

## Chapter 10

*Notes*

1. Roseberry (1986) begins with the outer colonies of the Roman Empire. The direct lineage of the family farm in Europe extends at least as far back as the conversion of land from common to private use in the sixteenth century.

2. And raw materials for industrial clothing. Both wool and cotton, however, involved larger scale capitalist, slave, or share-cropping organization. Sometimes, however, as in Indian cotton production, small-holding commercial family farmers were directly organized through merchant capital. See Banaji (1977).

3. These studies were anticipated in 1948 by the brilliant, eccentric work by Siegfied Giedion, *Mechanization Takes Command*. Part IV is "Mechanization Encounters the Organic," divided into two sections on agriculture and bread. Part VI is "Mechanization Encounters the Household," elevating the significance of domestic labor to that of other spheres. Indeed a separate part is reserved for the bath (the concluding section), but this focuses on matters other than labor. It is a most provocative and informative book.

4. The term is from Crouch and de Janvry (1980). They use it primarily to identify *crops* by their final users, thus distinguishing types of production which are self-provisioning from those which are commercial. I use it as a trace on labor-market growth from the side of consumption.

5. I develop the analysis of all the international complexes, plus the significant exception of dairy which has been consistently national (or continental in Europe), in my book, *The Political Economy of Food*, forthcoming from Verso.

6. This involved a different international redivision of labor. Typical of the Fordist period was an *inter-sectoral* integration across capitalist economies (Aglietta 1982); the world car is the most famous example. Agricul-

ture followed the same path, and a new international complementarity between Europe and the United States replaced the old food/manufactures trade. The soy/corn/meat complex was based on replacing extensive grazing with scientifically manufactured "composite feeds" of protein (soya) and energy (corn and other grains). The new feed industry in Europe imported soya, corn and other coarse grains, mainly from the United States, while substituting their own wheat for that previously imported. In anticipation of later third world import substitutions, with Green Revolution grain production, this created a greater demand for imported inputs than the imports of the final product. See Bertrand, Laurent and Leclerca (1983). Now that Latin America is being incorporated into the world meat economy, we face the prospect of the "world steer" (Sanderson 1986).

7. Calculated as five-year averages, 1948–52 and 1976–80, for the following countries: Third World—Asia, except China, Taiwan, Japan; Latin America; Middle East, except Israel; Africa, except South Africa. Advanced Capitalist—United States, Canada, Western Europe, Japan, Australia, New Zealand. Data are from FAO Production and Trade Yearbooks and United Nations Population Yearbook.

8. Concessional sales are commercial sales with special credit arrangements, financed by the government, in order to overcome inability to pay, usually because of foreign exchange shortages.

9. I am ignoring state socialism in this essay. The Cold War is a crucial part of the story, and the parallel development and crises of agriculture in the two camps came to be expressed in the grain deals of 1972–73, that at once expressed detente and signalled the world food crisis. While the shortage that led to the term crisis was temporary, there was a real if less dramatic crisis in the international food regime. The rules of the pre-1973 regime no longer operate, and no new set of rules has been devised to stabilize the present anarchy of international food relations.

10. The following argument is presented in greater depth and detail in an earlier article (Friedmann 1986).

## References

Adams, Jane H. 1988. "The Decoupling of Farm and Household: Capitalist Development and U.S. Agriculture," *Comparative Studies in Society and History* 30 (3): 453–82.

Aglietta, Michel. 1978. *A Theory of Capitalist Regulation*. London: Verso.

——— . 1982. "World Capitalism in the Eighties," *New Left Review* 136.

Banaji, Jairus. 1977. "Capitalist Domination and the Small Peasantry: Deccan Districts in the Late Nineteenth Century," *Economic and Political Weekly,* Special Number (August).

Bartra, Roger and Gerardo Otero. 1987. "Agrarian Crisis and Social Differentiation in Mexico," *Journal of Peasant Studies* 14 (3): 334–62.

Bates, Robert. 1981. *Markets and States in Tropical Africa.* Berkeley: University of California Press.

Bennett, John. 1983. *Of Time and the Enterprise: North American Family Farm Management in a Context of Resource Marginality.* Minneapolis: University of Minnesota Press.

Bertaux, Daniel. 1979. "Class Structure, Class Mobility and the Distribution of Human Beings," in J/A. Frieberg, ed., *Critical Sociology.* New York: Irvington Publications.

Bertrand, J-P, C. Laurent, and V. Leclercq. 1983. *Le monde du soja.* Paris: Maspero/La Decouverte.

Block, Fred. 1977. *The Origins of International Economic Disorder.* Berkeley: University of California Press.

Burbach, Roger and Patricia Flynn. 1980. *Agribusiness in the Americas.* New York: Monthly Review.

Buttel, Frederick H. 1986. "The U.S. Farm Crisis and the Restructuring of American Agriculture: Domestic and International Dimensions," Paper prepared for the Workshop on International Restructuring and the Farm Crisis, Centre for European Agricultural Studies, Wye College, University of London, 13–15 December.

Chevalier, Jacques. 1982. *Civilization and the Stolen Gift.* Toronto: University of Toronto Press.

Collins, Jane. 1986. "The Household and Relations of Production in Southern Peru," *Comparative Studies in Society and History* 28 (4): 651–71.

Crouch, Luis and Alain de Janvry. 1980. "The Class Basis of Agricultural Growth," *Food Policy* 5(1): 3–13.

Dewey, Katherine. 1981. "Nutritional Consequences of the Transformation from Subsistence to Commercial Agriculture in Tabasco, Mexico," *Human Ecology* 9 (2): 151–87.

deVroey, Michel. 1984. "A Regulation Approach to the Interpretation of Contemporary Crisis," *Capital and Class* 23: 45–65.

Ekins, Paul. 1984. *The Living Economy: A New Economics in the Making.* London and New York: Routledge and Kegan Paul.

Elson, Diane and Ruth Pearson. 1981. "The Subordination of Women and the Internationalization of Factory Production," in Kate Young, Carol Wolkowitz and Roslyn McCullagh, eds., *Of Marriage and the Market*. London: CSE Books.

Feder, Ernest. 1980. "The Odious Competition Between Man and Animal over Agricultural Resources in the Underdeveloped Countries," *Review* 3 (3): 463–500.

Fink, Deborah. 1987. "Farming in Open County, Iowa: Women and the Changing Farm Economy," in Michael Chibnik, ed. *Farm Work and Field Work: American Agriculture in Anthropological Perspective*. Ithaca: Cornell University Press.

Fowke, Vernon. 1957. *The National Policy and the Wheat Economy*. Toronto: University of Toronto Press.

Friedmann, Harriet. 1978. "World Market, State and Family Farm: Social Origins of Household Production in the Era of Wage Labor," *Comparative Studies in Society and History* 20:3.

——— . 1982. "The Political Economy of Food: The Rise and Fall of the Postwar International Food Order," *American Journal of Sociology* 88 (Supplement): 248–86.

——— . 1986. "Patriarchal Commodity Production," in Alison MacEwen Scott, ed., *Rethinking Petty Commodity Production*, special issue of *Social Analysis* no. 20: 47–55.

——— . (forthcoming[a]). "Agro-food Industries and Export Agriculture: The Changing International Division of Labor," in William Friedland, Larry Busch and Fred Buttel, *The New Political Economy of Agriculture*.

——— . (forthcoming[b]). *The Political Economy of Food*. London: Verso.

George, Susan. 1981. *Stratèges de la Faim*. Geneva: Grounauer.

Giedion, Siegfied. 1948. *Mechanization Takes Command, A Contribution to Anonymous History*. Republished 1969, New York: Norton.

Gilbert, Jess. 1987. Lecture, Seminar on U.S. Agriculture, Ann Arbor, MI, April.

Gramsci, Antonio. 1971. *Selections from the Prison Notebooks*, trans. and ed. by Q. Hoare and G. N. Smith. New York: International Publishers.

Greenhouse, Steven. 1986. "The Rise and Rise of Big Mac," *New York Times*, June 8: F1.

Hayden, Dolores. 1984. *Redesigning the American Dream*. New York: Norton.

Kenney, Martin, James Curry, and Todd Stockwell. 1987. "Contextualizing Agriculture Within Postwar U.S. Society: Fordism as an Integrative Theory," Working Paper #15, Technology, Innovation, Social Change Project, Department of Agricultural Economics and Rural Sociology, Ohio State University.

Kloppenburg, Jack, Jr. 1984. "The Social Impacts of Biogenetic Technology in Agriculture: Past and Present" pp. 291–321 in Gigi M. Berardi and Charles C. Geisler, eds., *The Social Consequences and Challenges of New Agricultural Technologies.* Boulder and London: Westview Press.

————. 1988. *First the Seed: The Political Economy of Plant Biotechnology, 1492–2000.* Cambridge and New York: Cambridge University Press.

Kohl, Seena. 1976. *Working Together: Women and Family in Southwest Saskatchewan.* Toronto and Montreal: Holt, Rinehart and Winston of Canada.

Lappe, Francis Moore and Joseph Collins. 1979. *Food First.* New York: Ballantine.

Lipietz, Alain. 1984. "Imperialism or the Beast of the Apocalypse," *Capital and Class* 22.

Maher, Vanessa. 1981. "Work, Consumption, and Authority Within the Household: A Moroccan Case," in Kate Young, Carol Wolkowitz and Roslyn McCullagh, eds., *Of Marriage and the Market.* London: CSE Books.

McMichael, Philip. 1984. *Settlers and the Agrarian Question: Foundations of Capitalism in Colonial Australia.* New York: Cambridge University Press.

Polanyi, Karl. 1957. *The Great Transformation.* Boston: Beacon.

Post, Charles. 1982. "The American Road to Capitalism," *New Left Review* 133.

Rogers, Susan Carol. 1987. "Mixing Paradigms on Mixed Farming: Anthropological and Economic Views of Specialization in Illinois Agriculture," in Michael Chibnik, ed. *Farm Work and Field Work: American Agriculture in Anthropological Perspective.* Ithaca: Cornell University Press.

Roseberry, William. 1986. "The Ideology of Domestic Production," *Labour, Capital and Society* 19:1.

Rosenfeld, Rachel. 1985. *Farm Women: Work, Farm and Family in the United States* Chapel Hill: University of North Carolina Press.

Rothstein, Frances. 1986. "The New Proletarians: Third World Reality and First World Categories," *Comparative Studies in Society and History* 28 (2): 217–38.

Sachs, Carolyn. 1983. *The Invisible Farmers: Women in Agricultural Production* Totowa, N.J.: Rowman and Allenheld.

Sanderson, Steven E. 1986. "The Emergence of the 'World Steer': Internationalization and Foreign Domination in Latin American Cattle Production," in F. Lamond Tullis and W. Ladd Hollist, *Food, the State and International Political Economy*. Lincoln: University of Nebraska Press.

Strasser, Susan. 1982. *Never Done: A History of American Housework*. New York: Pantheon.

Vail, David. 1987. "Unique and Common Aspects of Sweden's Current Agricultural Crisis," paper presented at the Rural Sociological Society, Madison, Wisconsin, August.

Weber, Max. 1958. "Capitalism and Rural Society in Germany," in H. Gerth and C. W. Mills, *From Max Weber*. New York: Oxford University Press.

Wessel, James. 1983. *Trading the Future: Farm Exports and the Concentration of Economic Power in Our Food System*. San Francisco: Institute for Food and Development Policy.

Whitehead, Ann. 1981. " 'I'm Hungry, Mum': The Politics of Domestic Budgeting," in Kate Young, Carol Wolkowitz and Roslyn McCullagh, eds., *Of Marriage and the Market*. London: CSE Books.

Wilkening, Eugene. 1981. "Farm Families and Family Farming," in Raymond T. Coward and William M. Smith, Jr., eds., *The Family in Rural Society*. Boulder, Colorado: Westview Press.

Yotopoulos, Pan A. 1985. "Middle-Income Classes and Food Crises: The 'New' Food-Feed Competition," *Economic Development and Cultural Change*. 33(2): 463–83.

Young, Kate, Carol Wolkowitz and Roslyn McCullagh, eds. 1981. *Of Marriage and the Market*. London: CSE Books.

# Contributors

JANE L. COLLINS is Assistant Professor of Anthropology at the State University of New York at Binghamton.

SCOTT COOK is Professor of Anthropology at the University of Connecticut, Storrs, Connecticut.

HARRIET FRIEDMANN is Associate Professor of Sociology at the University of Toronto.

MARTHA E. GIMENEZ is Associate Professor of Sociology at the University of Colorado, Boulder.

NONA GLAZER is Professor of Anthropology at Portland State University, Portland, Oregon.

RANDALL MCGUIRE is Associate Professor of Anthropology at the State University of New York at Binghamton.

SUSANA NAROTZKY teaches Anthropology at the University of Barcelona and is a member of the International Research Group on Processes of Transition.

GAVIN SMITH is Professor of Anthropology and Acting Dean of University College, University of Toronto.

JOAN SMITH is Professor of Sociology at the State University of New York at Binghamton.

DALE TOMICH is Associate Professor of Sociology at the State University of New York at Binghamton.

CYNTHIA WOODSONG is a doctoral candidate in Anthropology at the State University of New York at Binghamton.

# Index